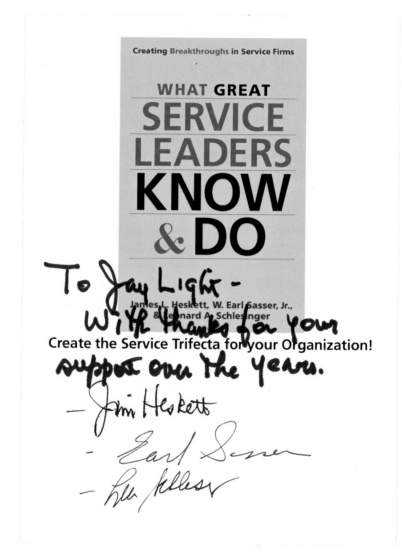

Creating **Breakthroughs** in Service Firms

WHAT **GREAT**

SERVICE
LEADERS
KNOW
& DO

James L. Heskett, W. Earl Sasser, Jr.,
& Leonard A. Schlesinger

Create the Service Trifecta for your Organization!

To Jay Light –
With thanks for your
support over the years.

— Jim Heskett

— Earl Sasser

— Len Schlesinger

More Praise for *What Great Service Leaders Know and Do*

"The ideas of Heskett, Sasser, and Schlesinger have the power to positively transform the strategy and the culture of your company. I have seen this happen repeatedly and in so many different cultural contexts. The world owes much to this trio of authors: their ideas are the seeds of a better socioeconomic world in which business and customers serve each other in enlightened ways."

—Luis Huete, Professor of Production, Technology and Operations Management, IESE Business School, Spain

"Nothing gets our juices flowing more than the topic of good and bad service. In this compelling read, Heskett, Sasser, and Schlesinger make an inspiring case for how the truly extraordinary experiences of the 21st century will come out of a new kind of leadership."

—Diane Hessan, CEO, Startup Institute

"A gem of a book that beautifully captures the collective, evidence-based wisdom of three of our best thinkers in service management."

—Leonard Berry, author of *Discovering the Soul of Service* and *Management Lessons from Mayo Clinic* and University Distinguished Professor and Regents Professor, Texas A&M University

"This book brings together the perspectives of customers, employees, and investors to deliver an outstanding practical guide to service delivery excellence. In times where service organizations like ours must take advantage of ever-faster technological change, this book provides a clear pathway back to the core of why we exist: our customers."

—Solmaz Altin, CEO, Allianz Turkey

"Based solidly in research, a wealth of concrete examples, and an insightful view toward the future, *What Great Service Leaders Know and Do* provides a rare combination of foundational knowledge and insightful advice for aspiring and established service leaders."

—Mary Jo Bitner, Professor, Edward M. Carson Chair in Service Marketing, and Executive Director, Center for Services Leadership, Arizona State University, and Editor, *Journal of Service Research*

"Heskett, Sasser, and Schlesinger are showing us the way ahead in service management and leadership. The discussion in *What Great Service Leaders Know and Do* provides cutting-edge thinking and practice on service leadership. More importantly, it gives service leaders the opportunity to realize what they don't know yet and how to face the challenges of service businesses in the years to come."

—Javier Francisco Reynoso, Professor, EGADE Business School, Tecnológico de Monterrey, Mexico

"Heskett, Sasser, and Schlesinger, pioneers in service management wisdom since the late '70s, now chart the path to the design and delivery of winning services in the future. Great service leaders will be those who can score a 'service trifecta' in which customers, employees, and investors all win."
—**David E. Bowen, PhD, G. Robert and Katherine Herberger Chair in Global Management, Thunderbird School of Global Management, Arizona State University**

"This book is an important read for all service leaders but a *must*-read for leaders who want to guide their companies through the changing landscape of what great service means. The authors provide practical and pragmatic data-driven advice on how to lead in the rapidly changing service economy."
—**Pattye Moore, Chair of the Board, Red Robin Gourmet Burgers**

"*What Great Service Leaders Know and Do* captures a fantastic wealth of experience and practical insights on building and sustaining world-class organizations that serve their employees, the customers they serve, and the investors who fund them. Peppered with current examples of well-cooked service wisdom on successes and failures, this is an excellent manual with all the necessary ingredients you need to work with to face the challenge of delivering world-class service in a sustainable and profitable way."
—**Ronan O'Farrell, Chief Executive, Timoney Leadership Institute, Ireland**

WHAT GREAT

SERVICE LEADERS

KNOW AND *DO*

WHAT GREAT

SERVICE LEADERS

KNOW AND DO

Creating Breakthroughs in Service Firms

JAMES L. HESKETT

W. EARL SASSER JR.

LEONARD A. SCHLESINGER

Berrett–Koehler Publishers, Inc.
a BK Business book

Berrett-Koehler Publishers, Inc.
1333 Broadway, Suite 1000
Oakland, CA 94612-1921
Tel: (510) 817-2277 | Fax: (510) 817-2278 | www.bkconnection.com

ORDERING INFORMATION

Quantity sales. Special discounts are available on quantity purchases by corporations, associations, and others. For details, contact the "Special Sales Department" at the Berrett-Koehler address above.

Individual sales. Berrett-Koehler publications are available through most bookstores. They can also be ordered directly from Berrett-Koehler: Tel: (800) 929-2929; Fax: (802) 864-7626; www.bkconnection.com.

Orders for college textbook/course adoption use. Please contact Berrett-Koehler: Tel: (800) 929-2929; Fax: (802) 864-7626.

Orders by US trade bookstores and wholesalers. Please contact Ingram Publisher Services, Tel: (800) 509-4887; Fax: (800) 838-1149; E-mail: customer.service@ingrampublisherservices.com; or visit www.ingrampublisherservices.com/Ordering for details about electronic ordering.

Berrett-Koehler and the BK logo are registered trademarks of Berrett-Koehler Publishers, Inc.

Printed in the United States of America.

Berrett-Koehler books are printed on long-lasting acid-free paper. When it is available, we choose paper that has been manufactured by environmentally responsible processes. These may include using trees grown in sustainable forests, incorporating recycled paper, minimizing chlorine in bleaching, or recycling the energy produced at the paper mill.

Library of Congress Cataloging-in-Publication Data

Heskett, James L.
  What great service leaders know and do : creating breakthroughs in service firms / James L. Heskett, W. Earl Sasser Jr., Leonard A. Schlesinger. — First edition.
    pages cm
  Includes bibliographical references and index.
  ISBN 978-1-62656-584-5 (hardcover)
    1. Customer services.   2. Service industries—Management.
  I. Sasser, W. Earl.   II. Schlesinger, Leonard A.   III. Title.
  HF5415.5.H474 2015
  658.4'092—dc23   2015016144

First Edition

20 19 18 17 16 15 | 10 9 8 7 6 5 4 3 2 1

Produced and designed by BookMatters, edited by Mike Mollett, proofed by Janet Blake, indexed by Leonard Rosenbaum, and cover designed by Nancy Austin

To John McArthur,
who enthusiastically supported our work
from its very beginning.

CONTENTS

Introduction

Why is it that customer service is still cited so frequently as being terrible, with evidence from your most recent bad airline experience offered up? It could be because a brighter spotlight on services has led to improved management and, with it, rising customer expectations. Airlines, for example, have never provided such dependable service to so many people. Good airline service, perhaps too fondly remembered 25 years later, is no longer remarkable or even adequate for customers who experience it much more frequently than their counterparts in earlier days. We still complain mightily when an airline service snafu occurs. Regardless of reasons why customers complain about the services they receive, or whether or not overall levels of service have improved, it's clear that there is room for a great deal of improvement in the way services are managed and consumed.

Meanwhile, some firms have become known for providing exemplary service. In every service industry, one or two organizations—breakthrough services—are leading the way. Whether we're talking about Whole Foods Market or Apple in the retailing sector, the Vanguard Group or ING Direct (now Capital One 360) in financial services, Disney in entertainment, the Mayo Clinic or Apollo Hospitals in medical services, Southwest Airlines in transportation, or a select group of other service organizations in their respective industries, they share one thing in common: they have all changed the rules governing how entire global service industries are operated. That's what is so exciting about them. It's what makes it important to understand how they are designed and led.

Over the past 35 years we've observed some of the world's most effective service leaders. Good leaders are good teachers. And they have taught us a lot. In the process, we have tried to get into the heads of these leaders to figure out how what they know influences what they do in creating successful services that have stood the test of time.

Through stories based on our collective experience, as well as an exploration of the underlying theoretical work in the field and its practical application, we present a narrative of remarkable successes, unnecessary failures, and future promise. We write with a definite point of view. The book seeks to provide a road map for the design and delivery of winning services for leaders entrusted with the task in the years to come.

THE RISE OF THE SERVICE SECTOR

The vast majority of the world's workers are employed in providing services to others. Despite the often-heard lament about the loss of manufacturing jobs, the proportion of people working in services continues to increase. It's time for a change in mindset about jobs that drive the developed economies of the world.

Jobs in just one service sector, professional and business services, have replaced manufacturing jobs as the mainstay of the middle class in the world's developed economies. In the United States, there are many more jobs in professional and business services than in manufacturing, they are growing at a faster rate, and they pay substantially more for work that is much less menial. All of this is documented in the appendix.

The simple fact that service jobs make up such a large proportion of available employment at present and in the future places added responsibility on the shoulders of leaders in the service economy. The way service jobs are designed and the way service workers are led will influence the job satisfaction of more than 80 percent of the world's workforce. The quality of their leadership will determine employees' loyalty to their employers and their customers; their productivity; the profits they help create for their employers; and the long-term economic development of cities, states, regions, and countries. It will have a profound effect on life for billions of people around the world.

REALIZING THE SERVICE TRIFECTA

Our objective is to sort out the most important practices that contribute to realizing the service trifecta—that is, positive results for employees, customers, and investors. Beyond the service strategies that fuel win-win-win outcomes, we'll look at the following:

1. Operating practices that produce employee and customer satisfaction, engagement, and "ownership"

2. The profit and growth that result from these practices

3. The effective hiring, nurturing, and retention of talent

4. The achievement of leverage and competitive edge through both/and instead of either/or thinking

5. The design of support systems that make the most effective use of technology, networks, and service facilities

6. The development of a small core of customers as "owners" who provide most or all of a firm's growth and profitability

7. The creation of organizations, policies, and practices that attract and retain talent capable of leading firms through the uncertainties associated with the next transformations in service

THE ORGANIZATION OF THE BOOK

Each of the eight main chapters is organized around what great service leaders have known and done—some for a long time. In addition, we look at some directions that we believe services will take in the future as well as what this will require of the reader as a service leader.

In chapter 1 we examine the evolution and underlying structure of service breakthroughs and the unique leadership beliefs and behaviors they require. Breakthrough service leadership is different from other types of leadership. It's important to understand the ways as context for the remainder of the book.

In chapters 2 and 3 we appraise the durability of the ideas we have long championed—ways of structuring a strategic service vision based on customer and employee value equations (chapter 2) and the design of specific elements of strategy around a service profit chain (chapter 3). These chapters explore the reasons why service strategies succeed and fail.

Chapters 4 through 7 discuss ways in which great service leaders achieve results through improvements in the quality of experiences for employees and customers along with a reduction of costs and an increase in value for both. Think of them as sources of competitive edge or leverage, ways of achieving superior value for employees, customers, and investors alike, the goal of well-designed and well-managed services. This is not necessarily about doing more with less. It's about that, but it's also about doing a lot more with a few more resources.

Chapter 4 discusses the most important challenge facing service managers, that of creating great places to work, places that deliver what we call "internal quality" and are fueled by effective cultures. These are workplaces in which workers are engaged and enthusiastic about what they do. The effort begins with hiring for attitude and training for skills, but it involves much more. We visit places in which work is organized around clusters of customers, often performed by teams, and controlled in large measure by frontline workers themselves, reinforced by such devices as service guarantees. Their work is measured according to predetermined desired behaviors, and it is rewarded and recognized in ways that ensure universal value for employees, customers, and investors. These are workplaces that provide a window into a future of service work and workers in which jobs are viewed positively; job satisfaction, trust, and engagement are high; and instances of worker ownership behaviors are frequent.

Chapter 5 is about achieving competitive edge through wins for employees, customers, and investors alike—the service trifecta. It's done by managing queues, customers, and the service "bookends"; "doing it right the second time" by means of effective service recovery; capitalizing on service co-creation by customers; and utilizing "both/and thinking" instead of settling for trade-offs. It leads naturally in chapter 6 to ways of enabling frontline service providers to be heroes and heroines in the eyes of their customers through effective support from technology, networks, and facility design.

We shift our focus from employees to customers in chapter 7 in the quest to achieve much more than just customer satisfaction. Instead, we settle for no less than developing a core of customers as "owners" invested in the success of the service. Typically, these customer owners account for more than 100% of profits. This is done by establishing a consciousness of a customer owner's lifetime value, putting in place processes for listening for and responding to customer needs, guaranteeing results, and putting the organization's best customers to work in building the business.

In chapter 8, we explore the most important challenges that service leaders will face in the future as well as possible ways of dealing with them. Increasingly, service leaders will be co-creating new services with customers who adopt an ownership mentality, partnering and sharing resources with customers and even competitors, crowdsourcing talent, designing services compatible with mobile technologies for an ever more mobile-driven society, delivering seamless service on a global basis, and contending with international competition in services previously thought to be immune to foreign competitors. These trends portend a world of more and more fleeting competitive advantage in which nonfinancial criteria, deep indicators of performance, take on greater significance for service providers, customers, and investors.

This final chapter explores the qualities of leadership that will assume greater importance in an uncertain and rapidly changing competitive world—a world that will require organizations to be adept at learning and fast reacting for the future while attending to current performance.

WHAT GREAT SERVICE LEADERS KNOW AND DO

From anecdotes, cautionary tales, and decades of research and observation, we have distilled here what great service leaders know and do. The summary in the sidebar provides the highlights of a rich story.

In reading this book, you will see that a growing number of practitioners and researchers have come a long way toward understanding ways of dealing with the challenges facing managers in the service sector today. There are many more examples of best practice on which to draw than when we first began examining the design and management of services nearly four decades ago. And there is more talent available to put them to work. It is an appropriate time to take stock, organize our thinking, and assess the basis for the further development of management practices in the service sector over the coming decades.

Chapter	What Great Service Leaders Know	What Great Service Leaders Do
1	Leading a breakthrough service is different.	They take steps to ensure repeated memorable service encounters.
2	Customers buy results and experiences, not services or products.	They focus on the few things that produce results and experiences for the right customers.
3	The best service operating strategies don't require trade-offs.	They foster both/and thinking in designing winning operating strategies.
4	Service starts with the frontline employee.	They hire for attitude, train for skills.
5	Effective operating strategies have to serve employees, customers, and investors.	They ensure the achievement of the leverage and edge that produce win-win-win results—the service trifecta.
6	The best uses of technology and other support systems create frontline service heroes and heroines.	They use support systems to elevate important service jobs and eliminate the worst ones.
7	Satisfying customers is not enough.	They take steps to develop a core of customers who are owners.
8	Their current beliefs about the future of services are wrong.	They build agile service organizations that learn, innovate, and adapt.

It is also clear that a lot of work remains to be done. A look at the data in the appendix regarding productivity and job satisfaction around the world leads us to conclude that service leaders are not doing well in living up to the magnitude of the task they face. The rate of increases in productivity lags manufacturing. Job satisfaction has rarely been lower.

Simply put, management has within its control the authority, and we think the responsibility, to improve service quality and productivity while increasing job satisfaction, employee engagement, and the bottom line for shareholders. It can be achieved through both/and thinking that rejects the popular notion of tradeoffs and leads to win-win-win results for employees, customers, and investors. This book is about ways it has been and will be achieved.

Reliance on stories about great service leaders involves a risk that we willingly assume. Our stories involve leaders whose organizations may not stand the test of time in spite of their efforts and ideas. For example, as we wrote the book, one of the leaders we profile, Gary Loveman, announced that he was stepping down as CEO of Caesar's chain of casinos. After putting together a service strategy based on pathbreaking ideas and practices, he saw a subsidiary of his firm driven into bankruptcy by the financial engineering of a private equity firm that purchased Caesar's for a high price and proceeded to load it with so much debt that its odds of success were greatly reduced, despite strong operating performance vis à vis competitors. An observer of Loveman stated "one of the drivers of his decision was he spent a lot more time on the balance sheet than he wanted to."[1] In cases like this, which undoubtedly will be repeated in the future, outcomes do not dull our admiration for the practices implemented in the organization.

We know what has produced success in service endeavors in the past. We have observed and documented strong service principles and even developed some service management concepts ourselves that have endured in practice over time. However, it is quite obvious to us that what it took to produce a winning hand in managing in the service economies of the 1970s and 1980s is in many ways different than it is today. While many of the same questions prevail, management's responses must be sensitive to future challenges facing service industries. With the help of the thinking—and doing—of outstanding practitioners, our goal here is to provide insights into what it takes to succeed now and in the future.

In every service industry, one or two organizations—breakthrough services—are leading the way. They are providing the blueprint for service excellence in the future. If they are to be emulated, we need first to understand what is so different about leading a breakthrough service organization.

CHAPTER 1

Leading a Breakthrough Service

Is Different

What great service leaders *know:*
leading a breakthrough service is different.

What great service leaders *do:*
they take steps to ensure repeated
memorable service encounters.

Robert Nardelli left General Electric to become CEO of Home Depot in 2001. Expectations were high for Home Depot, the home improvement retailer whose growth had slowed when Nardelli took over. After all, he had already led several GE manufacturing operations to great success.

At Home Depot Nardelli found that the stores were staffed with knowledgeable, full-time employees, sometimes more than were absolutely necessary. He led a move to hire more part-timers, many with less expertise in home improvement, in order to size the retail workforce to customer traffic patterns. The move backfired. Customers noticed immediately that their favorite employees on the floor were no longer there. Soon after, Nardelli was no longer there.

Nardelli found that leading a service organization is different from leading a manufacturing organization. In manufacturing, if the factory labor force is too large, there is a simple solution: downsize. Consumers are rarely aware a change has occurred. But at Home Depot, consumers did notice. Heading up a service organization proved to be very different from his previous job. In fact, there are many subtle differences in leading a breakthrough service organization which, if not understood, can pose real challenges for a manager with other kinds of experience.

WHAT IS A BREAKTHROUGH SERVICE?

Standards for judging a service are highly subjective. When we first explored service breakthroughs and the organizations that achieved them, we described them as

> those one or two firms in every service industry that stand out from the pack. . . . Firms that seem to have broken through some sort of figurative "sound barrier," that have passed through the turbulence that precedes the barrier into the relatively quiet, smooth zone beyond which a management action produces exaggerated results, results that often exceed reasonable expectations. Firms that alter the basis of competition in their industries.[1]

Based on our experiences in recent years, we can improve on that vague, albeit inspiring, definition. It requires an understanding of the way in which value is created for customers, the employees who serve them, and investors.

Value Is Central to the Idea

When we talk with consumers, business customers, and even recipients of social services about value, four topics come up, time after time, in conversations: (1) results obtained from a package of products and services, (2) the quality of the experience in obtaining them,

(3) the costs of acquiring them (other than price), and (4) price itself. Together, they make up a "customer value equation" (figure 1-1).[2]

Figure 1-1 Customer Value Equation

$$\text{Value for Customer} = \frac{\text{Results (or Solutions) + Quality of Customer Experience (or Process)}}{\text{Price + Access Costs}}$$

Other things being equal, as results and quality of experience increase, value for the customer goes up. As price or costs of accessing the service increase, value goes down.

Recent research has explored the relative importance to customers of results (the *what* of service) versus experience (the *how* of service) in the customer value equation. It leads to the conclusion that when the service is performed in a customer's immediate purview or is being recalled shortly after the service encounter, experience is a more important influence on customers' perceptions of value. Otherwise, customer perceptions of value are more likely to be influenced by the results they realized.[3]

The customer value equation reflects the extensive research on the topic of service quality carried out by Leonard Berry, A. Parasuraman, and Valerie Zeithaml in the past three decades. One of their early studies, based on interviews with 16 focus groups, concluded, for example, that customer expectations and the degree to which those expectations are exceeded or met on each of the dimensions of the equation determine customers' overall appraisal of service quality and value.[4]

The employee value equation is based on research and employee interviews and can be stated in a similar manner (figure 1-2).[5]

Organizations that deliver value provide employees with a reason to come to work (the nature of an organization's activities—its "business"—and its mission). They offer opportunities for personal

Figure 1-2 Employee Value Equation

$$\text{Value for Employee} = \frac{\text{Business/Mission} + \text{Capability to Deliver Results} + \text{Quality of Workplace}}{1 \div \text{Total Income} + \text{Access Costs}}$$

development, frequent feedback, and ultimately greater latitude to solve problems for valued customers, all factors that contribute to the employee's capability to deliver results. The quality of the workplace is determined by such things as the "fairness" of one's manager (whether the manager hires, recognizes, and fires the right people in a timely way), the quality of the work performed by one's peers in the workplace, and the degree to which good work gets recognized. High pay as well as easy access to, and continuity of, the job contribute to value. That's why pay is portrayed in the denominator of the fraction as 1 ÷ Total Income; when calculated this way, higher pay contributes to value for the employee.

The third of the three value equations (figure 1-3)—the investor's value equation—is widely known as simply return on investment.

Figure 1-3 Investor Value Equation

$$\text{Value for Investor} = \frac{\text{Revenue (Customer Price x Units)} - \text{Expenses}}{\text{Amount of Investment in Service}}$$

These three equations are interrelated. Revenue for the investor, other things being equal, means higher prices and lower value for the customer. Similarly, lower expenses for the investor, other things equal, means lower value for employees if the expense reductions come out of their compensation. But these zero-sum trade-offs need not be the case if a new policy or practice creates a way of delivering better results at lower costs while producing margins sufficient to create extraordinary value for customers, employees, and investors alike. That's largely what this book is about.

Breakthrough Service Redefined: The Service Trifecta

We've observed hundreds of service organizations in action, and we've seen what works and what doesn't work. We're convinced that breakthrough services are those that provide

1. extraordinary results and a high-quality experience for customers and employees alike

2. high value (not necessarily low costs) to customers

3. relatively high returns (for the industry) to employees and investors

Think of it as the trifecta of outstanding service design and delivery.

Breakthrough services share one other characteristic. They have all changed the rules governing how entire global service industries are operated. That's what is so exciting about them. It's what makes it important to understand how they are designed and led.

WHAT GREAT SERVICE LEADERS UNDERSTAND: THE "RIGHT SERVICE ENCOUNTER"

Many leadership practices have proved effective in any kind of organization. Still, great service leadership is distinguished both by the magnitude of its challenges and the priorities involved in addressing them.

Jobs in services involve personal relationships and require interpersonal skills to a greater degree than jobs in some other sectors. Unlike most manufacturing jobs, many service positions bring service workers into constant contact with customers in the service encounter.[6] In many service occupations, the service is both produced and "consumed" at the time it is delivered. As a result, the service provider is able to see the customer's reactions and take satisfaction from them. In the customer's eyes, the provider of a personal service has skills and a personality that are at least as important as the company and its brand. The provider is an important factor in the purchase decision. Although the encounter may be less personal in services such as retail and transportation, the service provider still has a strong influence on customer loyalty. For example, in an industry with minimal service differentiation, Customers often cite Southwest Airlines' Employees (*Customers* and *Employees* are always capitalized in the airline's communications) as one of the primary reasons they fly the airline whenever schedules and itineraries permit.

Service encounters often require face-to-face customer contact, customization of a service, and the co-creation of services by employees and their customers.

The Need for Face-to-Face Contact with Customers

Services that entail face-to-face contact with customers—hospitality, entertainment, professional services, education, personal services, and health care, for example—often require employees to be deployed over large geographic areas in order to provide customers with easy access. Organizations thus might have multisite operations with relatively complex organizational forms. Managers may need to ensure effective communication through a multilayered organization, particularly when change is being implemented. They may have to deal with real estate to house widely dispersed service personnel as well.

Degree of Customization Required

Some services are best performed with little customization. At Shouldice Hospital in Toronto, for example, surgeons fix hernias by a time-honored method that provides quality (measured in terms of operations that rarely have to be repaired) much higher than the average for North American hospitals. They are hired primarily for their enthusiasm for work in an environment that provides regular hours and good work/life balance—but one in which they have very little latitude in what they do. Surgeons who easily experience boredom have no place in Shouldice's operating rooms.

In the same industry, the Cleveland Clinic looks for surgeons with an interest in research and the ability to use good judgment in treating patients with widely varying medical histories and needs. Innovation is a natural part of the job description for many of the organization's professionals. This requires that the service provider use judgment in customizing the treatment of individual patients.

Both of these organizations benefit because they carefully hire their employees and give them good training, excellent support systems, and, where it is appropriate, more (Cleveland Clinic) or less (Shouldice Hospital) latitude to use judgment in the face-to-face relationship. These practices ensure both great results and a high-quality experience for the patient, meeting our standard for breakthrough service.

Co-creation of the Result

Customers at Shouldice Hospital participate to an unusual degree in co-creating the service.[7] They diagnose themselves and, if necessary, diet to make the weight limit that Shouldice doctors impose to qualify patients for surgery. Patients prepare themselves for surgery by shaving themselves, take charge of their own recovery by walking from the operating table, and counsel other patients who have not yet been under the knife. All of this helps Shouldice keep its costs to a minimum while offering jobs with more interaction with patients and fewer menial responsibilities. While it increases patient enthusiasm for the process and its results, it also requires that management hire and train people who can work with patients in ways often foreign to other hospitals.

WHAT GREAT SERVICE LEADERS DO

Organizations achieve excellent service on a consistent basis by recognizing and taking steps to address the determinants of repeated memorable service encounters, something for which there is no equivalent in manufacturing or other activities. The most important of these is employee loyalty, especially in an age when such loyalty is on the decline.

Manage for Employee Loyalty

The importance of the service encounter to the success of many service enterprises places a premium on the continuity of relationships between customers and the employees serving them. This continuity requires employee loyalty. Whereas high rates of labor turnover inflate costs and cut into profits, longer tenure reduces recruitment and training costs, preserves productivity gains, and creates a more positive experience for customers—making employee loyalty one of the most important deep indicators of future performance in a service organization.

Great service leaders understand that retention rates rise along with opportunities to advance. Leaders of a number of large service organizations realize the positive effects of frontline continuity on customer satisfaction and loyalty, and they are making significant efforts to expand frontline advancement opportunities for the best employees to keep them closer to the customer for longer periods.

Whole Foods Market, for example, has designed everything, from the rigor of the selection process, to the amount of latitude for self-management on the job, to methods of compensation to encourage frontline employees to stay. Teams at the global, regional, store, and store department levels manage the company. A store often has eight teams that are responsible for anything from produce to checkout. After a 30-day initial probation period, new employees must earn a two-thirds positive vote by members of their team—an endorsement by team members who regard their vote as one that directly affects the quality of their paycheck and work life. As team members, they set labor cost/sales or cost of goods/sales ratios for their store department, they are entrusted with decisions about how to achieve those ratios (including what food items to buy locally), and they are paid bonuses based on how well they do as a team. This often involves coming up with new ideas for increasing sales as one way of mitigating increases in labor costs.

At the same time, employees benefit from what CEO John Mackey describes as a "bias toward overdisclosure" of information on which teams base their decisions.[8] Every team member knows how other teams in the store are doing. Every member knows how the store is doing compared to other stores. Every member can know what other team members are paid. Employees have an opportunity to vote every three years on various items in the company's benefits package, from pay for community service to provisions in their health insurance. As employees reach the three-year mark on the job, they are given stock options to encourage them to stay with the company. All of these factors contribute to Whole Foods' turnover rate of less than 10 percent of full-time employees after the probationary period, a fraction of rates across the grocery retailing industry as a whole.[9] It's no surprise then that Whole Foods regularly is rated one of the best places to work by its employees, is known for its good service by its customers, and has in recent years had the highest profit per square foot of any major food retailer.

Reduce Customers' Perceived Risk: Make Service Visible and Tangible

Customers often fear what they can't see or feel. Making the invisible visible and the intangible tangible to reduce customers' perceived risks is a challenge faced by many service managers.[10] It's the reason car repair facilities wash and vacuum the vehicle after maintenance is completed. A clean vehicle exterior and interior signals that the car is now in great condition. Termite control service is provided around the foundations outside the home often with no one present in the home. The service technician leaves a personalized note on the door and later sends a report outlining the evidence to the homeowner. The service technician continues the personalized approach by addressing by hand the envelope containing the report to the homeowner. Similarly, lawn chemical services leave signs on the lawn after applications have been made to let the homeowner know that chemicals have been applied and to let neighbors and passers-by see a miniature billboard.

Reduce Perceived Risk through References and Referrals

Customers for personal services, in particular medical services, have until recently had little information on which to base their personal medical decisions. They perceive a high level of risk because of a lack of visibility of the work performed and the difficulty of measuring the quality of the results achieved. They therefore often use price as a surrogate for quality, resulting in a lack of price sensitivity on the part of customers for some services—as well as the high margins often generated by such services.

Today, when confronted with high perceived risks in purchasing a service, customers often seek reassurance through recommendations from people they trust. Internet-based networking and commercial websites have thrown open the doorway to more information than was available in the past. Not only are reviewers active on sites such as Amazon.com, Yelp.com, and AngiesList.com, but mechanisms are now being introduced that measure the reliability of such reviews. As a result, more people are trusting recommendations, for everything from cleaning services to medical services, than ever before. To anticipate the impact of social networking and other media through which accurate, and inaccurate, information is quickly and easily exchanged, service leaders in the future will supply more information to customers to provide greater transparency.

Manage the Customer Experience and Emotional Content

The fact that service organizations are often responsible for delivering a customer experience places nuanced demands on service leaders to define, measure, and manage the components of that experience, however intangible or invisible those components might sometimes be.[11] Customers should come away engaged with the brand that represents the experience, and loyal to it, as well as to the person who creates it.

Competing services often differentiate themselves by managing what is termed "emotional content." Patients at Mayo Clinic, for example, receive much more than just expert medical diagnosis and care. They quickly become aware that they are the center of attention for a team of medical practitioners that has organized its work around them. Scheduling of tests and appointments, for example, is designed to minimize a patient's time at the hospital. In addition to good results, the Mayo Clinic is also known for delivering outstanding experiences to sometimes reluctant clients whose time is valuable and who have traveled long distances to visit its premises under trying conditions.[12]

Some services have a higher level of emotional content than others. This is particularly true of personal services such as haircutting or cosmetic surgery—services whose results are "public." High emotional content also applies to such things as hospitality for special family events, the purchase of products such as lingerie, and even the daily coffee ritual. Here, managers have to subscribe to the idea that the quality of the service experience is as important as the results they deliver. But they have to do more than that. They also have to ensure that the organization hires people who can deliver such experiences, and see to it that it celebrates their ability to do so. They then must create a setting that conveys the nature of the intended experience, as well as provide employees with the support systems necessary to deliver a flawless customer experience. All of this requires that they pay attention to detail, as well as have a concern for the alignment of people, policies, practices, and technologies around a desired experience.

Take the Apple store, for example. The company puts young, tech-savvy people with great attitudes and customer-facing skills in a clean, bright, functional, exciting retail setting—one that reflects the design mentality of the technology they are being asked to sell. All of these employees are equipped with Apple-made handheld devices, enabling them to sell and serve customers more effectively—from checking inventory to scheduling service appointments. The result is sales productivity, more than $6,000 per square foot of selling space per year—a figure formerly unheard of for retail chains. By comparison, that is nearly 10 times the sales productivity of Walmart, a company that has been considered a leader in retail productivity.

Still, service leadership can't simply be put on autopilot. If Apple store productivity were to reach the point where it adversely affected the customer experience (say, as the result of large crowds or long lines keeping customers away), Apple's management would have to consider ways of restoring the experience. That is a complex task unrivaled in the world of manufacturing management.

Manage the Customer

Colleen Barrett, president emerita of Southwest Airlines, has told us, "Once people fly our airline two or three times, they keep coming back." Why? Because during the first and second flights, Southwest Airlines, an airline that has transformed the global airline industry, trains its customers. Customers are acquainted with Southwest's website through which its seats are reserved and sold. Next they go through a somewhat unusual boarding procedure that requires them to board in the specific order of their priority for access to seats that are not assigned. Once on board, they either respond positively or negatively to the over-the-top good humor displayed by many of Southwest's Employees, who are hired in part for their personalities.

Those who fly the airline only once often complain about its cattle-car boarding process and lighthearted Employees. They reject the Customer training process. Others, who respond positively and become knowledgeable and able to take advantage of the way things are done, become loyal Customers.

Dublin-based Ryanair, a low-cost airline that many regard, incorrectly, as a Southwest Airlines knockoff serving Europe, shares the challenge of training its customers. Ryanair's strategy is to provide as little service as possible for its basic (comparatively low) fare, charging extra for anything above and beyond basic air transportation between European cities. Ryanair's veteran, economy-minded passengers travel light with few or no bags, carry their own food, and are prepared to sit in seats with little legroom. Anything other than that incurs costs in addition to their fare. It's something that passengers unfamiliar with the airline's service have to either reject or get used to.

Ryanair's business model has been emulated by Spirit Airlines, a rapidly growing, profitable 2007 entrant to the low-cost, low-fare US airline competition. The loyal Spirit customer apparently values low fares above everything else, including reliable service. Spirit's on-time arrival record is regularly among the worst in the industry. It leads the industry in charging extra for everything from ticketing to carry-on bags and even seat selection. Recently, it was reported that fees composed 41 percent of the airline's revenue, by far the highest in the industry.[13] At Spirit, veteran customers know what to expect and act accordingly. The novice customer has an education awaiting him. Even CEO Ben Baldanza acknowledges the importance for first-time passengers of learning the routine. As he puts it, "You can't sleepwalk through the process."[14]

These are perhaps extreme examples of the ways that service organizations address the important task of managing customers (and their expectations). Leaders in breakthrough services understand that training is important, because customers often team with service providers. They build a competitive edge—co-creating great service (depending on how that is defined by the individual) at low cost—that customers enjoy. In many cases, they need to take special care in hiring and preparing employees to train, manage, and work with customers to co-create results.

Manage Service Quality: "Do It Right the Second Time"

The management of quality in manufacturing emphasizes "do it right the first time" or DRIFT—especially critical if the product in question is an airplane part and the manufacturer is Boeing. It has become a mantra of many manufacturing managers, mainly because it is much less expensive for manufacturing to get things right the first time.

Whereas for such services as medical care, getting things right the first time is important, but for the vast number of less critical services, perfection often goes unnoticed. "Doing it right the second time" often produces more enthusiastic customer satisfaction if the *service recovery* process is particularly effective and memorable.[15] Think, for example, of the last time your restaurant server made a mistake in your order and picked up the bill for dessert. This helps explain why service recovery occupies a higher priority than "doing it right the first time" in the tool kit of most managers in the service sector. Effective service recovery often results in greater delight for employees as well as customers than a service perfectly performed the first time. It casts the service provider as a hero. In combination, the outcomes represent a service breakthrough.

Manage the Entry-Level Workforce

The most effective service recovery occurs nearest the customer, by the frontline service provider. It often involves giving an entry-level employee wide-ranging latitude to correct problems, in a sense entrusting the business to someone who may be a teenager in her first job. Unless they are preceded by careful hiring, expert training, and the design of helpful support systems, recoveries can be risky.

More than half of all people hired by Walt Disney World are working for the first time in an organization of any kind. The company must select new employees in large part for their positive attitudes toward others, provide training that lets them know what to expect on the job—whether they are "on stage" or "backstage"—as well as the importance of punctuality, dependability, and appearance. It sets explicit rules, for example regarding facial hair as well as acceptable hairstyles. It allows no one to be seen "onstage" in a partial costume. It prescribes behavior, depending on the job. The result is a world-renowned experience for visitors to Disney's theme parks—one that is consistently memorable, and one that is largely delivered by a group of young people barely out of high school.[16]

Disney's challenge is not unusual. The vast majority of youth in developed economies enter the workforce through the service sector. This places a special burden on the shoulders of service management to serve society well by providing those workers with a favorable first impression.

Disseminate Best Practices in Multisite Businesses

While multisite management is not peculiar to services, no manufacturing organization compares with a large fast-food chain or banking company in the number of operating locations that have to be managed. Multisite management in services can require the supervision of literally hundreds of unit managers, leading to an organization where middle managers communicate important messages to customer-facing employees. This perhaps explains why many large retailers feel that they are fortunate if 90 percent of the stores receive and act properly on instructions regarding merchandising, store layout, and shelf appearance. As if that weren't complex enough, consider the rollout of a change in strategy. Whether at Bank of America or Westpac, one of Australia's leading banks, such an effort involves so many people that it requires that ideas cascade from one level in the organization to the next until the process reaches the front line.

Despite the challenges, a large number of locations also affords several opportunities. Breakthrough service organizations take advantage of multisite operations by measuring outcomes and circulating comparative data. Multisite management also offers opportunities for friendly competition among sites, experimentation at low risk at the unit level, and the sharing of best practices.

Government is encouraging best practice in entire industries. For example, all medical networks attain different success rates for various medical procedures. In the United States, Medicare costs per patient for roughly the same quality of outcomes can vary by nearly 100 percent in the same state.[17] Recognizing this, the 2010 Patient Protection and Affordable Care Act in the United States provides for the establishment of a Center for Medicare and Medicaid Innovation "to test innovative payment and service delivery models to reduce program expenditures."[18] The assumption here is that hospitals of a given type will be sufficiently similar to make it possible for administrators and practitioners to engage in the exchange of best practices.

Manage Unseen Workers and Work

Whereas most manufacturing is carried out by large groups of workers in facilities that offer managers at all levels proximity to, and visibility of, those being supervised, many service managers do not have the advantage of such proximity and visibility. Some must manage services that are carried out in scattered locations—even remote parts of the world—by one or two workers who can't be supervised economically. Thus, breakthrough service leaders have the unique challenge of managing unseen workers and work.

Consider, for example, the engineers of Schlumberger, the world's leading purveyor of support services to petroleum producers. Schlumberger provides wireline engineering services critical for detecting and accessing the world's oil reserves. Engineers operating in ones and twos in remote areas are responsible for rigs outfitted with expensive equipment entrusted to their care. The company cannot provide day-to-day supervision of what they do. Rather, it has to rely on hiring not only the right engineers in terms of skill set but also those with the kind of attitude under often lonely working conditions that will engender the trust of their superiors.

ISS, the Copenhagen-based provider of cleaning, catering, and other facility-based services around the world, has an army of low-paid cleaning people delivering hard-to-measure quality (what is clean?) at odd hours of the night, working either alone or in small teams. While the risks are not as great as those facing Schlumberger and its customers, the demands on management for careful hiring and training are much the same.

Manage General Managers

Unlike manufacturing organizations, which follow conventional ways of organizing by function, service organizations, particularly those operating in multiple sites, require the coordinated management of operations, marketing, and human resources at the level of the operating unit, typically the lowest level of management. As a result, much of service sector management takes place at the confluence of several functions (figure 1-4). Management scholars suggest that one of the criteria for identifying general management

Figure 1-4 The Locus of General Management (GM)
in Many Multisite Service Organizations

is responsibility for several functions in an organization. If this is the case, many service organizations, out of necessity, have to nurture general managers in large numbers in close proximity to customers. General managers managing general managers are the rule, not the exception, in services.

Measure and Manage for Results

Managers of breakthrough services also home in on different measures of performance than those in manufacturing enterprises. Whereas manufacturing management concentrates on productivity, product quality (as measured by the producer), cost per unit, safety, and on-time delivery, service management rightly focuses on employee engagement and loyalty, service quality (as perceived by customers), and customer loyalty. These are often components of a balanced scorecard for service measurement.

FIT THE STRATEGY TO THE SERVICE TYPE (OR DON'T)

Generalizations about services are inevitably oversimplifications. Differences among services are perhaps as great as those differentiating services from manufacturing activities. The sector is so diverse that it defies concise description. How, for example, can we compare the work of a hair stylist (highly personal, performed face-to-face, difficult for the customer to assess in advance, reliant on a high degree of trust and a certain amount of input from the customer) with a television network (simultaneous broadcast to viewers with many alternatives)? Rather than compare services one to one, we might think of them as falling along a spectrum with several important dimensions.

Scholars who have studied this challenge have come up with several generic types of service, each with different kinds of service encounters and needs. David Maister, Christopher Lovelock, and Roger Schmenner have provided what have proved to be the most useful ideas for "mapping" the service sector for our purposes.[19] They base their service typology on the degree of service customization, the amount of customer contact required, and labor intensity—the importance of labor costs in creating the service. Combining their ideas allows us to regard all services as *factory* (think low customization, low customer contact, and low labor intensity, as in fast food), *mass* (low customization and customer contact but high labor intensity, as in package delivery services), *technological* (high levels of customer contact and customization with low labor intensity, as in online banking), and *professional* (high customization, customer contact, and labor intensity, as in legal services). A "map" of these basic types of services prepared by Maister and Lovelock is shown in figure 1-5.

As shown in figure 1-5, each service type has its own particular goals and human resource challenges when it comes to recruiting, selecting, training, assigning, and rewarding people.

Figure 1-5 Important Human Resource Management Challenges in Various Service Enterprises

		Degree of Service Customization	
		Low	High
		The Mass Service	**The Professional Service**
Degree of Customer Contact	**High**	Recruiting and Selection: Broad-based effort, with criteria primarily based on human skills and attitude	Recruiting and Selection: Highly selective, based on technical and human skills
		Training: On-the-job, with little or no follow-up	Training: Professional schooling and on-the-job training, with periodic updates
		Assigning: To specific unattended tasks	Assigning: Given great care to facilitate personal development
		Rewarding: Modest, based on time on the job	Rewarding: High, on basis of value of output to client
		Goals: Minimize job complexity and training time required for frequent replacements	Goals: Build expertise through minimum turnover
		The Factory Service	**The Technological Service**
	Low	Recruiting and Selection: On the basis of criteria such as basic knowledge, health, and attitude	Recruiting and Selection: Selective, with criteria primarily based on technological skills
		Training: On-the-job, with limited follow-up	Training: Prior to selection, with technologically oriented update seminars
		Assigning: To cover unattended production tasks	Assigning: To specific unattended tasks
		Rewarding: Varied, often based on time on the job	Rewarding: Varied, based on technological skills
		Goals: Minimum training costs and minimum turnover only of key people	Goals: Minimum turnover to provide technological expertise and continuity

Source: Adapted from a framework first presented in David H. Maister and Christopher H. Lovelock, "Managing Facilitator Services," *Sloan Management Review,* Summer 1982, p. 22, as shown in James L. Heskett, W. Earl Sasser Jr., and Christopher W. L. Hart, *Service Breakthroughs: Changing the Rules of the Game* (New York: The Free Press, 1990), at p. 214.

Color outside the Lines

We've just delineated distinct types of services, which require different organization, staffing, training, rewards, uses of technology, and cost profiles, among other things. Conventional wisdom suggests that strategies that fit within these boundaries are the most successful. However, the opposite argument can be made, that there are real opportunities for service strategies that cross conventional boundaries on these maps. For example, organizations like LegalZoom.com have distinguished themselves from the competition by transforming a professional service into a technological service that makes low-cost legal documents and services for standard problems available online. L.L. Bean succeeded in catalog retailing by crossing the boundary from a factory service to what some would argue is a professional service with its service-center employees capable of providing advice about appropriate sporting goods to customers who shop by telephone or online. Using a kindergarten analogy, these are strategies crafted by leaders who "color outside the lines." Instead, they look for ways to bend the conventional boundaries of their service enterprises.

Address Different Management Challenges

One study of the management challenges faced in various types of companies in the service sector concluded that managers in service enterprises share certain challenges, such as maintaining quality (the number one concern), hiring, and training.[20] But the study also found some wide differences in the challenges faced by managers among various kinds of service businesses.

For example, for mass services that had high need for customization and contact with customers but low labor input, technology advances represented the most important management challenge. This would be typical, for example, for many Internet-based retailing enterprises. In contrast, for professional services (with high need for customization, customer contact, and labor input), "making service warm" was an especially important challenge.

LET'S GET DOWN TO BASICS

Over nearly four decades, we have contributed to an effort to understand how breakthrough services are created and led. We have observed hundreds of service practitioners at work and attempted to make sense of what we've observed. This effort has produced ideas that have, in the past, gained widespread application. However, changes in such things as the composition of the workforce, new technologies, and customers' expectations and behaviors can affect the applicability of these ideas. In chapter 2 we examine the effects of these changes and address ways in which great service leaders shape service strategies that deliver results.

CHAPTER 2

Shaping Service Strategies

That Deliver Results

What great service leaders *know*:
customers buy results and value, not services or products.

What great service leaders *do*:
*they focus on results and value for the right
customers, as well as on the employee and
customer value equations that produce them.*

Some organizations clearly know to whom they will and, more importantly, will not sell their services. Private banking organizations impose minimum limits on the available wealth of the customers they will accept into their investment counseling and management programs. The advertising agency TBWA\Chiat\Day passes up prospective clients who are not interested in its philosophy of "disruption" that the organization applies in designing and implementing marketing programs. These organizations have a clear *market focus,* something that is worth a great deal on the bottom line.

A growing number of organizations understand that their customers do not primarily seek products or services. Rather, they're looking for results and value. This is particularly true for manufacturers that add services to their product line to deliver a package of offerings designed to provide solutions to problems. GE Aircraft sells engine uptime and productivity rather than just the engines themselves. As we mentioned earlier, IBM centered its renaissance several years ago on its Global Solutions business. In some cases this has led the company to operate entire turnkey data centers for its customers. In other cases, it has encouraged clients to replace their data centers with cloud-based services supplied by IBM.

Too often, management concentrates on managing for effort. It's a throwback to the days of time-and-motion studies that produced odd behaviors at companies compensating for piecework. At Lincoln Electric, for example, office staff would spend their lunch hours eating with one hand while hitting the same typewriter key over and over with the other in order to gain rewards for effort. By contrast steelmaker Nucor Corporation has a policy of rewarding steel mill personnel only for tons of steel that meet quality standards, in other words, results.

Breakthrough service organizations define their businesses in terms of *results and value,* not products or services. Once employees are selected carefully and rewarded properly, management places more emphasis on results than on how they are achieved. The organizations assume that the results will be achieved in a manner consistent with their strategies and values. This is breakthrough service leadership at work.

Still other organizations have based their success on their *operating strategy and focus.* For years, United Parcel Service (UPS) would not accept packages above certain size dimensions and a weight of 70 pounds because those were the maximums that one driver and a UPS "car" could handle comfortably. A two-driver operation would have broken the focus and forced an increase in the operating budget, higher rates, and a degradation of the value for which UPS is famous. Here the emphasis is on *leveraging value over cost.* In order to do this, organizations like UPS search for the *operating edge,* whether it is achieved through people, technology (the UPS "car" design with dimensionally correct shelves and transparent roofs for better light), or other means.

Excellent support systems help fuel the success of yet other service organizations. Often, these systems involve data analysis and communication in support of decision making. In the case of Target Corporation, big data enables the company to analyze purchase patterns that help predict customer behaviors. For example, it helps identify prospects, such as pregnant women, for certain kinds of merchandise even before the prospects are aware of their impending needs. It allows careful, detailed analysis of individual purchase patterns to fuel marketing efforts targeted to the individual consumer. It also helps Target select and stock merchandise in ways that anticipate demand, helping to ensure successful shopping visits for its customers.

Taken together, market focus, business definition, operating strategy, and support system excellence are all elements of what we call the *strategic service vision.*[1] Service organizations that do all or even most of these things well—not only with regard to customers and investors but also employees—will continue to rewrite the rules by which competition takes place in their respective industries. TBWA\Chiat\Day, IBM, GE, Nucor Corporation, UPS, and Target are among the enterprises that are doing that. IKEA is, as well.

IKEA'S STRATEGIC SERVICE VISION

When hundreds of millions of people—typically students, younger singles, and married couples just beginning housekeeping—think of furniture, they think of IKEA.[2] Some individuals will even describe themselves as an "IKEA person," meaning they have turned over many decisions regarding taste and lifestyle to the company's merchants. But IKEA wasn't always a leader in assemble-your-own furniture. IKEA's strategic service vision helps us understand why a store selling everything from fountain pens and udder balm for cows in a small Swedish town in 1943 has grown into a global purveyor of a lifestyle through home furnishings, selling nearly 30 billion euros of home furnishings in fiscal 2014 through 315 big-box stores in 27 countries and pulling more than 11 percent of that to the bottom line. How did IKEA do it?

Market Focus

Over the years founder Ingvar Kamprad and his management team have had a clear picture of IKEA's target market—the profile of the customers IKEA targets with its offerings.[3] IKEA can fashion stories about these young people, single or married, furnishing their first residence on a limited budget. These are people with little time or patience—or money—to furnish a home. They may also lack confidence in their taste. For its target markets—primarily college students, singles, and young families—IKEA provides complete starter sets of furnishings at hardly believable low prices. This is offered to those willing to contain their creativity and furnish their living spaces in one or a mix of the four "style groups" comprising about 9,000 items and designed to be accepted anywhere in the world. They are also likely to be those who will shoulder some of the burden of getting their purchases home and assembling them. The company's website reminds us that "IKEA asks the customer to work as a partner."[4]

Of course, when it comes to furniture, not every consumer is looking for a partner. IKEA is not for everybody. Some bristle at the conformity implied by what one expert observer calls "IKEA's aesthetic 'global functional minimalism.'"[5] One former employee, writing about the company, describes the claustrophobia one can experience in shopping in an IKEA store on a busy day.[6] That said, a sharp dividing line between those giving a service organization high and low marks is an indicator of a well-focused strategy. Internet gripe sites targeted at organizations creating a desired experience for a clearly defined target market while repelling others are sure signs of focus. IKEA is no exception. In fact, its detractors have even created a Facebook group, "Official IKEA Is Hell on Earth."

There is general agreement at IKEA about the clientele for whom IKEA's experience is not meant. The company's management has addressed the question that most marketing people avoid like the plague: to whom won't we sell? As a result, it has achieved *market focus*.

Service Concept: Results and Solutions

IKEA's offerings are meant to provide a unique experience to its potential customers. IKEA does not sell furniture. Nor does it sell home furnishings. According to its website, it sells "affordable solutions for better living" and "a better everyday life for the many people." These are solutions sought by some customers. They constitute IKEA's business definition—its *service concept*. If it sold furniture, it would have to compete with thousands of other furniture stores. Instead, the kinds of merchandise required to deliver a lifestyle have to be designed, manufactured, and brought together in one place so that customers uncertain of their interior design tastes and skills can visualize how things will look in their own homes. If the lifestyle is to be affordable, all of the merchandise has to be designed and manufactured with an eye to low cost. IKEA is in business to prove that taste and better living don't have to be expensive. It has created an operating strategy to back up that claim.

Operating Strategy

With little time for shopping and an as yet unformed sense of design, customers drive—sometimes substantial distances—to get to one of the company's stores, which are often located on inexpensive land or in light industrial parks. There, they are invited to the Main Aisle, a clearly-marked path that ensures that customers miss nothing—starting with living room settings, proceeding through bedrooms, and ultimately ending in the kitchen. The unguided "tour" is designed to strengthen customers' trust in their own design preferences without the presence of a salesperson. "Stories" are provided about each room setting to personalize them for customers. All price tags point leftward and are easily readable. These practices are more than just indicators of founder Kamprad's legacy of management compulsion. Many are designed to reduce selling costs and contribute to lower prices.

In any number of other ways, the company has designed its *operating strategy* to deliver results and experiences at low costs—various forms of leverage that provide an edge over competitors. For example, purposely limiting design styles to four "style groups"—Popular, Modern, Scandinavian, and Traditional—reduces the costs of carrying inventory as well as markdowns on unpopular styles.

Many customers accept responsibility for transportation and assembly of furniture. IKEA can afford to pass on cost savings to them in the form of lower prices. Customers' transport and handling also frees IKEA store personnel from the dickering that results from alleged damages. It helps preserve the company's reputation for fair customer treatment.

Support Systems

An operating strategy directed largely to neophyte homemakers requires *support systems* with unique features. First, IKEA's retail stores need vast spaces for merchandise display. The facilities themselves are designed to provide a veritable seminar in outfitting a home. The Main Aisle we mentioned earlier is cleverly curved to obscure its length and encourage shoppers to explore fully furnished room settings at a leisurely pace (assuming the store isn't packed with shoppers). Displays are sequenced in the way that people often think of to furnish a home—large pieces and furniture settings first, smaller accessories and utensils later.

IKEA's operating strategy requires that customers have access to a large loading dock, devices for transporting merchandise to their vehicles, and ample parking space. Since this sort of real estate comes at a reasonable price if it is some distance from urban centers, the expected experience has to be sufficiently positive for customers to see the long drive as worth it. This is why IKEA seeks to provide a destination experience, one spanning several hours, for them. Customers are encouraged, for example, to take a break for a meal at the store, with specials that are priced lower than even those at the well-known fast-food purveyors. This too influences store layout and design.

The Strategic Service Vision and Competitive Edge

IKEA's high volume of sales for a limited number of styles and items allows it to achieve inventory turnover rates that support the same level of sales as competitors with two to three times as much stock. Although IKEA's management doesn't use the term, it has a highly-effective strategic service vision that does the following:

1. It defines customers that an organization desires to serve *and does not desire to serve*. It delivers market focus.

2. It is based on results or solutions—not products or services— delivered to these customers. It defines the business in terms of results or solutions.

3. It describes an operating strategy that delivers results for customers that they regarded as 3.3 billion euros—IKEA's profit margin—more valuable in 2014 than the costs of achieving them. It provides an edge over the competition by leveraging results over costs while preserving operating focus.

4. It provides support systems and resources needed to achieve the operating strategy. It is defined by the excellence of its facilities and their layout, networks, locations, and technology.

Great service leaders implicitly have to supply answers to a number of questions in putting together and sustaining breakthrough services. They include questions listed in the sidebar.

Questions for Management Raised by Components of the Strategic Service Vision

Target Market

- Who are our targeted customers, described both in terms of economics and demographics as well as how customers think?
- What results are sought by targeted customers?
- How well do we deliver (sell or rent) these results vis-à-vis competitors?
- Who don't we serve?
- How do we set expectations for customers that we can meet or exceed?
- How, if at all, can we train customers?
- With what clarity is our value concept (business definition) communicated to all?

Service Concept

- What business are we in (defined in terms of results, solutions, and value rather than products and services)?
- What results do we and don't we deliver?
- What are the stories we tell as part of the customer experience?
- What assurances do we give that results will be delivered?
- How do we know these results are delivered in the eyes of the customer?

Operating Strategy

- How does the operating strategy leverage results to customers over costs?
- What kind of edge does the operating strategy provide over competition?
- What assurances are there that the edge is sustainable?
- What kinds of people does the operating strategy require? Is this reflected in our selection process?
- What kinds of policies, practices, and organization help leverage results over costs?
- What makes the strategy scalable and sustainable?

Support Systems

- Are facilities, networks, and technologies aligned with the needs of the operating strategy?
- How do such support systems help provide an edge over competitors?
- What is being done to ensure that support systems don't constrain the operating strategy?
- To what degree are support systems replicable by competitors?
- What visible signs of service excellence do support systems provide to customers and others?

Now, think of all the elements of IKEA's strategic service vision, all the things on which it executes well, and how those elements fit together. They defy description on a bumper sticker or in a brief journalistic article. They provide the organization with the various sources of edge over competition that are mapped in figure 2-1.

Figure 2-1 Some Important Elements of IKEA's Strategic Service Vision

Target Market	Service Concept	Operating Strategy	Support Systems
Students	"Affordable solutions for better living"	High labor productivity	Large stores
Younger singles		Substitution of room groupings, "stories"	Store layout designed for systematic shopping
Married "starter" couples with little time, money, or patience to furnish a home	"A better everyday life for the many people"	Informative tags for salespeople	Warehouse attached to store
		Four basic "style groups" = less inventory + lower cost	Suburban/rural location
Willing to contain creativity		Shifting of high-risk transport and assembly to customers	Restaurant
Willing to work as a partner with IKEA for lower prices		Low real estate cost	
		Destination shopping experience	
		Boxed, knocked-down merchandise to fit in a private automobile	

How the Strategic Service Vision Creates Value for Customers

Strategic visions help organizations focus on a few important ideas. However, if those ideas don't translate into value for customers, they are essentially worthless. In the case of IKEA, the translation provides ways of delivering better results and solutions at lower cost for targeted customers—sources of leverage. In doing so, it also provides competitive advantage—or *edge*. As we discussed in chapter 1, the result from the customer's end is the value equation shown in figure 2-2.

The experiences and value that IKEA creates for customers are critical to the long-term success of the organization. But if the same thinking is not applied to employees, such a vision is doomed to fail. It involves thinking about employees in the same terms that the organization thinks about customers. In fact, it regards employees as customers.

Figure 2-2 IKEA's Customer Value Equation

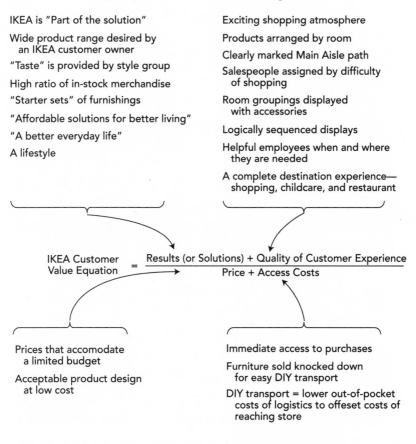

IKEA is "Part of the solution"

Wide product range desired by an IKEA customer owner

"Taste" is provided by style group

High ratio of in-stock merchandise

"Starter sets" of furnishings

"Affordable solutions for better living"

"A better everyday life"

A lifestyle

Exciting shopping atmosphere

Products arranged by room

Clearly marked Main Aisle path

Salespeople assigned by difficulty of shopping

Room groupings displayed with accessories

Logically sequenced displays

Helpful employees when and where they are needed

A complete destination experience— shopping, childcare, and restaurant

$$\text{IKEA Customer Value Equation} = \frac{\text{Results (or Solutions)} + \text{Quality of Customer Experience}}{\text{Price} + \text{Access Costs}}$$

Prices that accomodate a limited budget

Acceptable product design at low cost

Immediate access to purchases

Furniture sold knocked down for easy DIY transport

DIY transport = lower out-of-pocket costs of logistics to offeset costs of reaching store

A STRATEGIC SERVICE VISION FOR EMPLOYEES: THE INTERNAL BRAND

Many service organizations are distinguished from their manufacturing counterparts by the large numbers of people they employ (more than 130,000 at IKEA), who interact with customers as they simultaneously create and deliver services. This absence of a buffer between production and marketing poses significant challenges to those responsible for developing and executing service strategies. Just as customers seek results and solutions, so too do employees. These results and solutions comprise expectations that an employee has for the job. This is one side of what has been termed "the deal."[7]

Prospective employees know who the best employers are. They hear about them from friends, visit websites, and are conscious of favorable or unfavorable publicity. All of this determines the value of what is often called an organization's internal brand. Employers with strong internal brands have to do little recruiting. In a typical year, with little recruiting effort, Southwest Airlines receives more than 200,000 applications for what often turns out to be no more than 5,000 job openings. For the airline's management, the primary task is identifying precisely those who will fit with its operating strategy. In the case of Southwest Airlines, that means identifying prospects who are empathetic to others, Customers and fellow Employees alike, and can work well in teams—because that is the way the organization works.

Organizations that do a good job of focusing on the best talent for themselves accomplish this by enabling prospects to self-select through clear communication of the mission and values of the organization, as well as "how we do things around here." For example, working at IKEA is not for everyone, particularly those seeking to get rich quick. But for those to whom it appeals—often those seeking a structured, cooperative work environment—it is regularly named on lists of best places to work. It has no trouble filling its ranks with those who buy in to the company's mission and reasons to work there, shown in the sidebar.

When an organization fails to deliver on expectations, it can expect reduced employee loyalty, higher turnover, employees who decide to become unionized, or even legal litigation.[8] IKEA has not been exempt from these blemishes, having been charged with practicing mandatory overtime and having faced a vote for unionization in one of its stores. While the company's management appears to

---

**IKEA's "Top 10 reasons to work here
(Hint: Traveling first class isn't one of them.)"**

---

1. We hire the right people ("down to earth, hard workers with a genuine willingness to work together")
2. They're inspired! (Note: 90% of workers know "why" they work at IKEA; 80% are "inspired")
3. Making mistakes is okay—really
4. An up, down and sideways career
5. Sweden today, China tomorrow
6. Egos parked at the door
7. The rewards of a never-ending job
8. Learning by the seat of your pants
9. A parent-friendly environment
10. The original social network

Source: IKEA.com, October 7, 2011

---

have taken corrective action, these are cautionary warnings of the importance of "the deal" and whether or not it is kept.

Notice what IKEA does and does not promise. It promises interesting jobs; an opportunity for personal development and international experience; good, well-selected co-workers with a certain amount of humility; and a large social network, presumably for support. It says nothing about high compensation or perks like reserved parking and an executive dining room. They don't exist. No false expectations are created here.

Organizations that *focus on the right talent* enable prospective employees to determine whether or not they fit and to opt out early in the orientation process. Zappos.com goes one step further by providing an incentive to opt out, offering a trainee $2,000 to quit during the orientation and training process.[9] Zappos' management assumes that it is a test of a candidate's motivation—and it is worth a lot to avoid hiring the wrong employee. As Richard Fairbank, CEO of Capital One, has said, "At most companies, people spend 2% of their time recruiting and 75% managing their recruiting mistakes."[10] The extra effort to market an organization to talented prospects who are enthusiastic about "the way things are done around here" is equivalent to marketing efforts that focus on customers with specific characteristics and preferences.

How well does IKEA do in delivering on its promises, its *service concept* for employees? Several clues help us answer this question. IKEA's *operating strategy,* from the standpoint of its employees, simplifies many of the jobs they perform. For example, the need for selling is minimal. "Story" tags on the merchandise are intended to do much of the selling. This frees employees to spend more of their time in interesting activities like setting up rooms, albeit with rather specific sets of directions.

The warehouse is laid out to provide easy access to merchandise, nearly all of which is boxed and ready to go for easy handling. Equipment is designed for ease of operation and compatibility with the physical facility.

The company's *support systems* are designed to ensure a steady flow of merchandise to store warehouses so that customers rarely experience the disappointment of a stockout. This increases both sales and the incidence of customer satisfaction that is reflected back on co-workers. The successful delivery of results that this facilitates reinforces positive views among co-workers that IKEA is a good place to work.

EMPLOYEE VALUE EQUATION

The employee value equation, as we highlighted in chapter 1, is of particular importance in service delivery.[11] At IKEA, it comprises the elements shown in figure 2-3 and is based on research informed by employee interviews and surveys.

Figure 2-3 IKEA Employee Value Equation

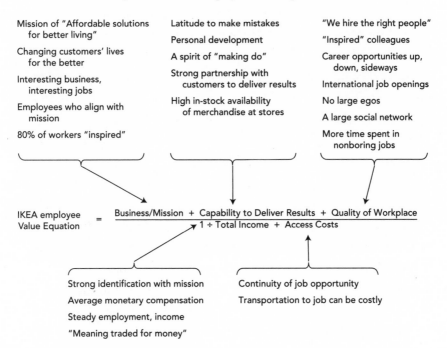

"Business"/Mission and Value

When we first conceived the employee value equation, we overlooked the importance of business and mission. Our research since then has caused us to change our minds. We are now more sensitive to the idea that some business opportunities offer jobs that appear more glamorous or purposeful than others. It helps explain why some young people are attracted to certain industries over others.

Similarly, mission has value for employees. It often influences their choice of a place to work. And it even influences the amount of pay they are willing to sacrifice in order to work there.

Organizations deliver value to employees through much more than the wages they pay. First, they provide a *business* activity (whether for-profit or not-for-profit) to which employees can relate and a mission in which employees can believe. An organization's mission—its *know why*—has the capacity to become an important source of satisfaction, and therefore something of significant value, for employees. That helps explain why outstanding talent is attracted to many not-for-profit organizations such as Médicins Sans Frontières (MSF, Doctors without Borders), a French-based organization devoted to providing health care in disaster-afflicted and war-torn areas of the world. Such altruism conveys a visceral sense of importance of mission that can be worth a great deal to the right person.

Years ago one of us (Schlesinger) researched and reported on the notion that the goal is to create jobs that provide "money and meaning."[12] Many service industries—such as entertainment, airlines, gaming, and education—satisfy employees seeking things like excitement or satisfaction on the job but have relatively low pay scales, especially for managers. Among administrators and educators alike in education, meaning is traded for money. Employees in other industries trade excitement for money. Anyone who has worked with Bill and Melinda Gates Foundation associates knows that they have skills and capabilities for which they are probably underpaid. At the same time, the enthusiasm they have for what they do in eradicating polio and other diseases from the face of the earth is irrepressible.

A mission that inspires also generates value by attracting the best talent in a given field and motivating employees to perform enthusiastically and well. ING Direct found this to be true when it founded a savings bank in North America—not exactly a groundbreaking business concept. But this savings bank was different. Its mission was not just to encourage savings, it was to "bring Americans back to savings" through higher interest rates made possible by lower banking costs, which resulted from, among other things, the elimination of traditional bank branches. In its hiring, ING Direct's management made a conscious effort to distinguish its mission from that of other financial institutions, such as credit card issuers, whose efforts, ING interviewers pointed out, are directed at encouraging customers to spend, not save, their money. Similarly, Google's mission of "organizing and making available the world's information" is a grand promise, much more inspiring to prospective employees than providing search capabilities or selling advertising. It has inspired young, talented, creative Millennials to join the ranks of Googlers. If these organizations are any indication, an organization's mission can be just as important as its business in attracting employees.

Other Elements of the Employee Value Equation

IKEA's business of providing "affordable solutions for better living," is one element of the employee value equation. Other elements include opportunities for personal development, frequent feedback, and ultimately greater latitude to solve problems for valued customers, factors that contribute to the employee's capability to deliver results. Still others are the quality of the workplace, which is determined by such things as the "fairness" of one's manager (often defined as whether the manager hires, recognizes, and fires the right people in a timely way), the quality of the work performed by peers in the workplace, and the degree to which good work gets recognized. Thus, value is enhanced for employees by the degree to which they consider their total income to be reasonable and their *access costs*, influenced by everything from the ease of the commute to the job to the continuity of the job itself, low. All of these elements are reflected to some degree in the employee value equation offered by our example company, IKEA.

THE STRATEGIC SERVICE VISION APPLIED TO MANUFACTURING

We have said that customers buy results and solutions rather than products and services. This has led a number of manufacturers to redefine their businesses from the manufacture of products to the delivery of solutions. CEMEX, one of the world's leading manufacturers of cement and concrete, now delivers solutions—airport runways, highways, and cement that absorbs pollutants in the air. GE Medical Systems, manufacturers of CAT scanners, delivers functional machine time to hospitals by remotely monitoring its machines and sending repair specialists to make repairs to ensure continued functionality. Otis Elevator Company sells the same kind of solution for the elevators that it manufactures and monitors remotely. Rolls-Royce's aircraft engines are sold on the basis of uptime, which requires the manufacturer to build dependable products and make sure that they are maintained in a timely and proper manner. These strategies, as Rogelio Oliva and Robert Kallenberg have pointed out, change "the focus of the value proposition to the end-user from product efficacy—whether the product works—to the product's efficiency and effectiveness within the end-user's process."[13]

Organizations that adopt a solutions-driven manufacturing strategy inevitably place as much emphasis on service as on manufacturing. Manufacturers establish a service organization that may become a separate business, either operated as a cost or profit center. This strategy also encourages manufacturing and service management to coordinate efforts to deliver solutions to customers.

Such a strategy essentially evolves through several stages. The first, primarily transaction oriented, is limited to the installation and occasional repair of a manufactured product. Responsibility for maintenance is the customer's, even though the manufacturer may perform it upon request. This becomes relationship-oriented when responsibility shifts from the customer to the manufacturer for maintenance, repair, and ultimately uptime. Manufacturers that lease their products and sell maintenance contracts essentially assume this kind of responsibility. It creates an alignment in incentives. What's good for the customer is good for the manufacturer and vice versa. In some cases, this kind of relationship may lead to a manufacturer taking over full responsibility for the operation of a facility, utilizing one or more of the products that it makes. Pitney Bowes, a manufacturer of postal processing equipment, offers to take over internal mail processing for large organizations. IBM offers turnkey information technology operating solutions instead of just hardware, software, or services.

According to Oliva and Kallenberg, this kind of transition involves several major challenges to manufacturers. First, it requires a cultural shift from a manufacturing mentality and an engineering orientation to one in which services and the activities they spawn become equally highly valued. As one of their respondents pointed out, "It is difficult for an engineer who has designed a multimillion-dollar piece of equipment to get excited about a contract worth $10,000 for cleaning it."[14] Second, in contrast to pure manufacturing, the strategy often involves the development of a global infrastructure populated with large numbers of service people, often scattered over great distances, requiring a different kind of supervision than in the factory. Third, it may require a large investment with an uncertain payoff some years later.

A manufacturer's migration toward the business of providing solutions inevitably leads to it realizing a greater proportion of its total revenues from services. Nowhere has this change been more dramatic than at IBM, where its Global Solutions Division, centered around providing solutions, often involves the turnkey operation of data centers or the provision of cloud computing capability. By 2011 IBM's systems and technology division (primarily manufactured products) made up only 18.5 percent of the company's total revenue.[15] And, not by accident, the head of Global Solutions, Virginia Rometty, became IBM's first female CEO.

The ascent of services in a manufacturing organization inevitably raises the question of whether the provision of services should be recognized as a separate business with its own leadership and profit targets. Perhaps the biggest influence on the decision is the extent to which services are performed in support of manufactured goods. In that case an organization may have a strong argument for retaining common leadership for the manufacturing and service operations. However, where services become an integral part of a solutions-oriented menu of services and products, as at IBM, a strong case can be made for creating a separate profit center for the solutions business.

DURABILITY OF THE STRATEGIC SERVICE VISION FRAMEWORK

The strategic service vision framework is as valid today as when we first proposed it. As organizations like IKEA and others show, enterprises that continue to apply the vision will contribute to a further blurring of the line between manufacturing and service activities—until they are hardly distinguishable. Organizations will increasingly formulate strategies that concentrate not just on manufacturing things or providing services but instead on achieving value for both customers and employees alike. Assuming an equitable division of bottom-line profits, this in turn will provide exceptional value for investors.

Increasingly, competitors will focus on more-definitive assessments of the results and experiences sought by employees and customers. They will seek to leverage value over cost in developing operating strategies that provide competitive edge. The strategies will require the design of support systems that enhance human capability to achieve operating breakthroughs.

Risks Inherent in Strategic Success

Service leaders effectively implementing these ideas nevertheless face certain risks. They may subject themselves to special risks if they fail to perform up to expectations. For example, both UPS and Target, two of our example organizations from this chapter, were taken to task by the public during the 2013 Christmas season. UPS was castigated for failing to provide adequate capacity for a deluge of deliveries created by online shoppers in the final days of the season. Target's credit card information, on which it relies for much of its big data, was hacked, fueling the distrust of its customers. Both organizations had to take extraordinary steps to restore trust among their customers.

Similarly, elements of service strategies like "affordable solutions" may give companies like IKEA a wide range of choices about what to merchandise. However, they can represent a trap, if, for example, the same merchandising approach is applied to something like food as to furniture. The world was reminded of this when inexpensive meatballs being sold in IKEA's European stores were found to contain horsemeat, apparently without management's knowledge.[16]

Addressing the Risks

Great service leaders have devised a number of ways of addressing the risks of breakthrough service success. They do such things as hire better and better talent that is naturally attracted to the organization, train them well, and raise the already high standards to which their organizations hold themselves. Note that the methods usually do not involve imposing more controls over the way a service is delivered. These leaders recognize that the solution lies in the talent, not the controls. As we will see later, a leader's primary task in such organizations is making sure that pride of accomplishment does not morph into arrogance in dealing with customers and others, and that good results can always be improved upon.

LOOKING AHEAD

Looking ahead, we believe that the design of the best service strategies will reflect elements of the strategic service vision framework, whether by this name or some other. In the future, this philosophy will spread to a larger number of organizations, including those creating packages of products and services designed to deliver results. We expect that it will be applied to an increasing extent to the strategies and management of not-for-profit and government organizations as well.

IKEA, the purveyor of a lifestyle centered around home furnishings, illustrates how elements of a strategic service vision fit together to produce remarkable results. To some, this exposition may sound like an ad for IKEA.[17] Rather, we intend to convey the idea that a strategic service vision has many moving parts and evolves over time. (For example, IKEA's practice of shipping and handling all furniture in knocked-down form was not formalized until 1951, when an employee took a table apart in order to get it into the back of his automobile.) This helps explain why few service organizations stand out in their respective industries. Do organizations like IKEA make mistakes? Of course. Do we agree with everything they do? No. But by means of strategic service vision thinking, whether it goes by that name or not, its managers have been able to bring many elements of strategy into alignment.

Organizations achieve a strategic service vision through an operating strategy that comprises a chain of relationships, which we have termed a *service profit chain*. Is that strategy still applicable more than 20 years after we first presented it? Does it hold promise for future service leaders? These are our next concerns.

CHAPTER 3

Designing Operating Strategies

That Support the Service Vision

What great service leaders *know*:
the best service operating strategies don't require trade-offs.

What great service leaders *do*:
*they foster both/and thinking in designing
winning operating strategies.*

One or two companies in an industry produce off-the-chart performance while changing the rules of the game by which competition occurs around the world. Each of these organizations exhibits a well-thought-out strategic service vision. You know these breakthrough service organizations when you see them, hear what their leaders have to say, and watch them act out their beliefs.[1] While they are not necessarily the largest in their respective industries, they do share a few things in common. For example, organizations producing outstanding performance on two important dimensions of breakthrough service, "best places to work" and "best customer service," show an unusually high, statistically significant overlap. In fact, 20 percent of the organizations found among *Bloomberg Businessweek's* Customer Service Champs from 2009 through 2013

Figure 3-1 Relationships between Best Places to Work, Companies Providing Best Customer Service, and Profitability, U.S., 2009 through 2013

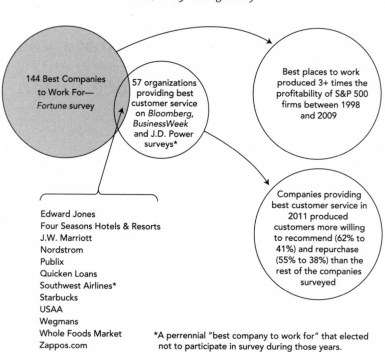

144 Best Companies to Work For—*Fortune* survey

57 organizations providing best customer service on *Bloomberg, BusinessWeek* and J.D. Power surveys*

Best places to work produced 3+ times the profitability of S&P 500 firms between 1998 and 2009

Companies providing best customer service in 2011 produced customers more willing to recommend (62% to 41%) and repurchase (55% to 38%) than the rest of the companies surveyed

Edward Jones
Four Seasons Hotels & Resorts
J.W. Marriott
Nordstrom
Publix
Quicken Loans
Southwest Airlines*
Starbucks
USAA
Wegmans
Whole Foods Market
Zappos.com

*A perrennial "best company to work for" that elected not to participate in survey during those years.

also appeared on *Fortune*'s 100 Best Companies to Work For, after eliminating manufacturers from both lists (figure 3-1).[2]

To understand the significance of this overlap, Michael Burchell and Jennifer Robin analyzed *Fortune*'s 100 Best Companies to Work For in the United States and concluded that companies on the list earned more than three times the market returns of companies in the S&P 500 between the years 1998 and 2009.[3] Another study concluded that organizations that provide the best customer service nurture customers who are 21 percentage points (62 percent to 41 percent) more willing to say they would "definitely recommend" their service provider and 17 percentage points (55 percent to 38 percent) more willing to say they would "definitely repurchase" the service.[4] Putting these findings together, one has to conclude that there is something going on here that should be of interest to anyone managing a service organization.

These organizations have figured out how to create outstanding operating strategies—ones that deliver a great deal of value to employees, customers, and investors alike. By and large, this is the way they have done it: first they create value for employees. That value encourages employees' commitment and ownership, drives employee loyalty, fosters productivity, and enhances value for customers. That value in turn produces similar attitudes and behaviors among customers. It results in customer loyalty—the single greatest contributor to revenue growth and profit. These are organizations managed by *dashboards* comprising deep indicators of success. One such organization is the United Services Automobile Association (USAA).

GREAT SERVICE LEADERS PRACTICE BOTH/AND THINKING

As you drive out of the main gate at the West Point Military Academy in upstate New York, the first building on the right is not a bar, a cleaning establishment, or a barber shop. It's a building housing a United Services Automobile Association (USAA) Financial Center. US Army officers in training get an early exposure to the centrality of USAA in their lives—that is, if they haven't already been exposed to it by a family history of military service. The company dominates in supplying insurance, investments, and other financial services to military personnel and their families (who are eligible to become members), roughly 8 million of them. Its ingenious strategy has frozen out most of the competition for this market; it has more than a 95 percent share of US active duty military officers. USAA is a mutual company that reflects its profits in low rates as well as rebates to its customers. The result? Great service at low cost—in other words, extraordinary value. USAA customers do not have to trade one for the other.[5] This is what we regard as *both/and*—both great service and low cost—results. It is the result of both/and versus either/or management thinking.[6]

USAA's operating strategy starts with hiring. The company hires many of its managers from the ranks of the people it serves: military personnel. As a consequence, management understands the needs and concerns of USAA's clientele. For example, rather than avoiding doing business with servicemen or -women going into battle, USAA may advise them to increase their life insurance. The military experience provides the military attitude—qualities such as devotion to duty, loyalty, and accountability that are important to those going into battle together—that is also important in staffing service jobs. USAA looks for these same qualities in its associates, even though many may not have served in the military. It also does what service leaders are best equipped to do: provide a clear message concerning the organization's shared beliefs, values, and behaviors, as well as training in the skills needed for the job.

USAA trains its associates both for the job and for life. It offers hundreds of courses on a wide range of topics to help personalize what otherwise could be a highly impersonal workplace—one with thousands of associates. One course is even designed to familiarize employees with military basic training, including push-ups, so they can better relate to the company's customers. It sanctions a four-day work week, which further emphasizes the importance of work/life quality for associates. Many members of management use the fifth day for concentration on more complex challenges, which are of increasing importance in today's hectic work environment. All of this helps explain why USAA regularly appears not only in the ranks of best places to work (especially for women) but also at or near the top of lists of companies providing best customer service, as shown in figure 3-1.

USAA's support systems are among the most sophisticated in the industry. For example, years before competitors, the company's frontline service representatives had multiple-screen capability to call up the documentation concerning a member's transactions with the company. Today, such systems provide a high level of transparency, helping to ensure no surprises on a two-way basis among both managers and associates. USAA is cited for its innovative practices in the use of technology.

Support systems also include the careful scripting of many interactions that USAA frontline personnel have with members. For example, when a member calls to inform the company that he's had an automobile accident, a triage process goes into effect, one that also endears the member to USAA. The first question he's asked is, "Is everyone all right?" While the member hears concern for his safety, the question is also designed to trigger triage. Accidents involving medical injury are referred to the most experienced of USAA's personnel, whereas injury-free accidents can be handled quickly by less experienced service personnel. This saves both time and money, while enhancing member satisfaction. Service breakthrough organizations like USAA don't settle for strategic results such as low cost or differentiation through outstanding service. They pursue practices that produce both/and results that are impossible for competitors with either/or strategies to top.

The things that drive both/and performance—what we have come to think of as *deep indicators*—are of prime importance. While some of the earliest work around deep indicators established links between employee and customer satisfaction and loyalty,[7] other studies have linked customer loyalty to profitability.[8] Although these studies merely associated one phenomenon with another, a more comprehensive study measured cause and effect. It indicated that financial performance was driven in at least one sample of marketing service organizations by quality and client focus, which in turn was a function of employee satisfaction and high standards.[9]

THE SERVICE PROFIT CHAIN
AND THE SEARCH FOR DEEP INDICATORS

In our search for deep indicators, based primarily on field observations and data analysis, we have found that measures of employee satisfaction, loyalty, engagement, and ownership are important predictors of customer loyalty, customer ownership, profit, and growth.[10] Years ago, we termed this the *service profit chain*—a set of relationships describing the operational ways in which an organization converts a strategic service vision (chapter 2) into profit and growth. As shown in figure 3-2, our early research led to the conclusion that the two concepts complement each other in important ways.

Think of the service profit chain as an effort to identify the deep indicators making up the management dashboard that helps explain and predict the ability of some organizations to achieve both/and results in service. The term *deep indicator* is used here to refer to the *what* that drives something else. Like Toyota's "six why's" of quality improvement, a deep indicator is what we find when we ask "what" several times. For example, if customer loyalty is one of the most important drivers of profit, what drives customer loyalty? What, in turn, drives that? And so on.

Since Version 1.0 of the service profit chain, our work, combined with that of others, has led us to a more complex view of the both/and management dashboard in the service profit chain (figure 3-3).[11] The strength of relationships shown there will vary from organization to organization and situation to situation. But we are convinced that the deep indicators of service success for nearly all services are shown there.

Figure 3-2 The Service Profit Chain, Version 1.0

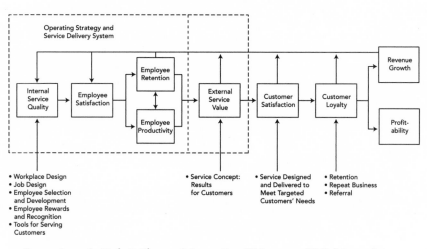

Source: James L. Heskett, Thomas O. Jones, Gary W. Loveman, W. Earl Sasser Jr., Leonard A. Schlesinger, "Putting the Service-Profit Chain to Work," *Harvard Business Review*, March–April 1994, pp. 164–174, at p. 166.

Factors leading to both/and results in service primarily progress from left to right in figure 3-3, with many interactions along the way, beginning with management practices that influence the quality of the work environment. This in turn leads to employee attitudes and behaviors that help determine the value delivered to customers, customer attitudes and behaviors, and finally financial measures. At numerous points elements interact directly to reinforce one another. For example, profit and growth both result from and confirm the rightness of the culture and other elements of the operating strategy. In an effort to provide explanations, scholars have examined relationships at various points in the chain, slowly connecting their findings in ways that help us dig deeper and deeper into the chain. But profit and growth merely describe what happened—not *how* it happened. We have a practical objective: to help managers in their efforts to construct management dashboards that explain and predict, not just describe.

Figure 3-3 The Service Profit Chain, Version 2.0:
Factors Leading to Both/And Service Results

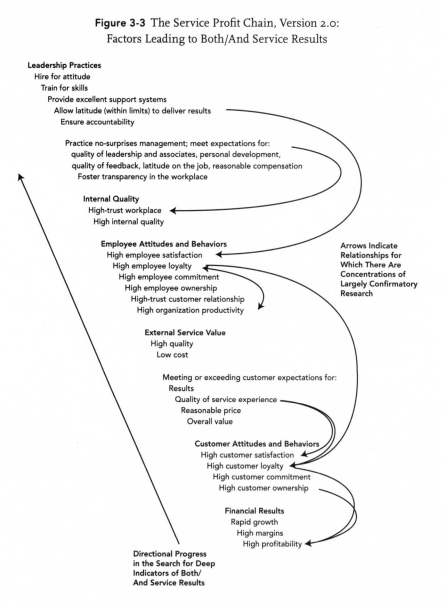

Leadership Practices
Hire for attitude
Train for skills
Provide excellent support systems
Allow latitude (within limits) to deliver results
Ensure accountability

Practice no-surprises management; meet expectations for:
quality of leadership and associates, personal development,
quality of feedback, latitude on the job, reasonable compensation
Foster transparency in the workplace

Internal Quality
High-trust workplace
High internal quality

Employee Attitudes and Behaviors
High employee satisfaction
High employee loyalty
High employee commitment
High employee ownership
High-trust customer relationship
High organization productivity

Arrows Indicate
Relationships for
Which There Are
Concentrations of
Largely Confirmatory
Research

External Service Value
High quality
Low cost

Meeting or exceeding customer expectations for:
Results
Quality of service experience
Reasonable price
Overall value

Customer Attitudes and Behaviors
High customer satisfaction
High customer loyalty
High customer commitment
High customer ownership

Financial Results
Rapid growth
High margins
High profitability

**Directional Progress
in the Search for Deep
Indicators of Both/
And Service Results**

THE PATH TO BOTH/AND SERVICE SUCCESS

Just how the service profit chain is being pieced together through research tells us a great deal about the potential impact on service management in the future. Stay with us here as we peel back the layers of this onion, starting with the outermost layer. The next several pages may be among the most important of the book.

In our field studies, customer loyalty and engagement are more strongly correlated with profit than is any other factor. If you accept this, you will be curious about the factors influencing customer loyalty, engagement, and ownership.

Customer and Employee Engagement and Loyalty: The Mirror Effect

If our beliefs about the service profit chain prove to be correct, customer engagement should be reflected in scores for employee engagement. The same should be true for loyalty measures. We call this the *mirror effect*. Our proprietary efforts for various clients suggest that the mirror effect is a strong presence in a wide range of service endeavors. We are convinced that it can be applied especially well to operating entities within the same organization as part of efforts to spread best practice to units with less success in engaging customers and lower profitability. Other studies confirm similar findings.[12]

Some have raised questions about the validity of the mirror effect. However, the questions are based on research that suffers from such things as inadequate sample size and the combination of data from facilities of varying size.[13] In addition, collecting comparable data from employees and customers has been difficult. The studies often compare employee satisfaction scores with what employees say about the quality of their relationships with customers.[14] As a result, they introduce a strong employee bias into their findings.

Employee Engagement and Loyalty

The service profit chain is based on the hypotheses that employee engagement (i.e., agreement with statements such as "I like my job" or "I would recommend my organization to a friend as a place to work") is directly related to loyalty, and that both are directly related to productivity and profitability. A growing body of research supports these hypotheses.[15]

The research shows that highly engaged employees are more loyal than less engaged employees. A Corporate Leadership Council study found that highly engaged employees say they are half as likely to leave as an average employee in the same organization.[16] Service Management Group regularly measures the relationship of engagement to an employee's intent to leave the job. Its most recent edition of the study concludes that employees with high engagement scores are 2.5 times more likely to remain on the job for the next six months than their less engaged counterparts.[17] Several such studies report similar findings.

These numbers alone help explain the difference between breakthrough and average performance in services. But when differences in productivity are added in, employee performance becomes pivotal in explaining success in the service profit chain.

Employee Productivity

Employee engagement levels are positively related to productivity. Because productivity reduces costs, it is an important factor influencing value delivered to customers. A study of Danish manufacturing firms concluded that high labor turnover negatively affects productivity.[18] The Corporate Leadership Council study cited above estimates that employees with high engagement scores are perceived as performing 20 percentage points better than those with low scores.[19] Perhaps most striking of all is a finding by Service Management Group that employees with high engagement scores were 21 percent more productive than those with the lowest engagement scores.[20] If ever there was an argument for hiring carefully, training well, and building engagement in a workforce, this is it.

What drives employee loyalty, engagement, and productivity? Internal service (workplace) quality.

Internal Service (Workplace) Quality

Research has shown that worker satisfaction with workplace quality has a significant impact on engagement (often measured by willingness to recommend the organization to prospective employees). For example, data compiled by Service Management Group from many organizations and thousands of frontline workers in retail services regularly shows that employees who are "very satisfied" are 2.7 times as likely to recommend their organization as a place to work as those who are merely "satisfied" and more than 9 times as likely to recommend their organization compared to those who are "neutral" when asked if they are satisfied with their job.[21]

An inspiring mission and set of shared values, combined with a shared belief in behaviors consistent with those values, are at the core of an organization's culture. When backed up with measures of behavior and, when necessary, corrective action, an organization's culture can be a powerful competitive force. It contributes to workplace quality along with the organization of work, incentives to perform it well, and the quality of the people hired to do it.

An in-depth study conducted by one of us (Heskett) illustrates the importance of workplace quality, which is generally equated to an organization's culture.[22] The objective of the study was to determine a method for calculating the economic value of an effective culture. Using a combination of internal data collected from several offices of a global marketing services company, combined with independent estimates for pieces of data not available in the company, Heskett developed a process for estimating the impact of culture on operating profit. The process employed measures of the kind shown in figure 3-3 along with assumptions drawn from service profit chain research.

Two findings from the study stand out. First, the study found that the internal quality of the workplace was responsible for nearly half of the difference in operating profit between pairs of offices operating in the same business. A high number might have been expected in a professional service organization in which most of its employees occupy frontline customer-facing jobs (as opposed to a "manufactured" service with little interaction between employees and customers). But a number this high? This should be enough to raise the curiosity of any manager.

The study sought an explanation for these striking results. Fortunately, all offices conducted the same employee engagement survey during the time of the research. Comparisons of survey data with operating data for a sample of offices showed that affirmative responses to the statement "In my office, management is trusted" were positively associated with high office performance.

Predictably, organizations with high levels of internal trust have a competitive advantage. To the extent that they combine trust with delegation of authority and accountability, they operate faster, less expensively, and more effectively than competitors. The result begs for consideration of how trust is developed.

Trust and Its Determinants

The study of the impact of culture on operating performance cited above suggests several possible factors that might contribute to high levels of trust that accompany breakthrough service performance.[23] These include transparency, delegation, and accountability for acting according to the commonly understood and shared values and behaviors of the organization. Also important is the practice of setting and meeting employee expectations in ways that eliminate surprises or unexpected behaviors or actions—in a sense, no-surprises management from the top down rather than bottom up in the organization.

Knowing and Meeting Employee Expectations

Managers who set out to meet expectations have to know what those expectations are. That means they have to be in close touch with associates, a behavior that itself contributes to trust.

Based on research in which Schlesinger has been involved, we have a good idea of what employees expect and how those expectations are shaped. The most frequently expressed expectations concern the quality of leadership and peers on the job, opportunities for personal development, the frequency and quality of feedback, latitude to deliver results, and reasonable compensation. The likelihood that expectations will be met is enhanced by a philosophy of hiring for attitude and training for skills, providing outstanding support systems, allowing enough latitude to deliver results to customers, and holding everyone accountable for the use of that latitude. These practices compose the very core of what it takes to create an effective workplace from which everything else, especially growth and profit, flow. They contribute significantly to competitive advantage, even in association with an inferior competitive strategy and position.

Trust as a Deep Indicator of Competitive Advantage at USAA

At USAA trust is at the core of its competitive advantage. It was an important element in the agreement among 25 military officers in 1922 to insure one another's automobiles, the agreement on which USAA was founded. USAA's current leaders, from CEO Josue Robles Jr. on down, operate with a distinct code of conduct derived from the organization (the military) from which most of them were hired. In the military they were trained to carry out a mission dependably, to meet expectations of those depending on them. At USAA, they have the mission to do the right thing for employees and members (customers).

Further, because USAA's members are selected from the same military culture, they are trusted by management. This trust saves time, eliminates costly verification, and reduces losses from default or fraud. It enables the organization to concentrate on the well-being of its members (who also happen to be "shareholders" in an insurance company with a mutual form of organization). For example, a USAA policyholder involved in an automobile accident can be advised to get her automobile fixed and send USAA the bill; there is no need for multiple estimates and documentation. Other insurance companies serving a diverse clientele don't have that luxury. If they trust, they have to verify first. At USAA, it may not work every time. But the instances of those taking advantage of the organization's trust are few.

WHAT FIELD-BASED STUDIES TELL US

Several studies of service profit chain phenomena shed additional light on findings discussed above.

Multilevel Linkages in the Chain

Studies link several elements of the service profit chain. One study recently performed at L Brands in its Victoria's Secret lingerie and beauty specialty retail chain found links between the quality of the customer experience and customer conversion (the proportion of customers entering the store who buy something), the likelihood to recommend the Victoria's Secret store to friends, and future sales.[24] The quality of customers' experiences reflected those of associates (employees) in the same store. Associates' experiences, particularly with their onboarding (hiring) process, appeared to have an influence on retention rates, which further contributed to the quality of customers' experiences.

Time Lags in Service Profit Chain Relationships

The L Brands study looked for a correlation between customer engagement (likelihood to recommend) and sales. When same-month data was used for both, no correlation was found. When customer engagement scores were related to the next months' sales, a strong correlation was found. One possible explanation for this is the frequency with which the typical Victoria's Secret customer visits the stores.[25]

One of the first efforts to lag results in service profit chain relationships was reported some years ago. It concluded that a 5 percentage point increase in employee satisfaction at retailer Sears led to a 1.3 percentage point increase in customer satisfaction and a 0.5 percent increase in sales. However, the relationship was not clear until increases in sales were lagged by nine months after increases in employee satisfaction scores.[26]

The findings of time lags make sense. The effects of increases in employee satisfaction, engagement, loyalty, and ownership behaviors can't be observed immediately. The lag in observable effects will vary from business to business, depending on such things as the "rhythm" of the business (seasonality or natural fluctuations), the nature of the management intervention to improve loyalty, levels of loyalty among employees and customers at the time of the intervention, and the amount of recent hiring or turnover among employees. Failure to lag service profit chain data has proved to be a shortcoming of work by researchers. It has also led to unrealistic expectations among practitioners, many of whom expect immediate results from their decisions.

From Correlation to Cause and Effect in the Pursuit of Deep Indicators

Nearly all of the research conducted to date on service profit chain relationships measures correlations, not cause and effect, between elements of the chain. The most extensive study of cause and effect in service profit chain relationships to date supports the nature of the relationships diagrammed in figure 3-3. In it, David Maister analyzed data provided by more than 5,000 employees of 139 offices of 29 marketing service firms. He found that the chain of effects leading to profit and growth does indeed begin with a culture of "enthusiasm, commitment, and respect" that infuses the coaching of employees.[27] He concluded that financial performance results from a combination of quality of work for clients and client focus (as judged by employees, not clients). This in turn was found to result from employee satisfaction levels, influenced by such things as empowerment, coaching, high standards, long-term orientation of the organization, training and development, enthusiasm, commitment, and respect for others, as well as fair compensation.

Studies of this kind inform managers about how strategic decisions and policies, when well-executed, affect service outcomes and ultimately financial performance. They influence the way services are designed and managed.

THE SPREAD OF SERVICE PROFIT CHAIN THINKING

Recent indicators suggest that service profit chain thinking is gaining acceptance among practitioners. Advertising campaigns are beginning to trumpet rankings on surveys of customer service or best places to work. One firm that develops software for "human capital management" (Ultimate Software) advertises itself as being on *Fortune*'s list of 100 Best Companies to Work For while promoting its latest software product for predicting the likelihood that an employee is likely to defect, terminating his employment.[28] A news report singles out a private-equity investment management company, Brentwood Associates, for its practice of investing in companies with "a fiercely loyal customer base."[29] These are real businesses applying service profit chain thinking to money-making pursuits.

Customers are now commonly asked the likelihood that they would repurchase a product or service or recommend their service provider to a friend. These are questions resulting from the spread of measurement practices using some form of a so-called Net Promoter Score—a score that indicates the likelihood that a customer would recommend particular services to others. The concept is a direct reflection of a belief in service profit chain relationships.[30] Service profit chain elements regularly appear in "balanced scorecards" (see chapter 4) utilized by a growing number of organizations to track their performance.[31]

One recent study of management practice found that among a sample of managers in 92 firms, 81.8 percent were aware of a positive relationship between customer loyalty and financial performance in their firms. Further, roughly one-third measured the relationship between employee and customer satisfaction (the mirror effect). All who were aware of the outcome of the measurement effort "reported the relationship . . . to be strong."[32]

Other anecdotal evidence also shows that many organizations are employing service profit chain thinking, whether they call it that or not. A comment by Ed Wise, chairman and CEO of the marketing services firm CDM Group, reflects this:

> It has been a long time since I actually read about the service profit chain, and I can't truthfully say that we have ever really used those three words widely within the company. . . . For me, the great insight from . . . the [service profit chain] was that there is a right way, a kind of system, for thinking about managing an agency. I was struck by seeing the proof that people were the key lever to growing an organization and making it excellent. . . . In short, service profit thinking will continue to spread because it works.[33]

ROADBLOCKS TO SERVICE PROFIT CHAIN IMPLEMENTATION

Even with the growing body of evidence that service profit chain concepts work in practice, many organizations still seek other means of achieving competitive advantage. We have to ask the question: why hasn't this thinking been implemented more extensively?

It's Not Simple

Tom Davenport has pointed out some of the complexity in the concept of service profit chains that inhibits its implementation:

1. The concept requires sustained effort to implement successfully.
2. Implementation has to be cross-functional.
3. CEOs have to be engaged in the process.
4. This is a way of life, not an individual program.[34]

One test of the relevance of a concept is that people begin to take it for granted. They express amazement that something so simple as "employee loyalty, engagement, and ownership drive customer loyalty, engagement, and ownership and ultimately growth and profitability" could command attention. The answer, of course, is that it wasn't always thought to be that simple. For years, the concept went unrecognized. Now that it is taken for granted by so many, it becomes the norm against which other strategies are judged.

It Requires the Right Data

In the study of the effect of culture on operating performance, cited earlier, Heskett confronted the absence of relevant data available to managers. Of the 35 key measures required to quantify the impact of culture on performance, only about one-third were readily available. Another one-third were obtainable with more effort than any manager would be willing to exert on a routine basis. And the final one-third simply did not exist in the organization. In terms of the measures shown in figure 3-3, the access of managers to data declines significantly as one moves from the lower right (profit, growth, and other financial measures) to the upper left (employee expectations and the degree to which they are met). Surprisingly, in our work we have found little effort on the part of managers to measure whether or not their employees trust them. Yet that may be one of the most important deep indicators they could be tracking!

We find it ironic that in an era of so-called big data, so little of the data relevant to the management of service profit chain relationships is available to managers on a regular basis. The growth of interest in a form of big data being called "people analytics" may foster attention to closing this gap.

It's Contingent on Employee and Customer Loyalty

Most service operating strategies reflect the belief that customer loyalty is the primary determinant of growth and profitability. A decline in the level of loyalty is a cause for grave concern. That's why the research of two marketing scholars, Itamar Simonson and Emanuel Rosen, is worth noting as we look to the future.[35] Based on their work, they have concluded, contrary to popular belief among their marketing colleagues, that the increasing capability of Internet search devices, combined with the reviews and recommendations of other users, will enable customers to cope effectively with the increasing amount of information, products, and prices they confront on a daily basis. As a result, they will know more about their options for everything from services to employment opportunities than ever before. They will place trust in reviewers whom they do not know. Their inclination to try new products and services and pursue new job opportunities will increase. The power of brands will decline. And of greatest interest to us: customer and employee loyalty, as well as the lifetime value of customer relationships, will decline. This is a lot to comprehend and contemplate.

Internet search, consumer ratings, and new apps clearly put more information and power in the hands of customers. What effect this will have on beliefs and practices based on the service profit chain is less clear. In part it depends on whether one believes the impact on the consumption of services will equal that for product purchase decisions. For example, sites such as Angie's List focus on recommendations of those who have experienced all kinds of services. Many shoppers for services use these recommendations in their purchase decisions. They do so particularly for the kinds of services that are not consumed regularly, such as furnace repair. Consumers who are disenchanted with their current service provider may also use such recommendations.

The development of Internet search and referral capability underlines the importance of a zero-defection mentality among managers, especially in services. To the extent that the Internet enables customers to recommend their service providers, a sign of ownership, we believe it will actually strengthen ties between breakthrough service providers and their best customers. While we may see a decline in loyalty among "passive" consumers (who tend to be less loyal to begin with; more about them in chapter 7) served by undistinguished service providers, the effect is not inevitable for all providers and their relationships with customers.

THE SERVICE PROFIT CHAIN AS A WAY OF LIFE

Think of the service profit chain as one set of deep indicators—one kind of balanced scorecard by which an organization's operating strategy can be tracked and controlled.

Service profit chain thinking has spread in recent years. It is characterized by the fact that a growing number of firms advertise high customer service rankings or citations as great places to work. Measures of links in the chain, such as relatively wide application of the Net Promoter Score to assess customer and employee engagement, have improved. Development has been encouraged as well by the adoption of a balanced scorecard of financial and nonfinancial measures (especially those tracking customer loyalty and employee retention) in a growing number of organizations.

This trend is somewhat remarkable in that the service profit chain comprises a demanding set of relationships and objectives. It requires significant organizational effort to implement the concept successfully. Much of the implementation is cross-functional in nature. In a sense, the service profit chain is a way of life, not simply another management program. For these reasons, CEO engagement and leadership are critical to any effort to introduce service profit chain thinking and action to an organization.

The goal of most service profit chain–based actions is to leverage value for employees and customers alike over costs in order to achieve a high return on investment for the service provider. It is a way that an organization attains an edge on competition. Ways that organizations have sought to achieve such edge include customer engagement (at organizations such as Build-a-Bear Workshop and Eleven Madison Park), service guarantees (Hampton Inn), innovative ways of organizing the work of frontline service employees (Caesar's Entertainment and Ritz-Carlton), team-based organization (Taco Bell), an effective organization culture (Whole Foods Market, Southwest Airlines, Zappos.com, and Disney), and resource sharing (Airbnb, Uber, and Instacart). That's what much of the rest of this book is about.

CHAPTER 4

Creating and Capitalizing

on Internal Quality—

"A Great Place to Work"

What great service leaders _know:_
great service starts with the frontline employee.

What great service leaders _do:_
they hire for attitude, train for skills.

It's fashionable for CEOs to proclaim that, in their organizations, "people are our most important asset." In the majority of service organizations, that is literally true. For these firms, people represent by far the largest cost—as well as the greatest opportunity—for differentiation. Employees are the heart, figuratively and literally, of the service profit chain. British historian Theodore Zeldin—who studies the history of work—commented to a reporter that, in the reporter's words, "the world of work must be revolutionized to put people—rather than things—at the centre of all endeavours." Zeldin continued: "I remember talking to some CEOs in London. One of them said, 'We can no longer select people, they select us.' If we want the best people and we want to attract them, we have to say: 'What do you want in your job?'"[1]

People are motivated by the quality of their jobs and the organizational cultures in which they work. Organizations are known among recruiters, current and prospective employees, and the general public by their "employer brands"—the internal quality of their workplaces. Mark Cuban, owner of the National Basketball Association (NBA) Dallas Mavericks provides an example:

> When I bought the Dallas Mavericks in 2000, they were coming off one of the worst stretches in NBA history. . . . One of the first steps we took was to invest in the product. Sure, that means paying more for player talent than most other teams. But we made our investments count in many other ways too. We spared no expense on player facilities, even in the visiting locker room. Players notice these things. Every time another team rolls into town, every player can see what we've built, talk to our guys, and file that knowledge away for the future. To refine players' skills, we also hired the biggest coaching staff in the league. That way, when a big man needs extra work in the post or a point guard needs to work on his ball handling, we've got specialized instructors who can take them aside and help develop their skills.[2]

Cuban was selling his organization to anyone who might be a "buyer"—potential players, employees, fans, and sponsors. It took 11 years, but the strategy apparently worked. Relatively modest expenditures to enhance the quality of the Mavericks' workplace probably paid dividends in attracting better talent at a more affordable price. It enhanced the quality of entertainment provided to the fans. It raised the esteem in which the organization was held in the community. And in 2011 it paid off in an NBA championship.

Whether the organization is a professional basketball team or a coffee shop, the internal quality of the workplace determines whether an organization is a great place to work. Great places to work tend to be favored organizations with which to do business, leading to profit, growth, or whatever measure of success is appropriate. This is particularly true for a service organization, in which a relatively large proportion of the employees are customer-facing.

How do outstanding employers do it? Knowing that great service starts with frontline employees, great service leaders hire for attitude, train for skills, and make theirs an environment conducive to both. There are one or two organizations in every service industry—even those with the most mercenary reputations, such as financial services—that point the way.

THE VALUE OF WORKPLACE QUALITY AT THE VANGUARD GROUP

Repeatedly, the management of the Vanguard Group of investment funds reminds its audiences that at Vanguard "the investor comes first." Of course, what financial services firm wouldn't do that? But at Vanguard, the claim has teeth. The Vanguard Group's strategy was built by founder John Bogle in 1974 on basic foundation blocks: (1) investment products featuring no-load (no sales charge) mutual funds composed of an index of a group of securities requiring little costly investment management (which has proved to deliver inferior net returns to investors more often than not), (2) efforts on every front to minimize costs that eat into long-term mutual fund returns, and (3) policies that discourage short-term trading and encourage long-term investments by loyal customers.

If the investor comes first, however, where does that leave employees, especially in an organization with a penchant for cutting costs?

Workplace Quality Yields the Right Employees

Vanguard puts the investor first by addressing the well-being of "crew members"—the term used instead of "employees" in a culture based on the values of Lord Horatio Nelson of the HMS *Vanguard* and British nautical fame. In addition to a comfortable, functional working environment in a suburb of Philadelphia, it also requires a set of values, policies, and practices of crew members. In particular, Bogle cites trust as a building block for the organization, as well as the need for leaders "at times of decisions" to "make contact with foundational convictions and with a sense of calling which comes from going deep within oneself."[3]

As anywhere, workplace quality starts with hiring. Vanguard looks for new crew members who have a sensitivity to customer needs but also who lean to the careful and conservative side in making investment decisions, and understand and sympathize with the need for frugality. Employee buy-in to the objectives of the organization is important. The central theme at Vanguard is, according to Bogle, stewardship. From the beginning, he set out a "solid system of human and ethical values" that include "integrity, discipline, honesty, quality, ambition, loyalty, competition, creativity, innovation, cooperation, continuity, even a sense of humor—in all, the *character* of our company."[4]

The work environment at Vanguard has fostered a high degree of loyalty among employees, which is of critical importance in an organization with a strategy focused on investor loyalty.

Careful Selection of Employees and Customers Pays Off: The Case of Mabel Yu

The careful selection of crew members has paid off handsomely at Vanguard. This was brought to our attention by an episode told and retold after the Great Recession of 2008.[5]

The story involves a recently hired investment analyst, Mabel Yu, who was assigned to examine the most credit-worthy (AAA-rated) derivative securities backed by mortgages and other debt that were being assembled by the most highly regarded investment bankers for resale to the public, pension funds, and mutual funds like Vanguard. Yu, a product of the careful Vanguard hiring process, could not assess the quality of the assets behind these derivatives and therefore couldn't understand what was being offered. As a result, she began recommending against derivatives as investments, and suffered the condescension and ridicule of her counterparts on Wall Street, many of whom couldn't adequately explain the nature of the securities either. Her management at Vanguard, who were hired by the same careful process, stood behind her. As a result, they passed up some hot issues and in the process endured returns lower than competing funds that were buying the offerings. That happened only until the US economy and the assets underlying many of these securities blew up in 2008, leaving Vanguard's customers with losses much smaller than those for many of its competitors. Vanguard, both because its investors own it (through a mutual form of ownership) and because of its conservative investment practices, required no bailout. Of greater importance for crew members, Vanguard didn't lay anyone off during one of the worst economic downturns in the past 80 years.

The overall result for investors over a longer period has been good as well. Vanguard's index funds, designed to produce investment results that are only an average for a bundle of securities, nevertheless often rank high among their peers on net returns to investors because of the low costs charged against individual account balances. Of perhaps greater interest for us, however, are clients' perspectives on Vanguard's services. Even though the typical Vanguard client requires little direct contact with the company, Vanguard regularly leads the mutual fund industry in investors' ratings of its services. The ratings are given particular validity by the fact that fully one-third of Vanguard's investors also have funds at its nearest competitor and can compare services directly.

As we can see from the Vanguard example, great employers have a clear and often inspiring mission. Even more important, they have a culture—a set of values, behaviors, measures, and actions—that is designed to ensure that the mission and its supporting strategy are both achievable and achieved. Most importantly, great places to work are often high-trust environments; high levels of trust enable an organization to do things faster, with greater confidence, and more profitably. Vanguard's management trusted Mabel Yu's judgment. Mabel Yu was secure enough in her job to make difficult decisions on her own.

ALIGN MISSION, CULTURE, AND EXPECTATIONS

The process of fostering great places to work, characterized by high-trust environments, starts by aligning the organization's mission and culture with the expectations of prospective employees. It helps if the organization has an impeccable global reputation. But global reputations don't just happen. They are the result of a clear mission, a performance-based culture, and a well-thought-out process for shaping and addressing manager and employee expectations.

Take the Mayo Clinic, one of the world's best-known medical institutions, for example. The Mayo Clinic is where patients from all over the world go for the treatment of complex ailments. Much of its fame is spread by former patients. Mayo patients talk. According to Mayo's estimates, on average each former patient tells 40 other people of his or her experience. Each one is estimated to generate about five new patients. One survey found that 85 percent of the Clinic's patients recommend that someone go there. That's real "ownership" behavior.[6]

For medical practitioners and staff, employment at the Mayo Clinic is prestigious. Its mission and "business" are the topics of conversation at parties. A job there wins admiration from others and is a source of self-satisfaction for associates. Still, that doesn't mean that recruiting new hires at the Mayo Clinic is easy. Like all organizations with a strong culture, the Mayo Clinic is not for every professional. It appeals to the team player, not the entrepreneur or aspiring star and millionaire. In a sense, everyone is a star at Mayo, but there, stars have to put their egos aside while working with others as a team.

Mayo is well known among medical practitioners, who either are enthusiastic about working there—or avoid even the idea of it. Doctors contemplating careers there know that they have to be prepared to show, by their attitude and the quality of their diagnoses and treatments, that they put the patient first, schedule their work around the patient rather than vice versa, and stand ready to share administrative duties from time to time. The clinic's research is conducted with a similar philosophy of interdisciplinary cooperation. While the organization may not reward its researchers on a star system, it has nevertheless produced remarkable research results, including the Nobel Prize for the development of cortisone, something that may have been impossible without the contributions of a number of professionals.

The Mayo Clinic manages the fit between mission, culture (values and behaviors), and employee needs carefully. Organizations seeking to capitalize on an effective culture start by finding out what the "right" prospective employees want, then come up with a human resource strategy that meets those needs, involve existing employees in the process of making the deal (establishing mutual expectations), and live up to the expectations created.

Sensitize Managers to What Employees Want: Internal Service Quality

If trust has significant bottom-line value and results from expectations that are met, we need to know the expectations that employees have for a job. We know from the research of others that customers' satisfaction depends on whether their expectations are met or exceeded.[7] The same goes for employees.[8] Great service leaders not only understand the expectations that form the basis for employee satisfaction and engagement but use that knowledge to inform management behaviors. Such an understanding can also provide the basis for altering expectations, finding a good fit between what employees want and what management can deliver.

What Employees Want. Service Management Group (SMG) periodically analyzes data on the service profit chain from the more than 20 million surveys it collects annually from employees and customers of more than 100 clients in the retail, restaurant, and service industries—a veritable treasure trove of information. Its analyses have consistently identified several aspects of management that are strongly correlated with employee engagement and loyalty, as well as outcomes such as employee satisfaction, customer loyalty, and sales.

The study by Service Management Group found that employees credit three management behaviors with having the greatest impact on their satisfaction, engagement, and loyalty:[9] (1) my supervisor is involved in my development, (2) my supervisor cares about me, and (3) my work is appreciated, in that order. Next is the amount of training received on the job, followed by how well the employee's team works together.[10] This study also found that management skills and behaviors are much more important in influencing employee satisfaction than policies and procedures.

A number of other studies have suggested other things that employees look for on a job:

1. *A boss who's fair.* Employees apparently judge fairness in terms of whether or not a manager hires, recognizes, and fires the right people. This suggests that every personnel decision made by a manager is judged by a jury of those who report to her.

Where such personnel decisions are left to self-managed teams, they serve as judge and jury.

2. *Opportunities for personal development.* Employees are interested in self-betterment. They want both access to job training and paths to positions with greater responsibility.

3. *Frequent and relevant feedback.* Employees increasingly prefer this type of feedback as opposed to the traditional annual review. This preference has a lot to do with the mentality of Millennials—those who have reached employment age after the year 2000—who exhibit a strong interest in personal development as opposed to immediate monetary gain. They are more confident than their predecessors that they'll be paid adequately throughout their working lives.

4. *Capable colleagues on the job.* Winners like to work with winners, but they don't like to work with losers. In fact, if managers are not sufficiently adroit at disengaging poor performers from the organization, winners will leave.

5. *Latitude (within limits) to deliver results to valued customers.* Latitude is of particular importance in service delivery, where unpredictable events requiring judgment and fast response are the order of the day. Employees need to know just how much latitude they have; it can be described in terms of the limits within which they appear to be comfortable in their jobs. A clear exposition of both latitude and limits is important.

6. *Reasonable compensation.* Employees exercise good judgment about what is reasonable. While an organization can't stray far from what is perceived as reasonable, employees' expectations regarding compensation are often surprisingly modest.[11]

One of the most extensive studies of the subject found that of the items on the list, just three caused nearly two-thirds of variation in employee satisfaction levels: (1) latitude (within limits) to deliver results to valued customers, (2) the authority given to employees to serve customers, and (3) the ability, gained in part through knowledge and skills gained on the job, to deliver results to customers.[12]

Why It Matters. If you recall, the Service Management Group study cited earlier found that as employee turnover increases, customer-satisfaction levels decline. Stores with the highest employee turnover are found to have the lowest overall customer-satisfaction scores. A significant relationship exists between the proportion of employees remaining on the job 12 months or more (remember, these are retail service jobs) and customer loyalty. More importantly, customer loyalty is significantly related (statistically) to 12-month comparative (year-to-year) sales increases.[13]

Shape and Meet Expectations: The Job Preview

For managers, understanding what employees want provides a basis for setting expectations for service jobs. Buckingham and Coffman have concluded that great managers make few promises to their employees but keep the ones they do make.[14] This kind of *no-surprises management* is the basis for the trust that makes execution easier.[15] It reduces management time and effort required in the implementation of changes in policies and practices.

Prospective employees form expectations about an organization from a variety of sources, including the organization's reputation, the actions of its leaders, the way its employees speak about it, its advertising and public relations, and of course the quality and value of its products and services. These sources of information are largely impossible to control. Given the so-called transparency afforded by new technologies, the best assumption is that the truth about an organization's values, beliefs, and behaviors will come out, for better or worse. An organization is advised, then, to encourage leaders to practice in a manner by which they would like to be judged.

Attracting potential employees to an organization under false pretenses, whether intentionally or not, simply doesn't make economic sense. Often doing so only promises misalignment, poor performance, and disengagement at a later date, all of which can be costly in both economic and psychological terms. As a result, the most effective communicators of the internal brand go beyond portraying the values, beliefs, and behaviors clearly to prospective employees. They also provide *job previews*—descriptions of jobs in their most attractive and unattractive terms during the recruiting process. Research suggests that job previews reduce employee defections and turnover by alerting prospective employees in advance to what to expect on the job. A preview, according to one interpretation, "vaccinates" people against disappointment.[16] Job previews have even been shown to be effective in improving retention after employees are hired. Job previews, according to one interpretation of this finding, inform new employees that what they are experiencing—irate customers, customer questions they can't answer, and so forth—is normal and just part of the job, not something to be overly concerned about.[17]

Measure and Take Timely Action on Nonbelievers

Cultures evolve by themselves without efforts by leaders to shape them. Still, culture building is not a process best left to chance. It requires a constant attention to behaviors that adhere to or violate values. Measurement of behaviors too often is neglected, subject to management "feel," and therefore subjective. Worse yet, these measures are often put aside when they identify managers who are *nonbelievers* in the culture—those not managing by the values, disruptive to the culture, and enabling counterproductive behaviors among their direct reports. This is especially true when the individual is a good producer, someone who "makes the numbers." Corrective action, whether it involves coaching or dismissal, is not something that many managers enjoy; as a result, they tend to put it off much too long.

The most frequent complaint we hear about managers is that they fail to take timely action to deal with those in leadership positions who can't manage by the values of the organization, regardless of their ability to meet bottom-line goals. Invariably performance improves when nonbelievers—or those simply incapable of managing by the values—are let go. Results from those remaining in the organization more than make up for those of the departed "good producer."[18] For example, Mayo Clinic gives a personnel committee responsibility for addressing problems with physicians who are not living up to the clinic's values or not "exhibiting respectful, collegial behavior to all team members. Some physicians have been suspended without pay or terminated."[19] This is essential to preserving this organization's culture.

HOW THE PROS MAINTAIN GREAT PLACES TO WORK

Cultures that foster high-trust environments provide the context for great places to work. But unless managers implement policies and practices that reinforce productive cultures on a day-to-day basis, internal quality can decline. Fortunately, we've had a chance to observe the best in action—and their policies and practices fit into clear patterns. The managers in each case may not reflect every behavior described here, but they invariably include most.

What we present here is a recipe, not a menu. Discipline is required in the order in which the "ingredients" are implemented.

Hire for Attitude

High-performing organizations invariably sort out prospective employees on the basis of whether they (1) are interested in the business, (2) are passionate about the mission, (3) relate to the organization's values, and (4) are comfortable with the behaviors associated with the values, in other words, "how we do things around here." We call that *hiring for attitude*. For example, at Lululemon Athletica, the manufacturer and retailer of workout clothing, those who are not passionately interested in personal fitness need not apply. According to its website, the company seeks to build "a community hub where people [can] learn and discuss the physical aspects of healthy living . . . as well as the mental aspects of living a powerful life of possibilities."[20] As if that were not definitive enough, the company "has a mission-oriented business model and expects its employees to have detailed personal and professional growth plans that are shared with other employees."

A word of caution is appropriate here, and Lululemon's leadership helps illustrate it. Organizations that are successful in hiring for attitude, as we've described it here, often foster in their members a great deal of pride in what they do. That pride can morph into arrogance, particularly toward customers. It's the role of leadership to make sure that doesn't happen. Unfortunately, that's not what happened at Lululemon when Chip Wilson, the company's founder and CEO, apologized to employees for introducing a fabric that, when stretched too tightly, became transparent, causing many customer complaints. Unfortunately, his apology was perceived as blaming customers, particularly those too large to fit comfortably in Lululemon's apparel, for the problem. Wilson's behavior was not surprising, given the strong emphasis on personal pride at Lululemon. However, customers who perceived his remarks as an insult ensured his early departure as CEO.[21]

Among those who strongly identify with a company's business, mission, and values, some candidates can exhibit the behaviors and some can't. A second screen is necessary for traits such as empathy, desire to work in teams, and other qualities critical to the effective delivery of outstanding service. Once issues of attitude have been resolved, other factors contribute to great places to work.

Train for Skills

Organizations know how to train for skills much more effectively than for attitudes. The training often starts with "how we do things around here." In organizations such as Google, it doesn't go much further than that. But other organizations may require more task-specific training. At Intuit, for example, subsequent training on the job may include the kind of education regarding both the company's tax software and the tax codes necessary for customer-service representatives in service centers to do their jobs effectively. This is followed by extensive observation and practice taking phone calls and responding to Internet messages. This training regularly includes the engineers who designed the software, because they are expected to take customer calls periodically to obtain information about improvements in their products.

Provide Effective Support Systems

Support systems—technology, networks, facilities, information systems—can be designed that (1) help make employees winners or losers in the eyes of their customers and (2) help make employers winners or losers in the eyes of their employees. Whereas solid support systems make things easier and better for employees and customers, technology requiring frequent maintenance, airline networks with poor connections and poorly designed or laid-out facilities make work harder for employees while negatively affecting customer service. While it's important to mention support systems here as part of creating a great place to work, we'll have much more to say about them in chapter 6.

Provide Latitude (within Limits) to Deliver Results

Too many managers assume that the key to creating a great place to work begins with more delegation and accountability. Nothing could be further from the truth. Only after having established a high level of alignment between the organization, managers, and their employees by setting expectations, selecting the right people, training them well, and providing them with effective support systems do organizations with great workplaces begin to expand the latitude given to frontline employees to use their judgments in delivering results. The sequence is clear: align expectations, hire for attitude, train for skills, provide effective support systems, and then extend latitude for decision making on the job.

Of course, latitude without limits can lead to anarchy. Employees prefer clarity on the limits under which they work. These limits can be explicit or implicit ("how we do things around here"). For example, the Ritz-Carlton organization gives its frontline employees, including housekeepers, the latitude to commit up to $2,000 in resources to correct a customer's concern on the spot rather than letting it fester into a bigger issue. Just the knowledge that they have the latitude conveys a sense among frontline employees that they have the support of their organization.

At Southwest Airlines the rule is "do whatever you feel comfortable doing for a Customer." It's up to the Southwest Employee (remember, at Southwest Airlines, *Employee* and *Customer* are always capitalized) to use judgment in deciding what is appropriate in a business in which quick thinking and action is important. This is illustrated by the following true story: A middle-aged man in a wheelchair approached a Southwest counter with a valid ticket. The agent immediately noticed, however, that the man was dressed in dirty, torn clothing and gave off a strong odor. Allowing him to board the airplane would create discomfort for other passengers; it was out of the question. Not boarding the passenger could possibly be grounds for a lawsuit. The agent had to think and act fast.

What would you do if you had no more than 10 seconds to react? What the agent did is a reflection of the care with which she was selected, trained, and given the latitude (within limits) by management to use good judgment. We'll pick up the story later in the chapter.

Extend Latitude to Include Firing Customers

The ultimate act of increasing delegation and latitude is that of granting authority to frontline employees to fire an occasional customer for good cause. Even though it's controversial, many outstanding service providers practice the art of firing customers. It is a way of correcting mistakes that result in the selection of customers who are rude or demeaning to employees or to other customers. It demonstrates to employees that management stands behind them. The following report of one such firing at jm Curley, a Boston restaurant, is illustrative:

> When a customer recently plunked a $20 bill on a table and told his server that he would deduct a dollar from the potential tip each time something went wrong, [jm Curley] restaurant manager Patrick Maguire took the man aside and explained— in so many words—that he was treating the wait staff like dirt. Maguire packaged up the entrees and escorted the man and his date from the restaurant.[22]

Restaurants aren't the only organizations that are firing customers, either. ING Direct, a provider of online banking services designed to deliver great service at low cost (acquired by Capital One), used to suggest to several thousand customers a month that they transfer their accounts elsewhere, simply because the company was not designed to meet their apparent need for frequent and extensive telephone or online service.

We can draw several conclusions from the sample of firms we've observed firing customers:

1. Employees immediately associate management's actions with a good place to work.

2. These practices take place in organizations with high employee engagement and loyalty.

3. Firings are generally viewed favorably by other customers for whom the service was designed.

4. Rarely does a fired customer complain to others about his experience.

5. Most often, fired customers not only are chastened but ask to be forgiven and served again. At jm Curley's, the restaurant cited earlier with the rude patron, the customer, when asked by the manager to leave, "became contrite, insisting on making a face-to-face apology to the server. Maguire (the manager) then reseated the couple. . . . And in the end, the patron left a 40 percent tip."[23]

All of this assumes, of course, that the fine art of customer firing is practiced well. This involves

1. Establishing clearly defined processes

2. Making sure that middle managers are involved and on board

3. Advising employees that the practice is implemented only in clear and extreme cases

4. Explaining unacceptable behaviors clearly to customers

5. Accepting some responsibility for the mismatch between customers and the organization (as at ING Direct)

6. In most cases, handling the situation as quickly and quietly as possible—but with the full knowledge of affected employees

New technologies will make firing customers both easier and less discriminating. New smartphone apps, for example, don't just enable customers to rate service providers. At Uber and Lyft, the Internet-based personal transportation services, drivers rate their passengers too.[24] Passengers receiving low ratings may find that the quality of the service they receive declines; fewer drivers will be willing to respond to their calls. While this feature places more authority in the hands of drivers, it also takes control over quality out of the hands of management. Whether this form of delegation will have a positive impact on service quality remains to be seen.

Calibrate Transparency

Open, two-way channels of communication contribute to no-surprises management, as well as the trust that follows. But transparency requires a policy regarding the amount and kind of information that will regularly be shared within the organization—one befitting the culture and strategy of the organization. Will limits on sharing be determined by what top management thinks employees "need to know"? Or will employees be allowed to pick and choose from a larger information base according to what they think they need to know? Vineet Nayar, vice chairman and joint managing director of HCL Technologies, a large India-based provider of information technology services, has a definite opinion on the subject:

> All HCL's financial information is on our internal Web. We are completely open. We put all the dirty linen on the table, and we answer everyone's questions. We inverted the pyramid of the organization and made reverse accountability a reality. . . . So my 360-degree feedback is open to 50,000 employees—the results are published on the internal Web for everybody to see. And 3,800 managers participate. . . . [Comments are] anonymous so that people are candid.[25]

In another venue Nayar said, "We are trying, as much as possible, to get the manager to suck up to the employee. This can be difficult for the top twenty or so managers whose ratings are posted. As one put it, 'It was very unsettling the first time.'"[26]

This degree of transparency may not be appropriate for all organizations and managers, but it has proved effective as a guideline in hiring and recognizing managers, fostering employee morale, and improving employee retention in a company that finds itself in a competitive labor market. Nayar and his organization have asked and answered important questions as part of an effort to establish a high level of trust.

Organize for Team-Based Work and Teaming

Many organizations that deliver outstanding service are organized around teams—and this is no coincidence. Team-based organizations have the advantages of making the workplace seem smaller than it really is, thereby enabling large organizations to deal with issues of scale and its negative effects on culture. They support notions of self-management as team members exert peer pressure on one another to do the right thing. Teams, particularly those with diverse members, are often more creative than individuals working alone.[27]

Amy Edmondson has coined the word *teaming* to describe the phenomenon of a group of people hired for their ability to work with others—to *team*—who come together to achieve a specific result, then move on to their next assignment with new team members. This is typical of what happens in the delivery of many services. As Edmondson puts it, "Teaming is a verb, not a noun."[28]

The effective deployment of teams—however narrowly or broadly defined—imposes certain responsibilities on management. Richard Hackman researched this and concluded that the successful deployment of teams requires that they have (1) a clear and compelling direction, (2) well-designed tasks, (3) norms that are enforced, (4) sufficient coaching in team processes, (5) a clear understanding of who belongs to the team, and (6) a team-based rewards system.[29] We'll have more to say about the last item later.

Create the Foundation for a Self-Controlling Organization

Teams can provide the foundation for self-control by employees that enables an organization to minimize traditional managerial inputs. As chairman and CEO of Taco Bell, John Martin discovered this when he concluded that he couldn't find or afford enough Taco Bell managers to staff his aggressive growth plans some years ago. Out of necessity as much as the desire to innovate, the company organized some of its units around self-managed work teams sharing a manager with several other units. With the proper training, such teams were able to carry out their own hiring, training, cash management, and problem solving. Invariably, they delivered better customer service ratings than units with dedicated managers.

We often think of control as the process of setting targets, measuring performance against those targets, recognizing those who meet the targets, and taking corrective action with those who don't. This process is not one of management's more pleasant and rewarding tasks. Just ask a manager attempting to complete an employee's annual review. In great places to work, leaders try to do something about this.

Integrate Control with Learning and Reflection. There is a trend toward replacing annual reviews—the traditional cornerstone for performance measurement and review—with ongoing observation and coaching. It is in part a response to the demands of a new generation of leaders and employees who typically value personal development and frequent feedback regarding their work (and sometimes their personal affairs) more than money. Frequent feedback has proved to work at all levels of a service organization.

A variation on this practice is the "team huddle" prior to every shift at a Caesar's Entertainment casino. The 10-minute meeting, on company time, returns many times the cost: employees have higher levels of problem awareness (what went wrong yesterday, what we need to do to ensure it doesn't happen today, information about the business, and so forth), development, and satisfaction, all of which lead to better customer service and more loyal employees.

A recent study measured the economic impact of the practice of allowing employees 15 minutes at the end of each day to reflect on their work and ways of improving it.[30] After testing the idea with students, these researchers replicated their study at Wipro, a large India-based business-processing outsourcing company. In the test group, Wipro set aside 15 minutes at the end of each work shift to allow employees to reflect on lessons learned that day. The test group exhibited a more than 20 percent increase in performance—even allowing for the fact that individuals in the control group were at their jobs 15 minutes more each day.

All of these practices suggest that for employees, time on the job devoted to preplanning or end-of-shift reflection may be more important than what we have traditionally thought of as work.

Staff and Organize for Self-Control. Organizational devices that foster learning and self-control have a powerful effect on the quality of the workplace. Foremost among these, as we have seen, are teams and teaming. To be successful, organizations carefully recruit people who are comfortable with getting more direction from peers than from the top. Working for Google, an organization that relies on people who are able to provide their own direction, is not for everyone. Remember also what we saw at Whole Foods Market: team-based incentives, recognition, and rewards matched with policies of transparency regarding information and teams with wide latitude to take charge of their own fate and exercise the corrective action necessary to achieve success. This team-based organization relieves management of some of its most distasteful tasks while better realizing the control function.

Emphasize Nonfinancial Measures and Balanced Scorecards

If the best predictors of future service success are nonfinancial measures such as employee and customer loyalty, engagement, and ownership, then organizations will find that it makes sense to highlight them in setting goals and measuring performance. A service organization can measure performance by a mix of financial and nonfinancial measures in a way that is both logical and effective. As we pointed out in chapter 3, the service profit chain lends itself naturally to the tracking of performance by means of employee, customer, and financial measures—a balanced scorecard.[31] These measures need not be equally weighted. Employee engagement, loyalty, and productivity measures may be among the most important ones on the *balanced scorecards* because much of service organization performance is driven by employees.

Decide on a Low- versus High-Retention Strategy

Management of service activities offers a fertile field for implementing basic notions about why people work. Leaders can choose from an underlying rationale for two basically different human resource strategies, one involving high and one involving low employee-retention rates. Basically, they can ask whether an organization functions more effectively with fewer, better-trained, better-paid people, or the opposite. The answer depends on the importance of such things as service quality and customer loyalty in achieving an organization's goals.

Our anecdotal, case-based research has led us to a point of view, summed up in a comment made by David Glass when he was CEO of Walmart. Our recollection of it is "Give me fewer, better-trained, better-paid people and they'll win every time."[32] Our views on the choice are best expressed in the names we have in the past attached to the low-retention strategy (a cycle of mediocrity)[33] and the high-retention strategy (a cycle of success). But let's be clear: both can be winning strategies if they are pursued relentlessly with a logic that is internally consistent.

The Logic of a Low-Retention Strategy. At the core of a low-retention strategy are simplified jobs, limited attention to selecting from a pool of job applicants, little training, and relatively low pay (figure 4-1). All of these practices, when combined with reasonable productivity resulting from practices that may be a reminder of the Taylorism movement of the early twentieth century,[34] can result in low prices that will appeal to certain customers. The results may be repetitive, boring jobs that have been designed to accommodate a low skill level; relatively low levels of employee satisfaction; a poor attitude in the service encounter; high turnover; and relatively poor service quality. But employees can be replaced at relatively low costs of selection and training. If the service is regarded by customers as noncritical, they may not defect. The outcomes for the organization are relatively low costs from lost business, reasonable margins, and acceptable profits. All of this can lead to the conclusion that the strategy is working.

Still, the consequences of this strategy may also be a low-quality service encounter, a high rate of customer turnover, a high level of customer dissatisfaction, substantial effort devoted to replacing departing customers, and a lack of continuity in customer relationships. These are costs that are frequently ignored in economic analyses of low-retention strategies. In the wake of the adoption of the Affordable Health Care Act in the United States, for example, many employers are opting for a larger proportion of jobs with less than 30 hours per week of work—the point at which health benefits have to be provided. This will inevitably lead to a higher rate of turnover among customer-facing employees. In some cases, this low-retention strategy will lead to unintended, adverse results.

Figure 4-1 The Logic of a Low-Retention Strategy in Services

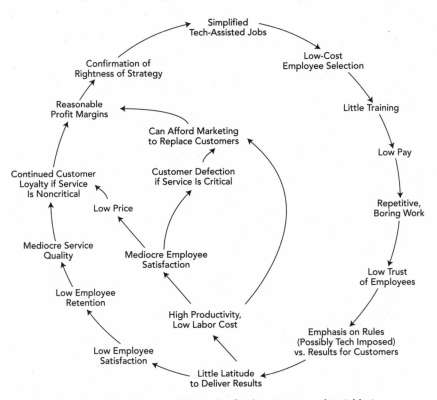

Source: Adapted from Figure 1, "The Cycle of Failure," in Leonard A. Schlesinger and James L. Heskett, "Breaking the Cycle of Failure in Services," *Sloan Management Review*, Spring 1991, pp. 17–28, at p. 18.

The Logic of a High-Retention Strategy. The second of these strategies, one that we originally thought of as "the cycle of success," is designed for relatively complex jobs requiring employee judgment (figure 4-2). This strategy entails careful employee selection, extensive training, and above-market pay, all of which can lead to relatively high labor-associated cost. It requires the delegation of a great deal of latitude to the employee to deliver results to customers, a factor that is thought to lead to relatively high service quality and high loyalty among customers who regard the service as critical.

Figure 4-2 The Logic of a High-Retention Strategy in Services

Source: Leonard A. Schlesinger and James L. Heskett, "Breaking the Cycle of Failure in Services," *Sloan Management Review,* Spring 1991, pp. 17–28, at p. 19.

It leads to fewer costly defections of customers. It may influence customers to help with the marketing effort to new customers by providing referrals, thus reducing marketing costs. Other customers, who do not regard the high quality of service worth paying for, may depart. They are not replaced, again avoiding unnecessary costs of marketing.

High costs of selection, training, and wages for employees may be offset by high levels of employee loyalty, which are also critical to the delivery of high-quality service.

All of this results in the retention of targeted customers (as well as the loss of those not targeted), reasonable margins, and confirmation of the rightness of the strategy. Note that the primary objective here is a high retention rate. It is seen as an element in a purposeful strategy to retain customers and the profit they bring.

One result of this strategy is reasonably high productivity delivered by loyal employees to offset high wage rates. When it works, it results in lower overall labor cost/sales ratios. On other occasions it may require premium prices to defray higher costs while maintaining profit margins.

Case Example: Costco versus Sam's Club. The irony of David Glass's comment when he was at Walmart is that his organization has not followed the high-retention strategy while one of its competitors, Costco, has. At Costco, the starting wage at the time we write this is about 40 percent above the national minimum wage. Average wages are nearly three times the minimum wage. In commenting on the policy and advocating an even higher national minimum wage, CEO Craig Jelinek said,

> At Costco, we know that paying employees good wages makes good sense for business. We pay [high starting wages] . . . and we are still able to keep our overhead costs low. An important reason for the success of Costco's business model is the attraction and retention of great employees. Instead of minimizing wages, we know it's a lot more profitable in the long term to minimize employee turnover and maximize employee productivity, commitment and loyalty.[35]

An analysis several years ago of the Costco strategy compared with that of Walmart-owned Sam's Club, a direct Costco competitor, supports Jelinek's argument.[36] Its author, Wayne Cascio, attempted to cost out the turnover of employees for the two chains. He concluded that added costs of recruitment, training, and lost productiv-

Table 4-1 Cost and Productivity Comparisons, Costco and Sam's Club, 2005

	Costco	Sam's Club
Stores	338	551
Full-time employees	67,600	110,200
Average pay/hour, 2005 (2013*)	$17 ($20.89)	$10 ($12.67)
% covered by health insurance	82%	<50%
Average cost of health insurance/employee	$1,330	$747
Employee turnover, all employees	17%	44%
Employee turnover after one year, 2005 (2013*)	6% (5%*)	n/a
Cost of turnover, % of annual salary (assumed)	60%	60%
Cost per replacement	$21,216	$12,617
Total cost of turnover	$244 million	$612 million
Cost of turnover/employee	$3,628	$5,274
% of employees unionized	15%	0%
Rates of shrinkage (loss and theft)	Lowest in the industry**	Unknown
2005 sales	$37 billion	$43 billion
Operating profit/hourly employee	$21,805	$11,615

Sources: Adapted from data presented in Wayne F. Cascio, "The High Cost of Low Wages," *Harvard Business Review* 84, no. 12 (December 2006), pp. 23–33.
* Source: Brad Stone, "How Cheap Is Craig Jelinek?" *Bloomberg Businessweek*, June 10–16, 2013.
** Source: Annual reports of Costco and Walmart.

ity from a low-retention strategy far outweighed the costs of paying higher salaries under a high-retention strategy. He found that even though Costco paid its employees about 70 percent more than Sam's Club did and spent nearly twice as much for health insurance, its higher employee retention rate and higher productivity enabled it to earn nearly twice as much per employee. His productivity and profit comparisons for Costco and Sam's Club are shown in table 4-1.

Although both organizations are notoriously frugal in the ways they operate, they have distinctly different strategies when it comes to the workforce. Costco, while not embracing the union movement, has not discouraged employees from joining it—about 15 percent have. Sam's Club, on the other hand, has avoided unionization. Although Costco has had to weather criticism from investors that the company pays its employees too much, both Costco and Sam's Club are successful. This fact, combined with the herculean task of converting from one strategy to the other, explains why the two organizations pursued separate ways.[37]

Relationships to Success or Failure. Equating our low-retention and high-retention strategies to success or failure would be a mistake. Each appeals to the needs and psyches of a different group of potential employees. Some may be motivated by self-realization and some by money, regardless of the management process by which it is earned. Both groups, if matched properly to organizations that serve their primary needs, can produce good results for customers, investors, and themselves.

Foster Heroic Service Capability: Back to Mabel Yu

Our discussion of performance feedback and recognition would not be complete without a parting look at the way in which Vanguard Group recognized Mabel Yu's remarkable work in guiding its investors away from complex investments that turned out to be unsafe. During the years that her conservative recommendations resulted in returns to investors lower than those enjoyed by Vanguard's competitors, Yu said, "Management didn't give me any trouble. I got only average reviews those years, but there was no big problem."[38]

As a result of her determination to help Vanguard avoid problems that befell almost every other financial organization investing in derivatives, Mabel Yu became something of a media star, cited in print media and interviewed on national radio. At Vanguard, she received a typically muted recognition by an organization that doesn't support a star system for talent and generally downplays individual performance. But she did get invited to lunch by founder John Bogle. As you might guess, the lunch took place in the "crew member galley." Bogle picked up the bill, but Yu is said to have ordered "a salad and a drink, following the Vanguard $5 lunch coupon celebration tradition." As she put it, "He is very frugal, so I wanted to do things his way."[39]

The message of this story is clear. An organization's values and behaviors may evolve from all parts of the organization, but their communication and preservation start at the top. The clarity with which they are communicated and the consistency with which they are practiced go a long way toward creating a workplace capable of attracting the best talent and allowing that talent to make sometimes courageous decisions. This brings us back to the Southwest Airlines agent facing a ticketed passenger in a wheelchair badly in need of a shower and some presentable clothing.

Foster Heroic Service Capability: The Airline Example

The first thing the Southwest Airlines agent said was, "I will get you on your flight [an assurance that quickly diffused the customer's anxiety], but I would like you to cooperate with me." She asked him to cooperate by accompanying another employee to the employees' lounge for a quick shower and change of clothes donated by other employees. The man agreed, boarded his flight on time, and filed no complaint about discriminatory treatment.

The first words out of the mouth of this employee saved what could have been a disastrous service encounter. What happened here is testimony to the value for employees, customers, and investors of a high-retention strategy. Imagine what would have happened if the agent had been recruited haphazardly, had not been selected for a passion for the business as well as good judgment and had been given little training about what to do in hard-to-script circumstances. Worse yet, what would have happened if the agent had not been led to understand that she had the latitude to do what she felt necessary under the circumstances without checking with her supervisor. You can't make these stories up. They happen all the time on the front lines of a service organization that hires for attitude, then trains for skills.

WILL HIGH-RETENTION STRATEGIES FOR SERVICE GAIN MORE FAVOR IN THE FUTURE?

As we look ahead, a question confronting us is whether or not we will see trends in the use of low-retention and high-retention strategies for service delivery. Our biases are evident, or we wouldn't emphasize stories about the remarkable use of good judgment by frontline service employees who are carefully selected and trained, fully supported by management, and given the latitude (within limits) to act quickly when confronted with unusual situations.

To some observers the future for high-retention strategies appears bleak. One study of managers from a number of countries found that about one-fourth planned to leave their organizations in the coming year. In the United States, where the problem appears to be most severe, only 14 percent of companies responded that retention was not an issue. This was a proportion lower than in Asia and roughly half that of Europe.[40] As economies continue to recover from the depths of the Great Recession of 2008, alternatives for employment will expand. Better information about job opportunities and better technology for accessing it are available than ever before. The supply of talent will not outpace the demand. All of these factors will make retention a greater and greater challenge.

This prospect may have prompted Walmart's leadership to take at least modest steps toward a high-retention strategy as we finished this book. Walmart announced early in 2015 that it would raise both minimum and average wages paid to its employees. What is more significant is Walmart's announcement that it will be providing more-regular work schedules, offering more opportunities for advancement, and focusing on recruiting and retaining "better talent so it can improve its business . . . (with) better-run stores, more satisfied customers and an increase in sales and profits."[41] Given Walmart's size and influence in ranks of retailers, its action has called attention to at least the possibility of a high-retention strategy.

What this means is that for those organizations seeking to achieve service breakthroughs by means of high-retention personnel strategies and willing to apply the effort to do it, the opportunities for differentiation will only increase as fewer organizations find themselves up to the task.

By now it should be clear that great places to work have many moving parts. Some of those parts have to be put in place in a careful sequence. And all are dependent on the most important element of all, the quality of an organization's leaders. Together, these moving parts are designed to make work easier and more enjoyable, to the extent possible freeing up frontline service providers to become heroes and heroines in the eyes of their customers.

Great places to work and their employees are central to delivering value to customers. When led by leaders with effective policies and practices and aided by supporting technology and systems that provide competitive edge to an organization, they can deliver world-class service. In the next two chapters, we turn to these elements of the service delivery process.

CHAPTER 5

The Nuts and Bolts of
Breakthrough Service Operations

What great service leaders *know*:
effective service operating strategies have to create
value for employees, customers, and investors.

What great service leaders *do*:
they ensure the achievement of the leverage and edge that
produces win-win-win results—the service trifecta.

Caesar's Entertainment, the gaming company, has a policy for its high-lifetime-value customers (called Diamonds and Seven Stars in the company's Total Rewards customer loyalty program) that calls for them to always be next in line for whatever service they seek at a Caesar's facility. Additional lines will be created for them if necessary. Thus, at cashiers' windows, if the line for high-value customers has two or more people in it, another line for customers of lower value (Golds or Platinums) will be closed, and the Diamonds and Seven Stars will be ushered to the front. If Gold customers complain, Caesar's associates are advised to counsel them that if they increase their loyalty to the Caesar's casino, they too may someday qualify for Diamond or Seven Star status. What they can learn from the Total Rewards brochure is that they will have to raise their value to Caesar's from $2,000 lifetime as Golds to $100,000 lifetime as Diamonds or $50,000 a year as Seven Stars by increasing their patronization, regardless of whether they win or lose at the slot machines or gaming tables.

This policy requires that employees know who the organization's high lifetime value customers are, and that requires (1) a state-of-the-art information technology support system, (2) effective front-line "listening posts," (3) a facility equipped with mechanisms, such as easily changeable signage, to build flexibility into the service encounter, (4) a set of strategies for fostering customer loyalty, (5) selection and training of employees capable of managing the dynamics required to enforce the policy, and (6) training of customers in what to expect in using the rewards program.

Ensuring Diamond and Seven Star customers that they will always be next in line is a source of competitive edge for Caesar's Entertainment. It is also illustrative of the countless number of ways, often employed together, in which competitive edge can be achieved. The trick is to choose those that fit with an organization's purpose, culture, strategy, and capabilities. The organization provides the context within which sources of edge can be established.

What distinguishes places like Caesar's from lesser service organizations is the fact that its managers understand that their operating strategies need to serve both customers and employees. The design and implementation of those operating strategies also deliver both leverage and edge.

Leverage involves doing more with less. *Edge* is competitive advantage. Sources of leverage may or may not provide edge. For example, there are a number of technologies that can be employed in service delivery to achieve more results with less effort and cost. But most technologies are not proprietary to their users. While they offer great opportunities for leverage, they rarely provide long-term sources of edge.

Compared to the grand, sweeping topics of leadership, service strategies, culture, and workplace, the sources of leverage and edge that we'll discuss here are the nuts and bolts of a service operation—ones that can be tightened or loosened to meet the needs of a particular operating strategy.

EVALUATE SOURCES OF LEVERAGE AND EDGE: THE SERVICE TRIFECTA REDUX

The first tracking devices tested years ago by Federal Express (now FedEx) generated information important to both the company and to its customers. The idea enhanced the value of the service for customers, and, through better package tracking, meant lower costs and higher profits for investors. But the devices were hard to use and perceived by Federal Express's associates as making their jobs more difficult. Employee objections mounted to the point that the program had to be halted, and the process and technology were redesigned. The service trifecta that we first described in chapter 1—one involving benefits for employees, customers, and investors—was not achieved.

Important sources of leverage and edge are related to the value equations for employees, customers, and investors that we introduced in chapter 1. They can be found in ways to deliver results more effectively, as well as in ways of enhancing the service experience for employees and customers alike. For employees, they are those hard-to-replicate elements of culture and organization that foster best places to work. For customers, they are those things that ensure results as well as positive and unique experiences associated with a service. For investors, they are innovations that help grow returns on investments.

Consider the seemingly simple act of managing queues at Caesar's casinos from this perspective. Employees are given the training, information, and tools to delight Caesar's best customers while motivating (educating?) many of Caesar's other customers.

Their jobs have added substance and provide greater self-esteem. Some customers receive service whose value is enhanced, without serious damage to the perceptions of others. Investors gain what should be greater revenue and profit for their company. Perhaps most important of all, the competitive advantage provided by this service trifecta is sustainable. Caesar's competitors don't have the information or ways of organizing it that are necessary to replicate the policy. That's competitive edge.

When appraising whether or not new ideas are opportunities for leverage and edge, always keep in mind the service trifecta. Ask yourself: do these ideas increase value (measured in terms of results and a high-quality experience when compared to costs) for employees and customers alike while increasing returns to investors? If so, these ideas for sources of leverage meet the standard for a service breakthrough. If the differentiated value is sustainable, they also provide competitive edge.

DEVELOP OPERATING STRATEGIES
FOR TACTICAL AND STRATEGIC ADVANTAGE

Creative elements of operating strategies for achieving leverage and edge range from the tactical to the strategic. We have selected several—requiring various degrees of investment of effort—that have proved to provide high return and positive impact on performance in the right context. All have their limits and have to be employed carefully in creating value for customers, employees, and investors. Failure in implementing them can nearly always be traced to the failure to take into consideration the needs of one of these parties— a failure to achieve a service trifecta.

Make Services Visible and Tangible

Many services, like cleaning services, are invisible and intangible. That's why the management of ISS, the global cleaning services company whose employees clean offices in the middle of the night, out of sight of their occupants (and often each other), instructs them to leave evidence that they have been working through the night. Neatened desktops and carefully folded ends on rolls of toilet paper are just a couple of reminders they use to show that services were provided.

By a similar logic, increasing numbers of restaurants are being designed with kitchens that are visible to customers. Restaurant patrons like to see their food being prepared. It is a natural source of interest to many. To others, it provides assurance that their restaurant has nothing to hide from its patrons. Airport design has also changed over the years to make the airplanes more visible from inside the terminal. It is based on findings that show that travelers' anxiety is reduced by the knowledge that their plane is at the gate. Anxiety drops even further if they can see the plane.

In each of these examples, different benefits are being provided. In the first example, the cleaning service is furnishing evidence that a service has been provided, of value to both management and customers. In the second example, the restaurant demystifies the food preparation process and provides assurances of quality and safety to the customer—the implicit control over quality that results from making a service process visible. In the third example, the airport reduces customer anxiety through design of the terminal. All three examples illustrate how the quality of the service experience (and hence value) for employees and customers alike can be enhanced—sometimes with little added investment.

Manage Queues

Queues are a feature, for better or worse, of many services. They reflect the inability to match demand and supply exactly, even when efforts to avoid them, say through reservation systems, are employed. The Disney organization, known for its ability to engineer service experiences, confronts queues every day at its theme parks. They are a fact of life in an organization that seeks to balance the efficient use of expensive and elaborate equipment and properties with a memorable experience for its visitors. One solution is to make the inevitable wait for rides and other services part of the experience.

The way queues are designed and managed influences perceptions of the quality of a service. The key word here is *perceptions*, because the way we perceive service in a queue may have little relationship to the actual time spent in waiting, as described some years ago in a landmark article by David Maister that dealt with the psychology of waiting.[1]

Reduce Perceived Wait Time. Perceived wait time is reduced if those entering the line (1) are recognized immediately, converting a "pre-process wait"—the worst kind according to Maister—to an in-process wait, (2) experience reduced levels of uncertainty and anxiety, (3) are able to occupy their time while waiting, and (4) experience shorter wait times than they expected.

Airline personnel work the back end of long lines at busy airports to recognize customers as they enter a queue. People with high anxiety are made to feel that their needs are being recognized, even if they are not immediately acted upon. These passengers, after being recognized, feel that they are no longer waiting to begin a process.

Entering a queue is an uncertain proposition. To reduce levels of uncertainty and anxiety, restaurants tell us how long the wait will be for a table. Traffic signs on busy highways now inform us how long the driving time will be between two points. And at Disney theme parks, visitors in a queue are informed progressively about the time of the wait by signs placed strategically along the queue, estimating the length of wait based on recent experience.

Studies have shown that occupied time passes more quickly than unoccupied time. It follows that any effort to help customers occupy their time while waiting will reduce the perceived length of a wait. Mirrors are often placed in waiting areas, encouraging those in line to check out their appearance, something few humans can resist. Sales or other information is presented during wait times to help customers occupy their time. It's important, however, that whatever selling is done be perceived by the customer as useful.

As we said, Disney posts wait times at various points in the lines managed at its entertainment parks. The times posted are conservative estimates, ensuring that the actual wait will be shorter than expected. Because the tactic of exceeding expectations is one of the basic rules of good service, this is a must: underpromise and overdeliver. In the long run, this will prove to be good advice even if, in underpromising, some customers may be discouraged from entering the queue. A misled and dissatisfied customer can create enough negative word-of-mouth to more than outweigh the lost business caused by his departure.

Make the Line Seem Shorter Than It Is. Lines spilling out the door and down the street are often perceived as signs of business success—the price customers are willing to pay to participate in an entertainment or other service. Such lines are not, however, the hallmark of good service.

Worse yet, few facilities are designed to accommodate single long lines of customers. That's why queues at airport security checkpoints and Disney entertainment venues are designed to double back on themselves. It's also why facilities are constructed to conceal portions of the waiting space from those at the end of the line.

Care has to be taken to ensure that the customer doesn't feel deceived by too many attempts to conceal the length of a line. While customers will tolerate a modest number of efforts, after several such experiences, the customer begins to associate a service provider with deceptive behavior.

Ensure Equity or Manage Inequity. If given a choice, we always get into the wrong line. At least that's the way it seems. Single queues are perceived as being more equitable. They also move faster, creating the notion that service is somehow better. Single queues are the norm at Disney. They have the added attraction of enabling Disney's personnel to interact with visitors in a more organized way. Over the past decade, single-queuing tactics have replaced multiple queues in any number of services, including those at airline counters, banks, and movie-ticket kiosks.

While equal treatment for customers may be important in some cases, an alternative strategy purposely treats customers differently depending on their loyalty. It's pursued by many service organizations whose offerings are purchased frequently. It's nearly universal in the travel industry, for example, and has resulted in a wide range of preferential prices and services for loyal, versus casual, customers. Whereas some organizations try to avoid creating perceptions of differentiated service, others may display service inequities as part of a strategy to up-sell those not receiving preferential treatment. That's what we saw happening at Caesar's Entertainment, where employees are trained to turn customer complaints of inequity into opportunities to sell the benefits of the higher status attained by increasing their business with Caesar's.

Manage the Bookends

In recent years automobile dealers have come to the realization that their service departments are important sources of profit. As a result, some have assigned their most personable, knowledgeable people to jobs welcoming customers as they arrive at the service entrance. Why? When you think about it, automobile service facilities are a kind of hospital. As in all hospitals, diagnosis of the problem is a critical step in good service. In service operations, expert performance of first steps can pay off in terms of better outcomes and lower costs to the provider. First impressions also count in customers' appraisals of service.

At the other end of the process, last impressions count as well. Research conducted by Nobel Laureate Daniel Kahneman found that research subjects preferred to repeat a medical procedure that left a better memory even though it involved more pain. The memory was heavily influenced by the procedure's best and worst points and how the experience ended, something he called the "peak-end rule."[2] They may not have read Kahneman's work, but that's why automobile dealers are likely to have washed your automobile at the end of your last service visit.

Huggy Rao and Robert Sutton describe a student experiment to test these ideas. Students measured the effect of an effort they made to help JetBlue passengers with one of the last and most anxiety-ridden elements of an air-travel experience: their trip-ending baggage collection. Rao and Sutton report that "the positive responses the prototype generated from customers and JetBlue employees impressed company leaders, who redoubled their efforts to make the baggage-claim experience as smooth for passengers as possible."[3]

Our late colleague D. Daryl Wyckoff called these beginning- and end-of-service opportunities *service bookends*. The concept helps explain why diners tend to remember the first (salad and bread) and last (dessert) courses more than the rest of the meal. Diners also respond to the introductions and the farewells. Of course, great bookends are not a substitute for quality in other steps in the service encounter. They are not a substitute for poor results or service experiences. But they may condition customers to think more favorably about the quality of the service experience as they remember it later.

Manage Customers

Many service organizations leverage value over cost by engaging the customer in the service-delivery process, thereby reducing cost. If the customer and even the employee can have fun in the process, bingo! That's leverage. It's what happens at a Build-a-Bear Workshop as customers move from station to station purchasing skins, materials for stuffing, and other accessories for the teddy bears they make themselves in the store. Instead of engaging in selling, employees assist customers and entertain those waiting in line at the busiest sales stations. This operating strategy—encompassing elements ranging from the kind of people hired, to the nature of the do-it-yourself process, to the layout of the store—provides Build-a-Bear Workshop with a sustainable competitive edge. Replicating the brand loyalty of the organization would prove difficult for a potential competitor.

There are limits to what customers will do to cooperate in creating operating leverage. Eleven Madison Park, a gourmet restaurant (with average checks of $225 a person) in New York, found this out.[4] Owners Will Guidara and Daniel Humm, in response to the downturn in business due to the Great Recession, made changes to increase profits, including simplifying their menu and limiting seating to accommodate just 88 guests in greater comfort. Just as they were considering downscaling the entire operation, their restaurant received the highest rating awarded by an influential *New York Times* reviewer. The award led almost overnight to a long nightly waiting list of diners in a restaurant that now seated just 88. Overnight, the name of the game shifted from filling the seats to "turning tables," the term used in the business for speeding up dining time.

To provide an incentive for guests not to linger after their meals, thereby increasing table turn, Guidara and Humm began offering guests a visit to the kitchen shortly after the conclusion of their meal. The visit included a special cocktail followed by an invitation to imbibe a glass of cognac in the lounge and take home a small gift on their way out of the restaurant proper (a bow to the importance of service bookends). Although some customers were delighted by the table-turn strategy, soon repeat customers began objecting to their loss of control over the dining experience. As a result, the owners revised their strategy yet again to eliminate the kitchen and lounge visits, instead offering only a 12-course, four-hour dining experience with no limit on table time. The required increase in price did not appear to dampen the enthusiasm of Eleven Madison Park's largely price-insensitive customers. The service trifecta was restored once again.

Put Customers to Work

Going back many years, customers have shown a willingness to work when they perceive it to be in their self-interest. For example, self-service has been a way of life in supermarkets and other retailing for nearly a century. Customers can be put to work in diverse ways—co-creating a service, controlling service quality, and generating new business, to name just a few.

Involve Customers in Co-creating the Service. One of the most brilliant decisions at Amazon was to invite customers to review books (and subsequently other items) that they had purchased and to make it easy for them to do so. Customers willingly and in unexpectedly large numbers volunteered with reviews that are "published" on Amazon, increasing the site's value to other customers. The review feature of the site took on a life of its own, generating valuable traffic and sales. It has been emulated by a number of other online service organizations. The supply of customers willing to join in delivering services in this way appears to be limitless.

Most websites these days enable some kind of customer co-creation, most commonly the act of reserving everything from airline flights to seats for various entertainment and sporting venues.

Not all efforts to involve customers in delivering a service have been unqualified successes, especially those that ignore the service trifecta concept. For example, self-service checkout is being employed in a growing number of retail environments, such as grocery stores and drugstores, but not with complete success. As Frances Frei points out, it "is currently problematic for the simple reason that shoppers receive little if any benefit for their effort."[5] Under some conditions self-service checkout not only does not save customers time, but it doesn't eliminate jobs or produce long-run returns to investors either. It can be an example of the service trifecta in reverse. The problem is that checkout requires the kind of constant practice that employees get as part of their job. Customers, on the other hand, have to relearn the process, sometimes by making mistakes, starting over, and becoming frustrated with a task that has in the past been performed for them and with less expenditure of time. To correct for this, some retailers station employees near the self-service checkout area to assist customers, thereby reducing the economic advantage of the process to investors.

Regardless of these cautions, customer co-creation can be an important source of leverage and, in some cases, even competitive edge. We will return to this phenomenon later.

Let Customers Help Control Quality: The Service Guarantee. Guarantees have traditionally been employed to enable manufacturers to market their products, particularly those that represent high levels of perceived risk in the minds of buyers. That's why automakers introduced warranties on their products early in the development of the automobile industry. And so-called money-back guarantees long ago became a staple strategy among product manufacturers.

More recently, purveyors of services have employed the concept of the guarantee as a device for assisting in the control of quality.[6] Hampton Inn, for example, was one of the first hospitality companies to introduce a guarantee that could be invoked for any reason by a dissatisfied guest.[7] Its message was "If you're not completely satisfied, we don't expect you to pay." It required only that the guest provide a reason, which furnished information that was then used to track the performance of each inn along with measures of financial performance. It became part of an early-warning system that enabled Hampton Inn's management to identify inns requiring attention as part of a continuous quality-improvement effort.

One year after establishing the guarantee, Hampton Inn's management carried out an economic analysis of results. Among other things, they found that (1) 2 percent of frequent guests—those staying 11 times or more a year—stayed at Hampton Inn because of the guarantee, (2) relatively few guests invoked the guarantee, but (3) the test provided enough information to enable management to take actions to improve quality at a number of the company's inns. Even when expenditures used to promote the guarantee were charged to the test, management concluded that for every $1 spent honoring and promoting the guarantee, Hampton Inn received $10 in increased revenue. Given the high operating profit on each dollar of incremental revenue in the hotel business, they easily concluded that the guarantee, in addition to providing information needed to improve Hampton Inn's controls, was a financial success as well.

Customer complaints resulting from a service guarantee trigger a quality-control process that is often superior to more conventional means of managing quality discussed later in this chapter.

Plan for Service Recovery: "Do It Right the Second Time"

We mentioned in chapter 1 that "do it right the first time" is a mantra for the management of quality in manufacturing. It is critical where the failure of components or products can lead to death or injury. Fortunately, for most non-life-threatening services, "doing it right the second time" will often suffice to meet or exceed customers' expectations. In fact, doing it well the second time may actually enhance customer-satisfaction levels. Particular processes and results especially impress customers.

Make Service Recovery Fast, Customized, and Personalized. For some years we asked students in our MBA service-management classes to write two letters, one commending a service organization for a positive experience they had had and one complaining of poor service they actually had experienced. All letters were to be constructive. They were to be evaluated on the degree to which they indicated an understanding of the business and whether or not they contained knowledgeable recommendations about how the process could be improved. Extra credit was awarded for those letters that actually prompted corrective action among respondents.

We, along with the students, then waited for responses, many of which included free services in recognition of service complaints. What we found was this: About two-thirds of service organizations bothered to respond to critical letters. But given the poor nature of many of the responses, respondents garnered roughly the same marks on customer satisfaction as nonrespondents. For the responding organizations, their responses represented a lot of wasted effort and resources. What was wrong with the responses? Many failed to contain an apology. Many were slow in coming. Some were clearly form letters with little effort at personalization. Others contained premiums or gifts but provided little indication that anything would be done as a result of the complaint. Others even failed to accept the word of customers making allegations.

As a result of the experiment, carried out over several years with hundreds of students, we have concluded that service recovery, if it is to be effective, should in most cases (1) start with an apology (something often discouraged by legal advisers), (2) recognize the elements of the complaint, (3) indicate what, if anything, might change as a result of the complaint, (4) be timely, even if that means sending an informal e-mail or fax, and (5) contain a personalized and customized response. If recovery has to be carried out in real time, for example a waiter spilling a drink on a restaurant customer, it requires "latitude within limits."

Make Maximum Use of Latitude within Limits. A number of the practices and examples described above require the concept of *latitude* for frontline employees to take corrective measures. As we've seen, you address mistakes and complaints in a timely fashion before a poor service incident is allowed to fester into customer dissatisfaction and long-term bad will. You do it through the person in the organization in the best position to do it—the frontline service provider. But you impose limits on the service provider.

Limits may not always be explicit or exact, and they should be set in ways that reflect the kinds of recovery efforts that customers may require if their perceptions of service quality are to be maintained. Most often, they are described in terms of expenditures. The cost limits for a high-end fashion store, for example, have to be higher than for Waffle House. But in organizations with particularly strong and effective cultures, the limits may be treated with more subjectivity.

Before providing latitude to frontline employees, managers will need to satisfy some prerequisites. They will have to make sure that employees have the appropriate information on which to base their decisions. In a Caesar's Entertainment casino or a Ritz-Carlton hotel where large transactions take place, this may require information systems that tell the employee just how valuable a particular customer may be. Training will be needed for those information systems, as well as for other skills that employees need to be successful in their jobs. And, of course, the employees will need to be hired with a great deal of attention to their attitude, their interest in delivering results to customers, and personalities that enable them to succeed in doing so.

If these steps are taken, the risk of abusing the latitude given to frontline employees is low. In our experience, the problem is not that employees might "give away the store" with their newfound latitude. It is rather that, having been taught in previous jobs to be too protective of the company's assets, they won't give away enough.

Identify, Track, and Manage by Deep Indicators

Craig W. Fugate, the head of FEMA, uses what he calls the "Waffle House matrix" to gauge the severity of some disasters.[8] The matrix works because Waffle House, a chain of fast-food stores found primarily in the southern part of the United States, has a policy of never closing. Joe Rogers Jr., chairman and CEO of Waffle House, is fond of saying that once a store opens, "we throw away the key."[9] If a Waffle House closes during a disaster, Fugate knows that a community is really in trouble and needs help. According to Fugate,

> It's a shorthand for us to get in there and quickly get a snap-
> shot. . . . Is the Waffle House open? Everything normal
> there? . . . Waffle House has a very simple operational
> philosophy. Get open. They never close. They run 24 hours
> a day. . . . They have a corporate philosophy that if there is a
> hurricane or a storm, they try and get their stores open. It don't
> matter if they don't have power, it don't matter if you don't have
> gas. They have procedures that if they can get a generator in
> there, they'll get going. They'll make coffee with bottled water.[10]

A deep indicator is most often a nonfinancial measure that can have a strong influence on an organization's performance. It can sound an alarm that something is wrong, help a manager in taking corrective action, and provide a tool in predicting future performance. In the case of FEMA, the Waffle House matrix is Craig Fugate's deep indicator.

Deep indicators are often developed intuitively by managers. Because they are the product of many elements of a business strategy, they are often identified by managers with extensive experience and knowledge of a business. Too often, either by mistake or design, they are not made explicit and communicated to others. An organization's time to try to identify them is well spent—and there is a relatively simple process for doing so.

First, management will need to determine the primary drivers of profit in a business—those assets that are most important in conducting the business. In a service business, these are invariably frontline employees, but they may also be high customer loyalty, high-traffic locations, or the overall design of the experience offered to customers. Once these primary profit determinants are identified, the most important influences on each of them are next identified. By the time this exercise is carried to one more specific level, its participants will begin to get a clear idea of the few things that truly drive the organization's performance. A deep indicator exists for each of them.

Of course, merely identifying a deep indicator is not enough. It is just a first step. The organization will need to develop ways for measuring it and adding the results to the dashboard that every manager uses to control, learn, and execute for results.

A deep indicator is a barometer for the health of a number of ongoing practices, the way they are interrelated, and the degree to which they are internally consistent—the way they fit together. In this sense it is also a measure of the health of a strategy. In a service organization, candidates for deep indicators can be found among the elements of the service profit chain. In particular, employee and customer loyalty are good predictors of future performance. They also provide an early-warning system that things may not be going according to plan. These measures are often superior to the usual financial measures that appear on the management dashboard.

Robert Kaplan and David Norton have pointed out in their work with the balanced scorecard that financial measures, because they are typically historical, need to be supplemented with other measures.[11] Financial measures rarely predict the future. That's why the best financial analysts are turning away from strictly financial data in a search for the kind of information that will help predict future performance—deep indicators. Managers will increasingly be paying attention to them as well.

Produce Results and Experiences That Exceed Expectations: Service Quality

The degree to which the service experience exceeds expectations is directly related to a customer's perceived satisfaction. This has been referred to as the *service-quality gap*.[12] It suggests that (1) service quality is relative, not absolute; (2) it is defined by the recipient of the service, not the service provider; and (3) it can be managed by improving what is delivered, reducing a recipient's expectations, or both.

Service-Quality Gaps. According to researchers the service-quality gap may be caused by several other gaps. These include the knowledge gap (the difference between what management thinks customers want and what they really want), the perceptions gap (actual versus perceived service differences caused by a customer's inability to measure what was delivered), the policy gap (caused by management policies that set service standards below customer expectations), the communication gap (resulting from misleading communications that create unrealistic customer expectations), and the delivery gap (resulting from the inability of an organization to meet customers' expectations).[13] When management ignores one or more of these gaps, the consequences can be severe, as the management at Circuit City found out in 2007.

The leadership of Circuit City, at one time the leading US retailer of electronics, may have been a victim of its success. Management apparently assumed it knew what customers wanted: low prices.

Circuit City rode its strategy of good shopping experiences and low prices into being one of only 11 US companies meeting Jim Collins's stringent criteria for performance improvement, described in his 2001 book, *Good to Great*. These were the only US companies with "fifteen-year cumulative stock returns at or below the general stock market, punctuated by a transition point, then cumulative returns at least three times the market over the next fifteen years."[14] In fact, on this criterion Circuit City's performance far outdistanced the other ten.[15] Whether or not this recognition had any influence on the company's leadership, in March 2007 they confidently announced a move that would further reduce costs, replacing 3,400 higher-paid sales veterans with lower-paid newcomers, confident that their customers would not notice. Apparently their customers did notice. Circuit City's same-store sales over the holidays in 2007 fell 11.4 percent from those of the previous year. According to one account, "Shoppers quickly noticed and fled . . . [posting] their frustrations with the retailer online, in blogs and chat rooms. Many tell of a noticeable apathy among Circuit City's workers."[16] The service-quality gap between the store visit that customers expected and actually experienced clearly was working against the company.

Clearly, management didn't know what Circuit City's customers really wanted—closing the knowledge gap. They set service standards below customers' expectations—a policy gap. They understandably failed to communicate to customers what to expect from the new workers—in all likelihood, an intentional communication gap. And the new workforce was unable to meet customers' service expectations—particularly customers' needs for information about some of the more complex products being sold by Circuit City—a delivery gap as well. No wonder the company declared bankruptcy and closed its last store in 2009. Things were so bad that its owners were unable to find a buyer willing to keep the company's once-proud name alive.

Dimensions of Service Quality. Important dimensions of how a customer perceives quality have been identified, in the order of their
importance, as *reliability* (Did the service provider do what was
promised?), *responsiveness* (Was the service provided in a timely
manner?), *assurance* (Did the service provider elicit a feeling of
confidence in the mind of the customer during the service delivery process?), *empathy* (Was the service provider able to take the
customer's point of view?), and *tangibles* (Was evidence left that the
service was indeed performed?).[17] These are dimensions of the most
widely accepted method of measuring service quality.[18]

At times an additional dimension of service quality, "procedural
justice," can be important. It's what happens when, for example,
an organization does or does not enforce implicit rules of behavior
when someone cuts in to the front of a line. Various research efforts
have shown, for example, that "procedural justice" determines how
people feel about outcomes ranging from court decisions to medical
treatments—they care about how they were treated more than the
actual outcomes.[19] The perception of fairness has been found to
help explain such things as why we obey the law or why we sue for
medical malpractice, indicators as well of the regard we hold for
the quality of such services.[20] It helps explain why airlines go (or
should go) to great lengths to clearly identify why some passengers
have privileges—priority boarding, wider seats, and so forth—not
enjoyed by others. It's why it's so important, as we saw earlier, that
Caesar's employees be able to explain clearly and carefully why
their Seven Star and Diamond guests enjoy privileges other patrons
don't. If management identifies negative service gaps on any of
these dimensions, their role is to take corrective action.

To date much of the work on service quality has been associated with a field labeled "services marketing." It has largely been
applied in market research efforts by those primarily interested
in marketing challenges. But the implications of this work for the

more general management of services are so great that it deserves much more widespread attention among general management practitioners.

Align Operating Strategy
with Mission, Culture, and Overall Strategy

The management of Whole Foods Market could probably negotiate better prices from suppliers if the company were to place blanket chain-wide orders for as many items as possible. Purchasing at the division level might even be able to provide the advantage of getting some quantity discounts while reflecting the customer preferences in various regions of the United States. Instead, Whole Foods places an emphasis on delegating as much purchasing as possible, particularly for locally produced goods, to the store-based departmental teams. Why? Because doing so helps support shared values concerning self-determination for every employee—at the core of the company's culture. In the long run, management has concluded that the benefits of self-control and increased effort and productivity gained from allowing employees to make purchases at the store level far outweigh the disadvantage of higher purchase prices. It's an important way that Whole Foods aligns policies that are part of its operating strategy with its mission, culture, and overall strategy.

CREATE WIN-WIN-WIN EDGE

Most academic research has focused on service quality for customers. But if you believe in the service trifecta, quality is just as important for employees and investors as it is for customers. The likelihood of the success of an innovative policy or a new service depends on whether unexpected value is created for all three of these important constituencies.

Successful efforts to leverage value over cost often involve small investments. The cost is negligible for an ISS employee to neatly fold the end of a roll of toilet paper in the bathroom of the office he's cleaning in the middle of the night in Denmark. The cost is much less than the value of the evidence it provides to the office occupant that an invisible cleaning service has been provided. It's a *win for the customer.* The satisfaction it provides to cleaning personnel hired for their positive attitudes may not be substantial, but it exceeds the cost of the time spent in folding the paper and is hence a small *win for the employee.* In addition, it provides a "paper trail" (or should we say a deep indicator) for the employee's supervisor that a room has been cleaned properly. If it helps retain just one customer, the return on the effort is more than worth its costs, representing *a win for investors.* It represents win-win-win service quality.

A $2,000 problem fix by a cleaning person at the Ritz-Carlton is far more costly than a cleaner's folded toilet paper. But it probably is equivalent to the margin on perhaps $4,000 of incremental business, representing perhaps 10 nights of occupancy. Over a lifetime relationship with a customer, 10 nights of occupancy are easy to recover. The housekeeper invokes his latitude to make the fix on behalf of the hotel, an action reinforcing an employee's positive feelings about his job. All told, the guest wins, the investor wins, and the employee wins, becoming a hero in the eyes of the guest.

At Caesar's Entertainment, the cost of switching a line from Gold to Diamond customers is negligible, given the way that facilities have been designed to enable the rapid change. The service delights the Diamond customer, who after all is paying most of the bills at Caesar's. Hence, it should also delight Caesar's investors. Although employees must make the effort to overcome the concerns of Gold customers, it gives them a chance to sell the advantages of Diamond status and provides a demonstration of the latitude they have to make the switch. Again, every major player wins. It's a service trifecta.

In cases where the result for certain stakeholders is mixed, invariably the innovation or change will fail, at least for those stake-

holders, regardless of whether the net result across all three is positive. The lesson of the service trifecta is so important that it is worth
repeating. If there is one perceived loser in the employee-custom-
er-investor triad, the chances of success in implementing a change
in operating strategy decline precipitously. In fact, failure to delight
any one of these core stakeholders can spell doom for new ideas.
Remember Circuit City. When customer experience suffered—even
when the cause of the suffering was motivated by cutting costs to
potentially increase investor benefits—the result was lose-lose-lose:
a loss for employees who lost their full-time jobs, a loss for customers experiencing a lower quality of service, and the ultimate loss for
investors, bankruptcy.

Sources of leverage and edge in an operating strategy are often
complex and sometimes difficult to identify clearly. Rarely do they
result from any one thing. Instead, they result from the alignment
of a number of small innovations, careful implementation, and a
lot of hard work with a clear mission, carefully shaped culture, and
cleverly designed strategy. That helps explain why organizations
such as Zappos.com and Disney are willing to share what they do,
even with potential competitors. They understand that the employment of hard assets, most often associated with new technologies
and explicitly described practices, to achieve leverage and edge
might easily be copied. But those activities associated with efforts to
shape an organization's culture and attract, develop, and retain the
best talent are difficult to copy. These organizations are confident
that their results can be replicated only with great effort, over time.

CAPITALIZE ON CO-CREATION
BY CUSTOMERS AND EMPLOYEES

Co-creation by customers and employees has always been an
important feature of service delivery. But the Internet has accelerated the rate at which responsibility for, and costs of, service

delivery are being shifted to customers. In some cases, the incentive provided to customers is tangible. Airline travelers who book their own tickets online without the assistance of an agent pay no booking fee, whereas booking over the phone incurs a fee. This works to the advantage of the customer and the airline if the airline's website facilitates easy booking. If it doesn't, the customer stands to lose valuable time (and end up paying the booking fee for a telephone call anyway), and the airline loses standing in the eyes of the customer.

In other cases, customers are not rewarded either for the time they might spend on the Internet or for the information they provide about themselves as they browse and help design a service or buy a product. One apocalyptic view of this trend suggests that value is flowing from consumers, who provide information gratis to support "free" Internet-based services, to a small number of designers and operators of information exchanges such as Facebook, Google, and others. This view maintains that unless something is done to redistribute the economic benefits to those providing the information, the result will be a small number of people with huge concentrations of wealth and large numbers of people whose jobs manufacturing things have been lost and left without incomes and without the means to consume goods and services.[21]

As we saw earlier, there do appear to be limits on the amount of effort customers will contribute to the co-creation effort without adequate compensation. Co-creation has noneconomic benefits for many customers. But there are limits to their patience and available time. The solution is not greater compensation for their efforts but greater investment in the design of tools, such as websites, that makes co-creation nearly foolproof for the customer. Amazon has led the way in this process with its "1-Click" feature, but too few organizations have followed its example. Sooner or later, the investment will have to be made if an organization's service reputation is to be preserved.

SUBSTITUTE THE SERVICE TRIFECTA
FOR TRADE-OFFS

A service trifecta rarely emerges from a process of balancing trade-offs. More often, it is the result of a combination of new technologies, policies, procedures, and people that reduce costs sufficiently or produce enough new business that there are sufficient increases in margin to reward everyone. It's a non-zero-sum game that is being played here. The purpose is not to reduce costs to their bare minimum. Rather, it is to align operating strategy with an organization's mission, culture, and overall strategy in such a way that employees are highly motivated, performing their work with an enhanced sense of mission—one that is clearly perceived by customers.

Clearly, a win-win-win approach to the design and adoption of ways of leveraging value over cost and gaining edge over competitors is not rocket science. But if that is the case, why do so many innovations in operating strategy fail? Why, for example, is self-service checkout still a concept whose future is in doubt even as it is being implemented by seasoned managers in a number of large retailing organizations? The answer may well lie in whether customers conclude that they are getting a fair share of the benefits in the service trifecta.

Looking to the future, well-known service practitioners are predicting the ascendancy of various uses of new technologies such as service robots in their industries. Using criteria described here, we (and you) can begin to assess the likelihood that these innovations will in fact gain widespread use.

Breakthrough service providers don't stop with the development of operating strategies that provide sustainable competitive edge. They give special emphasis to the design of support systems—technology, networks, and servicescapes—that reflect strategic needs and contribute to achieving the service trifecta. They try to avoid the mistakes made at Starbucks several years ago, a subject to which we turn in the next chapter.

CHAPTER 6

Develop Winning

Support Systems

What great service leaders *know*:
*the best uses of technology and other support systems
create frontline service heroes and heroines.*

What great service leaders *do*:
*they use support systems to elevate important
service jobs and eliminate the worst ones.*

Technology, networks, and facilities are as important to services as they are to manufacturing operations. However, for service leaders, decisions regarding the design and application of support systems comprising these elements become more complex because they often have to take into account the impact the decisions have, not just on investors but on service providers and their customers.

Too often service leaders get priorities wrong or leave out one of the important constituencies of change, most often employees. Those who have studied the problem have concluded that "it is tempting to blame poor quality on the people delivering service but frequently the real culprit is poor service system design."[1]

Service leaders who design support systems that emphasize positive employee, customer, and investor experiences and value—the win-win-win philosophy of the service trifecta—can save untold amounts of operating costs while enhancing revenues. Support system design deserves the best effort from an organization's leadership.

Technology can enhance service jobs or drain them of their content and attendant employee satisfaction. It can empower customers or leave them feeling powerless. And it can eliminate service jobs altogether, either adding to or detracting from the customer experience. By connecting employees and customers with wider networks of resources, it can foster the remote delivery of even personal services. The outcome the organization achieves depends on the degree to which technology fits within the context in which it is being applied. It also depends on those responsible for the process being aware and in agreement with an organization's strategy and the service experience that it seeks to offer to both its customers and its employees. When implemented well, support systems can be a huge asset to service organizations; when implemented poorly, well, let's ask Starbucks.

TECHNOLOGY AND THE STARBUCKS EXPERIENCE

The pressure on Orin Smith was undoubtedly high when he assumed the role of ceo of Starbucks (titles are not capitalized at Starbucks), the world's best-known purveyor of coffee, in 2000.[2] He had had extensive experience, but he was following the company's "father figure," Howard Schultz, in the job. As chairman of the board, Schultz would be looking over Smith's shoulder. The company was growing rapidly and racking up earnings that pleased Wall Street and its investors. Its share price was at an all-time high. This was a mixed blessing for Smith. It meant that expectations would be even higher for Starbucks' growth in the future. Under Smith's leadership, Starbucks responded by opening more stores faster, at one point five stores a day around the world.

Despite the rapidly increasing number of company stores, Starbucks' customers experienced longer and longer waits for their lattes. This slowdown was the product of a number of incremental changes, such as the introduction of a wider range of products and types of coffee to increase sales. But in part it was because of some things that hadn't changed, such as the quaint but outmoded slow, manually operated La Marzocco espresso machines that—while integral to the perceived artistry of the experience—slowed service. Customers loved the product but were becoming impatient with the wait time. Baristas were also experiencing increasing physical problems with the repetitive motions required to operate the machines. The Starbucks management team clearly saw that new technology was needed.

After Schultz's retirement as ceo in 2000, his successor took the largely unnoticed step of creating an industrial engineering division. Given its new challenge, it responded by coming up with a new semiautomatic espresso machine from La Marzocco that was faster and made the job of the barista much simpler. There was only one problem with the new machine: its size. The Verismo 801, because of its capacity and internal grinding and portioning mechanism, required more space on the counter.

The technology worked just as claimed, but something was wrong. In effect, the Verismo 801s had literally and figuratively come between baristas and their customers, who were accustomed to a daily visit to Starbucks and their favorite baristas performing coffee magic. First, the new machines were faster than their predecessors, speeding up the contact between baristas and customers and allowing less time for chatting. More importantly, the machines were so large and tall that they obscured the baristas, making it all but impossible for them to carry on conversation with customers while they prepared espresso. The machines hid whatever barista magic was left in the process. All of this eroded the experience that Starbucks' customers had come to expect. It didn't happen overnight, but customers slowly began to find other ways to get their morning fix. It became clear that the experience was at least as important as the coffee, and Starbucks' new system wasn't delivering it.

In the quest for growth, Starbucks incrementally lost its distinctive ability to meet its promises to employee-partners to deliver to them interesting jobs involving satisfying customer interactions. The jobs were being dumbed down. They required less training. The equipment had taken over much of the relationship. The experience became dispiriting for both baristas and their customers. As Schultz put it, "If the barista only goes through the motions . . . then Starbucks has lost the essence of what we set out to do 40 years ago: inspire the human spirit."[3] With the new automation, something else was lost. Gone was the artistry of achieving "the perfect shot."

By 2007 the situation had become so critical that Schultz, observing from the sidelines, could stand it no longer. He wrote a memo pointing out how and why the customer's experience had deteriorated. Several months later, he returned to Starbucks as ceo in an effort to turn the company's performance around. In our terms, he returned to restore the service trifecta that Starbucks had once enjoyed. We'll return to the story later to find out what happened next.

THE SERVICE TECHNOLOGY SPECTRUM

Several factors determine whether and how technology can be deployed effectively in the service encounter. These include (1) the importance of a human "face" in the service encounter, (2) the need for flexibility and judgment in the service encounter, (3) the level of anxiety and perceived risk—often mitigated by human intervention—with which a customer enters the service encounter, (4) the impact of technology on service personnel's perceptions of the quality of their jobs, (5) the degree to which customers' service quality perceptions can be enhanced by technology, and (6) the importance of low costs afforded by technology in customers' perceptions of service value. A seventh and increasingly important dimension is the degree to which customers desire the opportunity to co-create services with providers, a process often facilitated by technology.

Options for employing technology range from complete disintermediation, in which human input is replaced, to the use of technology in subtle and creative ways that make service providers heroes in the eyes of customers. Any of these strategies can be justified as long as they enhance results and value in the eyes of employees, customers, and investors. Inappropriate uses of technology in service delivery, however, can frustrate customers, enervate and demoralize employees, and destroy value that productivity-enhancing technologies are introduced to create. Where and how to employ technology depends on where a service fits on the service technology spectrum (figure 6-1). At one extreme is the use of technology to replace service labor altogether.

Replace Service Labor: Disintermediation

As we write this, the Massachusetts Turnpike Authority is in the process of replacing toll takers with electronic readers designed to enable it to bill turnpike users. Cameras will record each transaction and provide proof that the transaction happened in order to discourage reluctant payers. The technology will reduce toll-taking costs, speed traffic on its way, and reduce automobile pollution. It eliminates boring jobs that have little or no future, that are performed in cramped quarters and often in uncomfortable conditions, and that rarely enhance the service encounter in the eyes of drivers, whose primary need is speed. Savings are so large that employees

Figure 6-1 A Service Technology Spectrum

The Role of Technology in the Service Encounter

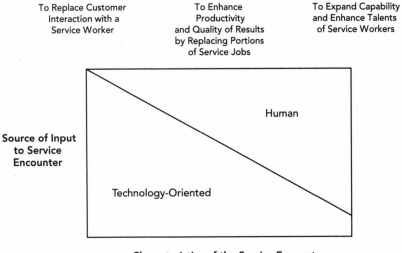

To Replace Customer Interaction with a Service Worker	To Enhance Productivity and Quality of Results by Replacing Portions of Service Jobs	To Expand Capability and Enhance Talents of Service Workers

Source of Input to Service Encounter

Human

Technology-Oriented

Characteristics of the Service Encounter

Low	Need for human "face"	High
Low	Need for flexibility and judgment	High
Low	Customer-perceived risk	High
?	Negative impact of technology on service worker self-perceptions	High
High	Degree to which service quality can be enhanced by technology	Low
High	Importance to customer of low-cost afforded by technology	Low
High	Degree to which technology can enhance customer co-creation of service	Low

who lose their jobs can be amply compensated and given training in the skills demanded by more interesting jobs.

Invoking our service trifecta criteria for value, we see that it is a win-win-win for employees, customers, and investors. Disintermediation, a la the toll-taking example, is at one end of a service technology spectrum. Here, all of the criteria calling for human intervention in the service encounter register low to nonexistent on the dashboard. Although some regular commuters on the Massachusetts Turnpike may welcome a particular face in the toll booth every morning, the perceived costs to them in higher taxes to support what appear to be unnecessary jobs are not worth it. Further, there is little need for judgment in the service, it evokes little or no fear or perceived risk, the quality of the job is not improved by the technology, and customers' perceptions of quality are raised by the technology. The scorecard dictates disintermediation by means of technology.

Disintermediation creates strange bedfellows. For example, not far from the turnpike toll takers on the service technology spectrum are college professors who lecture with no student-professor interaction. In these professors' classes, attendance, unless required, is often low. Instead, notes from the lectures are shared among students. While the professors' particular skills and knowledge may be irreplaceable by technology, the fruits of those skills and knowledge can be distributed without actual face-to-face communication. In fact, by means of streaming, students can experience the classroom lectures of some of the most highly renowned instructors in the world. For this reason the lecture as a form of instruction, when delivered with a less-than-stellar effort, is a threatened species in the world of higher education.

The traditional lecture eliminates the need for judgment and flexibility, generates little or no anxiety of the kind provoked by interactive teaching, and produces economics that are improved greatly with the use of technology. This would suggest that at least this one form of teaching may be ripe for the application of technology. The fact that results to date have not been uniformly positive may be testimony to the inappropriate application and execution that have characterized many of these efforts, a subject to which we will return.

Enhance Quality and Productivity

Technology that simplifies work, enhances quality, and increases the productivity of service workers is epitomized at McDonald's by the "four-by-four system"—a technique of cooking hamburgers, 16 at a time, with the grill set at a temperature that cooks the 16th hamburger the right amount (according to management at McDonald's) on one side at precisely the moment it is turned by the grill operator flipping the burgers in a precise sequence. It is complemented by the "two-by-two" ketchup and mustard applicators that increase productivity by a factor of four in applying condiments.

Note where this technology falls on our service technology spectrum. Here, there is a need for judgment in the cooking process that technology improves. Because the output from the four-by-four system is the same nearly every time, a customer's anxiety and perceived risk when purchasing a McDonald's hamburger is low. The burger is cooked the same every time. The technology improves the quality of the job and helps enhance customers' perceptions of both the product—just what is expected every time—and service quality, because it speeds up production. Its impact on economics is muted by the fact that a grill operator is still required, although the operator can control the rate of output under the system.

Expand Human Capability

Estate planners fall somewhere near the opposite end of the service technology spectrum from toll takers. They often form close relationships with their clients, relationships that result in highly customized service encounters and outcomes. Perceived risk is high. Therefore, trust in the investment adviser and her judgment is important. It's something that is hard to replicate with technology.

At the same time, the better the data and the information at the disposal of the adviser, the better the service experience (if not the result). Here, technology can play an important role as a support system while complementing the skills of the service provider. Technology can allow her to evaluate many more estate planning scenarios, trust vehicles, and alternative investments according to various criteria and what-if alternatives. Technology can make the estate planner look (and feel) like a heroine in the eyes of her clients. When combined with human talent and judgment, it can help produce remarkable results.

Enhance Human Talent

Think about the kinds of teaching that require an almost constant interaction between pupil and teacher. We're not talking about the traditional lecturer, whose job was discussed above. We're talking, for example, about tennis coaching. While the tennis coach may employ video for review purposes and an automatic volleying machine, these uses of technology merely enhance the visual, verbal, and physical interaction required to coach tennis. Actual play as well as the trained eye of the coach are irreplaceable ingredients in the service. That's why, like estate planning, tennis coaching will be enhanced but not replaced by technology.

None of the roles for technology described above stand alone. In any application technology may, and invariably does, play several roles at once. And whether or not a technological application makes sense always has to be determined by the win-win-win criterion. Failure to include employees, customers, or investors in the calculation of benefits has led to the downfall of many applications in the past.

Overcome the Negative Effects of Technology on Human Behavior

The introduction of even the best, most reliable technology alongside human inputs can lull workers into a false sense of security on the job. Several years ago, when an Asiana Airlines captain asked his co-pilot to land the plane with a visual approach (rather than using automatic pilot) into Los Angeles, the co-pilot froze. According to the pilot, who had to take over the controls to avoid a crash, the co-pilot told him, "I don't need to know this. We just don't do this."[4] This incident provides evidence that the introduction of automation to the cockpits of airliners has led to laxities in training that pose safety problems of their own.

Recently, efforts to create an automated subway line in Paris by the RATP (Régie Autonome des Transports Parisiens) were made more difficult by memories of the crash of a train at the Notre-Dame-de-Lorette subway station in 2000. The cause of the accident was attributed to both a malfunction of the automatic pilot and the inattentiveness of the driver.[5]

When many of their tasks are put on automatic, workers relax; this can be a bad combination. Because it's never wise to assume that technology is foolproof, the design of the service requires strategic human input combined with careful selection, training, recognition, and incentives to produce a good result.

Neutralize Opposition from Organized Labor

Even with the best of intent, organizations that introduce technology into the service process often become lightning rods for opposition from organized labor unions. Here is where win-win-win thinking and the service trifecta come in handy.

The RATP had to negotiate with eight different unions in the process of obtaining support for an effort to automate one line on its Paris subway service, a move that would eliminate 630 jobs. The subsequent reduction in payroll on Paris's busiest subway line, with about 12,000 trains a month, generating more than $15 million in monthly revenue, gave RATP's leadership access to several options for making sure that the lives of displaced drivers could be improved, and produced a reasonable return on investment for investors without adversely affecting customer service. According to Laurent Souvigné, deputy director of the Social Relations Unit of the RATP at the time, automation presented "a social challenge which is more important than the technological one."[6]

Recognize the Importance of Individual Customer Needs and Preferences

Rarely is the role of technology in services limited to only one point on the service technology spectrum. Often, different customer needs and preferences allow technology to be brought to a given service in ways that fall at all the points on the spectrum. For example, personal trainers are multiplying in numbers at precisely the time that fitness centers are being equipped with smart exercise machines—machines that provide some of the same advice as, and more precise feedback than, a personal trainer. Some people benefit from the customized coaching, personal interaction, and moral suasion that come with working with a trainer. Others, who need these things but can afford only interaction and moral suasion, work out in fitness classes. Still others simply join a fitness center and replace what a trainer has to offer with personal discipline and technology.

Ask the Right Questions

When assessing the value of a potential technological addition to any service operation, an organization will need to take a number of things into account. Before introducing any new technology to the service setting, service leaders will want to ask the following questions:

1. What is the role of service in the overall strategy of the organization? To what degree and at what points in the service delivery process can it be performed best or enhanced by technology or by human input?

2. What effect will the technology have on the service experience

for the customer? Will it, for example, require more customer input to the process? If so, will this improve the service experience enough to warrant asking customers to contribute?

3. What effect will the new technology have on the nature of work? Will it relieve workers of boring tasks? Will it free up their time for more interesting work? Will it enable workers to be more productive? Will it enable less stressful work? Will it enhance or degrade self-esteem on the part of employees? Will it enable them to deliver results to customers that were previously impossible?

4. In terms of bottom-line results, will it reduce costs? Will it enable lower prices and/or higher margins and operating profits?

In short, does the technology create a win for employees, customers, and investors alike? In introducing new espresso machines, Starbucks' management, in the case described earlier, managed to create a loss for the baristas and their customers. As a result, the inevitable result was a loss for investors as well. It flunked the test on every important dimension other than the ability of the technology to perform as advertised.

TECHNOLOGY AND EDGE

By itself, technology is not an important source of competitive edge over the long term. It is too easily replicable. Good ideas are impossible to contain and monopolize. However, when the successful application of a technology is so complex that few competitors are inclined to implement it, technology may provide an intermediate-term competitive edge.

Take, for example, the experience of world-renowned architect Frank Gehry in implementing 3D technology in the design of large, complex buildings. These buildings have to meet stringent requirements for environmental sustainability. They require extremely detailed and clear plans, which are important for the seemingly mundane but critical approval process for building permits.

Gehry's designs rarely feature square angles and corners. Instead, they are characterized by flowing, curving elements that defy conventional architectural thinking. They constitute Gehry's brand and competitive edge. Prior to 3D software, these elements were time-consuming to design and difficult to communicate through traditional drawings. Worse yet, they often resulted in designs that were misinterpreted and mispriced by contractors, elements that didn't connect with one another when constructed on the job site, and conflicts between contractor and architect. These deficiencies led to job shutdowns while the problems were worked out. This is where Building Information Modeling (BIM) comes in. Developed by IBM, it incorporates techniques that solve such problems, resulting in more cost- and time-effective projects and freeing up designers to exercise their creative abilities. Or do they? Gehry's experience suggests that they may not.

Gehry and his team have been able to use the technology effectively. But he emphasized to a reporter that

> "BIM is not something that you can 'just buy in a box.' Instead it is a change in the way projects are organized and in the roles, responsibilities and cultures of each party involved. Adopting a new tool will get you part of the way there, but the really big advances come from using these tools to work and think differently," he says. One of the most significant benefits of BIM is encouraging a project team to work in a more collaborative way—by setting goals and improving coordination of activities.[7]

When supplemented by the right organization, policies, practices, and culture, this technology can provide a sustainable competitive edge. Alone, it provides nothing of the kind.

TECHNOLOGY AND SERVICE CO-CREATION

Service co-creation can be mundane. For example, at the checkout counter of our local supermarket, many of us go to work with our grocery checker to co-create a service with the help of information technology. After we unload our selections and place them on the moving belt, items appear on a screen visible to us as they are checked, along with a running total of our purchases. Customer and checker go to work together to speed up a checkout process that is faster for both, provides more assurance to the customer (us), and yields adequate returns on the store's investment—win-win-win.

Co-creation can also be incredibly complex, as seen in the work of architect Frank Gehry. Here, technology can help clients picture complex architectural designs with more flexibility and timeliness than ever before, involving contractors in a conversation with the architect and the builder about materials, angles, and construction challenges that could never before be addressed during a project, at least not with any speed. The results of this co-creative process are designs that could barely be conceived, let alone communicated to those responsible for building them just a few years ago. The technology makes possible for the first time a complex co-creative conversation that results in building designs never before seen in built form.

REMOTELY PERFORMED SERVICES
AND THE INTERNET OF THINGS

In some service industries, even those with high levels of personal content, technology allows competitors to extend their reach. This has brought services formerly performed on a face-to-face basis into global competition with one another. This is especially true of two service industries with high information content and professional knowledge and expertise: education and medicine.

Remotely Performed Educational Services

Education delivered by means of the Internet through MOOCs (massive open online courses) represents a potentially game-changing application of technology in an industry that is to some degree in a state of denial. Even after the explosive early growth of online education, many doubters still underestimate its potential, usually citing the importance of face-to-face interaction in the educational process. Based on our personal experience, few limits apply to remote educational experiences. But quality will come at a cost. Paramount among the conditions necessary to enhance remotely performed education is the need for an occasional in-person, face-to-face meeting between an instructor and students to foster a learning relationship, which is so important to the educational process.

Periodic face-to-face contact also helps establish the norms and peer-group pressures that motivate remotely located students to complete what they've set out to do. Where face-to-face contact is lacking, early initiatives in which large numbers of students have enrolled with no opportunity for in-person interchange have produced high dropout rates. The courses will have to be redesigned to raise the psychological, if not economic, costs of dropping out.

Institutions of higher learning will inevitably provide official credit for MOOCs. When that happens, it will open a floodgate of users eager to obtain credit for courses taught online and by streaming techniques by some of the world's preeminent experts on a range of topics. The next step, of course, will be the displacement of a number of classes, instructors, and even entire institutions by complete curricula offered by the Internet-based services, in an industry currently characterized by high costs, rapidly rising tuitions, too many bricks, and too much mortar.

The technology will be misused as well. In the rush to adopt it, many institutions will forego the value of combining online and classroom instruction. It will not displace all face-to-face teaching. But it will change the role that people play in the educational process at all levels, affecting a wide range of methods and jobs.

Education is no doubt one service lying in the natural path of evolution in which information technology will play an increasingly significant role vis-à-vis human inputs in the service-delivery process. Medicine is another.

Remotely Performed Medical Services

Apollo Hospitals is a hospital chain headquartered in Chennai, India. The experiences of its management illustrate both the joys and frustrations of what often seem like natural opportunities to employ technology to deliver desired results remotely.[8]

In 2000 the environment seemed ideal for the introduction of telemedicine at Apollo Hospitals to extend the reach of its medical expertise to rural areas of India. After all, the organization had developed a worldwide reputation for the quality of its work in several specialties, but especially in cardiac medical services. Through prudent financial management, it had been able to develop state-of-the-art facilities equipped with the latest medical technology. Its training program, initiated by founder Prathap Reddy, had produced a staff of practitioners on par with those of the cardiac care units of the world's best hospitals, a staff current on research findings from institutions elsewhere in the world. It delivers world-class quality in the treatment of heart ailments at low cost. As a result, it has contracted with hundreds of organizations, both inside and outside India, for the long-term provision of cardiac services. Medical tourists more and more frequently come to Apollo from around the world for high-quality, low-cost treatment.

Apollo's services were also needed in remote reaches of the state of Andhra Pradesh in which Apollo is located. Patients unable to obtain emergency advice and services, most of them quite poor, were literally dying while awaiting treatment. In response to a critical need, Apollo obtained funding to launch an experiment in telemedicine in Aaragonda, a remote village. It installed computing and communications equipment capable of facilitating the exchange of text, sounds, pictures, and videos (digital convergence) between local medical attendants and remote medical experts.

As it turned out, the technology itself—other than its initial cost and the creation of sufficient volume of use to defray the cost—was the least of the concerns of Apollo's management. Much more formidable were the concerns of patients about the efficacy of remote diagnosis and prescription. But even this paled in comparison with the need to overcome any perceived loss of face on the part of remote practitioners who would have to admit to the need for advice, often in front of their patients. As a result, in an effort to encourage them to install and use the communications technology critical to the service, Apollo took steps to make remote practitioners feel like members of a team quite naturally delivering its services by the latest methods. It appears to be working. Today, Apollo operates more than 150 telemedicine centers in India.

Telemedicine will have application wherever medical specialties are in short supply. It will be administered from geographic centers of excellence to provide outstanding medical diagnosis and guided treatment to outlying medical service centers accessible to patients who can't afford expensive travel and treatment. Whether it is in India or the United States, the technology will perform well. However, the problems of implementation will be the same as those encountered by Dr. Reddy in India.

The Internet of Things

At its most basic level, the Internet of Things is an emerging category that represents a broad array of products that can connect to the Internet and to each other with the objective of providing customers with smarter, more efficient, and more personalized experiences.

According to the information technology consulting firm Gartner, nearly 26 billion devices will be on the Internet of Things by 2020. All sorts of devices will be able to collect information in all sorts of physical environments. Most relevant to service providers is the ability of the Internet of Things to be responsible for taking action after the devices' sensing. We have seen the beginnings of intelligent shopping systems that monitor customers' shopping habits in a store by tracking their mobile devices. This data transmission and collection could instantly translate into special offers, repair services that anticipate imminent product failures, or a portfolio of service opportunities that have yet to be imagined.

The Internet of Things represents an enormous opportunity to create new and compelling service businesses out of tired product-based enterprises. As a simple example, GE's lighting business redefined itself from a mature product organization with few growth opportunities to a large-scale service enterprise using the embedded intelligence in its lighting and electrical monitoring devices to dramatically reduce electrical consumption in homes, offices, and government buildings.

Service leaders looking to build their Internet of Things capabilities will need to recognize the importance of a carefully designed service interface that targets the needs of specific target groups. The capacity to process enormous amounts of data from these devices represents a huge challenge to those attempting to create positive customer experiences.

DESIGNING NETWORKS:
MANAGE THE COST/VALUE CURVE

Networks represent the core of the support systems for many services, including social networks, airline route structures, and retail chain store operations. They have the property of taking on added value with the addition of each new participant, or "node." The cost of growing a network, however, may create an economic limit on size. It's the relationship between the value and cost of additions to a network—what we term the "cost/value curve" (figure 6-2)—that is at the heart of network management. As long as the value of incremental network size outweighs the cost, the network will be grown. Theoretically, at the point that these costs are equal, the network's optimum size will have been reached. But enough of the theoretical world. Let's get back to the real world.

Utilizing Pull or Push Networks

We like to think of the task of network expansion as having *pull* and *push* characteristics that influence scalability. For example, Facebook's social network expands through the efforts of those who desire to be included. It's a pull process driven by participant demand. Because the labor involved in expanding and maintaining the currency of the information on the network is provided by participants, the value of adding one additional member (to at least some of the existing network members) far exceeds the cost of adding that person, as shown in figure 6-2. As a result, there is no real limit on the size of the network, no point at which the cost of adding a member exceeds the general benefit, even though the benefit to each existing member may vary widely. These economics have supported the get-big-quick strategy that drives most social networking businesses.[9] They have resulted in vast amounts of value being added quickly. Unfortunately, that value can be adversely affected if the network falls out of favor with participants, something we have witnessed with the rapid rise and fall of social networks that are directed to younger audiences. Contrast this with characteristics of push networks.

When John Jamotta, head of route design at Southwest Airlines, has to select the next city to be added to the airline's network, he

Figure 6-2 Cost/Value Curves in Pull and Push Service Networks

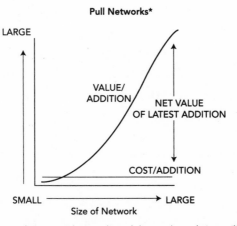

Pull Networks*

*Examples of pull networks are social networks and direct-sales websites utilizing the Internet.

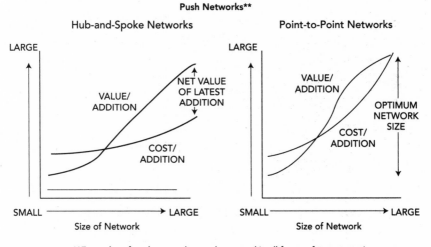

Push Networks**

Hub-and-Spoke Networks   **Point-to-Point Networks**

**Examples of push networks are those used in all forms of transportation,
including the highway system.

has to take into account not only the positive impact on the company's revenue but also the considerable costs of establishing and operating a new station. These are costs incurred by the network's operator in a push network, and they limit both the growth rate and the size of the network, as figure 6-2 indicates. Not only does Jamotta have to take into account costs to his company, but he also has to assess the value and costs to the airline's Customers involved in a given design. He does so by using Southwest's bank of data of Customer travel volumes and habits to decide how the new city will be connected to the network, especially in relation to the other cities that will be serving it directly.

How Much Connectivity to Provide

In Internet-based pull networks, the amount of connectivity—the degree to which various points and people in a network are connected—may be vast. Theoretically, every Facebook member is connected to every other Facebook member. But the service had to recognize that not all network members want to be connected with one another. Therefore, it had to design means ("friending") to enable Facebook members to put limits on their personal connectivity.

The same is not necessarily true in push networks. Southwest Airlines, since its founding, has pointed out the benefits to its Customers of a point-to-point network that enables many of them to reach their destinations with a nonstop flight. As a result, it operates a network with a great deal of point-to-point connectivity. When John Jamotta adds a city to the airline's network, he and his colleagues have to decide whether the city will be connected to just one other city through which the passenger can connect to other points on the network. Or they can do it by means of multiple connections between the new city and the existing network, something that academics term increased *connectivity*.

Because an airline has to populate a network with expensive terminal operations as well as even more expensive "links" (airplanes), a point-to-point network has a relatively steep cost curve unless a decision is made to limit connectivity in an effort to control costs. By contrast, the cost curve for a hub-and-spoke network is less steep, as shown in figure 6-2. It is governed by the number of hubs that are created—as well as the adverse impact on operating costs that occurs at some point in the expansion of a hub beyond a certain size.

While a hub-and-spoke network is less expensive to expand than one attempting to link all or most other points on the network to the one being added, there are offsetting costs to the passenger, who may have to negotiate several connections and plane changes to get around. This creates another kind of trade-off and a potential competitive advantage to the airline offering direct point-to-point service as opposed to service through a hub. The word *potential* is important here. If direct service costs more to operate than hub-and-spoke service, it either has to command higher fares or be operated at high levels of capacity usage, called the "load factor" among airlines. In the case of Southwest Airlines, its management has regularly chosen to keep fares low and bet that it will be able to attract enough passengers to achieve a high load factor on a network that is largely point-to-point. Testimony to its success in building demand to meet supply is the fact that the airline continues to be in great demand among airport authorities around the United States. They know that Southwest's fare structure will increase traffic through their facilities by a factor of two or three.

Impact on Network "Health"

In any network, organizations must take care to ensure that new additions will not adversely affect the quality or operations of the existing network. This is especially true in a push network, such as a retail franchise chain. At McDonald's, for example, a franchise agreement sets high standards for operation, requiring that a new franchisee work in an existing McDonald's for a specified amount of time in addition to attending the company's Hamburger University.

In contemplating a move to add air service to New York's LaGuardia Airport in 2009, John Jamotta had to take into account the impact of the airport's congestion on the rest of Southwest's network and the poor record for on-time performance for flights into and out of the airport. Some means had to be found to shield the rest of the airline's route network from the uncertainty introduced by serving LaGuardia. This was done by ensuring that, as often as possible, equipment was scheduled to shuttle in and out of LaGuardia from only one connecting city rather than expose other stations to the uncertainty.[10]

Impact on an Organization's Culture

When it comes to company culture, organizations always run the risk of growing the network too fast. These risks are particularly high for organizations reliant on strategies based on posh networks, such as airlines. Southwest Airlines, an organization protective of its culture, has resisted requests by dozens of cities for access to its network, preferring to grow at a measured pace. In addition, in considering the LaGuardia addition, Southwest Airlines' leadership had to ensure that it could find a supply of New Yorkers compatible with a corporate culture influenced by Southwest's Texas roots. In this case, the decision to initiate the service was accompanied by a decision to staff the new station with a mix of New Yorkers and existing Employees from other stations.[11]

Effects on the Customer Experience

Regardless of the nature of network design, the most important element of design in services is the customer experience that it produces. Some Facebook customers want to be connected to as many other users as possible; some of them may have something to sell. Still others may want to be connected only with "friends" with whom they communicate frequently. They need a feature that enables them to select their friends and filter out other members of the network. The switching required to accomplish this takes place nearly instantaneously and invisibly at no cost to the user and very little cost to the network operator.

As we pointed out earlier, an equivalent process of switching in the airline travel experience is much more costly when measured in terms of the inconvenience incurred and time spent by the traveler. As a result, a hub-and-spoke airline route—one that requires passengers to transfer repeatedly from one plane to another in order to access any city on the network from any other city—will suffer in the face of competition that provides a nonstop, point-to-point alternative.

Importance of What Is Being Moved through the Network

Up to this point, we've assumed that our network is being designed to move messages or passengers, or somehow to serve consumers through a chain of retail stores. Instead, what if the task of the network is to move freight from one point to another? Here the concern is for total transit time and dependability. This in turn varies with the value of the cargo being moved. For example, fashion merchandise moving from the Far East to the Spain-based retailer Zara will move directly, often by air, in order to minimize transit time and potential damage. The value of such a network far exceeds the high cost. On the other hand, Mittal Steel, in transporting its output from its mills in India to its far-flung customer base, will employ the lowest-cost transport network, even if it requires making several time-consuming stops of a ship in several ports to off-load portions of a shipload of steel.

Standardization versus Customization in the Network

Walk into the Swissair terminal in Nairobi, Kenya, and you immediately think you're back in Switzerland, given the signage, crisp uniforms, and attentive service that you experience. Regardless of the local customs and practices, that station looks and operates like any other on the Swiss airline's network. It has to if the airline is going to project a brand that speaks to its customers with assurance that they're going to travel safely and securely from one part of the world to another, all while experiencing Swiss hospitality.

Walk into an office of advertising agency DDB in Shanghai, however, and you might think you are entering the premises of a typical Chinese service business. Services provided, as well as policies and procedures, reflect local needs and customs, especially if the Shanghai office wants to serve local clients as well as Chinese representatives of multinational clients. In this case some core functions such as finance are standardized. But functions such as legal services and human resource management have to be decentralized and customized to fit the local laws and culture.

The issue of standardization is particularly vexing where the variance in local customer preferences is especially wide and the service organization typically has maintained a high level of standardization, often shaping customer preferences rather than catering to them. This was the case at McDonald's, the organization that taught Americans what to expect in fast food. This was not the place to "have it your way," as a competitor, Burger King, once advertised.

McDonald's franchisees were the ones who convinced management that their global offerings could not be standardized completely. As a result, McDonald's menus in Hong Kong include items such as soy green tea and dinner rice. There are core menu items like hamburgers and French fries that have to be offered under the McDonald's franchise agreement. But McDonald's franchisees around the world now offer menu items not found in the United States—items that reflect local preferences.[12]

FACILITIES DESIGN: CREATE THE SERVICESCAPE FOR THE SERVICE ENCOUNTER

The Sunday services at Willow Creek Community Church, one of the largest of the US megachurches, located in a Chicago suburb, are conducted in a large sanctuary devoid of the usual religious symbols and artifacts. Typical features of the services are soft-rock numbers performed by the church band or dramatic or humorous skits that suggest the importance of faith-based beliefs. The sermon, more like a performance, is delivered from a lectern made of a transparent material. These features are all intended to bring the speaker closer to the congregation while suggesting accessibility to the ideas being conveyed.

The services are intended for the "seekers" who may be searching for a church to join. The "seekers" may be accompanied by "believers" who also attend Wednesday evening services in the same sanctuary, but with symbols and artifacts as well as elements of a more traditional religious service. Willow Creek employs signs, symbols, and artifacts as part of a conscious strategy to create what has been termed a *servicescape*—a setting that both creates expectations and communicates some idea of the way in which a service will be delivered.[13]

Servicescapes were first cited by marketers as important ways to create an image or brand. Mary Jo Bitner then pointed out that the influence they have on employees in a service encounter is just as significant. She grouped elements of a servicescape into three categories: ambient conditions (such as temperature and sound); space and function (layout); and signs, symbols, and artifacts.[14]

Servicescapes serve many functions. They communicate the nature of the service, engender trust among potential customers, and facilitate the delivery of the service, whether it involves personal interaction or self-service applications.

Design Communicates the Nature of the Service

Servicescapes "speak" to a potential restaurant customer, suggesting the kind of dining experience she might have (white tablecloth or more casual, silver or plastic tableware, soft or bright lighting, oil paintings or travel photos on the wall). They communicate a great deal about the philosophy of the service, for example, whether or not the restaurant's kitchen is visible to the diner. They include the cleanliness of the restaurant and attitudes of its employees, which convey a lot about the quality of its management. These are all signals that our diner seeks on her first visit to the restaurant. They provide what marketers have referred to as important cues about what to expect and, in fact, whether the restaurant is for her or not.[15] Servicescapes also influence employee perspectives on such things as the quality of the restaurant as a place to work, the amount of prestige that will be associated with the job, housekeeping standards, and the quality of the restaurant's management. Research has suggested that these in turn influence employees' satisfaction, motivation, and productivity on the job.[16]

Design Engenders Trust among Potential Customers

Trust in a service encounter is especially important when a customer perceives risk, has little information about what to expect, is a first-time user of the service, and is unable to obtain recommendations from a trusted source. It helps explain why a website such as Yelp.com, on which reviews are posted of encounters with all kinds of service providers, generates so much traffic. When customer uncertainty is high, the servicescape—in combination with such things as service-provider behaviors, customer-assurance procedures, and policies regarding such things as service guarantees—can engender needed trust.

Recently, one of us (Heskett) had to find a dentist in a community unfamiliar to him. Not knowing whom to ask, the next best thing was to get the name of the nearest dentist from Delta Dental, the insurance provider. Knowing that the treatment would probably involve that most dreaded of all procedures, a root canal, the first visit to the dentist raised some apprehension. Visual cues would be important. And the visual cues were not encouraging. The waiting room was well-worn and somewhat dreary. The equipment visible from the waiting room appeared not to be the latest. And supplies looked as though they had been stashed in an unorganized fashion in a small break room. The cues didn't foster the trust that is so important when customers enter service encounters with high levels of perceived risk. As it turned out, the service quality was quite adequate. But the patient hasn't returned for additional treatment.

Design Facilitates the Delivery of a Service

Servicescapes may spell the difference between the success and failure of self-serve services, where layout, signage, and instructions are critical if a customer is to successfully negotiate the servicescape and complete a transaction. Websites are servicescapes that many of us visit with increasing frequency. Their design can spell the difference between a successful transaction or a frustrated customer.

Where the service is interpersonal, any number of features may make it easier for a service worker to provide heroic service. For example, at Caesar's Palace, several features have been built in to its high-stakes slot machines to ensure that the company's policy of providing differentiated service to its highest-value customers is implemented. At the time that a customer swipes his Total Rewards card to begin play, the machine lights a color signaling the customer's value to employees on the floor of the casino. Because slot machine players typically do not like to have to surrender their machines to get food or beverages, they are able to summon service to the slot machine, all paid for by means of preauthorized charges to a credit or debit card, saving the player the trouble of digging through his pockets while the machine waits. In this case, the servicescape enables Caesar's employees to deliver differentiated levels of service to its customers, thereby reinforcing the value of Total Rewards program loyalty in their minds.

Of course, servicescapes often have to be redesigned to support the introduction of new technologies. Technology, network, and servicescape design and use can make or break a service depending on the degree to which they are consistent with one another and with the nature of the service strategy they are intended to support.

BACK TO STARBUCKS: TECHNOLOGY GONE AWRY

To pick up from where we left off, after hearing quite enough from Starbucks's partners (employees) about how they were losing touch with customers, Schultz composed and sent a confidential e-mail to the company's ceo and his team outlining his concerns. It was titled "The Commoditization of the Starbucks Experience"—and it was leaked by one of its recipients to the world, creating a firestorm of comment from financial analysts, investors, and partners. Financial performance of the company was still good, but Schultz was frustrated by things he saw going on in its stores. His fellow board members, with concerns about the impact of gathering storm clouds in the global economy, asked him to return as ceo at the beginning of 2008.

By the time Howard Schultz had resumed the job of ceo, a new espresso machine, the Mastrena, was in the final stages of design at Thermoplan, its Swiss manufacturer. He approved the rollout of the Mastrena but asked that it be "more artfully designed" to contribute to the Starbucks in-store customer (and barista) experience. One goal was to reduce the height of the machine on the counter to restore eye contact between barista and customer—so critical to the Starbucks service encounter. If that could be done, losses for employees, customers, and investors could be converted to wins, using our criteria for judging support systems. Schultz's description of the result tells us a lot about the subtleties of design, his passion for the nature of the business and ideas that contribute to the coffee experience, and the complexities of fitting technology into a service strategy:

With its dusted copper and shiny metal skin and ergonomic design, the Mastrena is truly elegant. On top, a clear chalice holds fresh espresso beans waiting to be ground. Inside, every component had been engineered with Starbucks' beans in mind. The Mastrena also, to my great joy, sits four inches lower on our counters, so baristas and customers can visually and verbally connect. By perfecting the coffee's grind size and pour time, a barista can proudly "own" every shot.[17]

Schultz's description borders on poetry. No wonder we're still willing to pay a premium price for a Starbucks experience that incidentally includes coffee. It illustrates the subtle differences in employing technology in the delivery of experiences—the importance of visual aesthetics, communication, and employee ownership of the process for both customer and service provider—as opposed to just products and services.

Howard Schultz distanced himself just far enough from the business to become more objective about what he saw happening. What he saw was that Starbucks stores were losing their distinct "flavor." Their servicescape was sending the wrong cues. For example, the smell of ground coffee was being displaced by the smell of cheese from the newly introduced breakfast sandwiches. Many new products were being sold. The point-of-sale equipment was outmoded.

Refocusing Starbucks required the company to drop products, restore the in-store coffee ambience, close every store for several hours so partners could be retrained, and bring back technology that reconnected baristas with their customers. As a result, nearly 20,000 of the old machines were replaced with new Mastrena machines, helping to bring back the art of the barista while restoring relationships critical to the service experience. Partner loyalty, so critical to the quality of interactions with customers, increased almost immediately. And with it, customer loyalty and profits increased as well. The company was well on its way to regaining the in-store experience that had distinguished it for so many years.

LOOKING AHEAD

Technology, network, and facility design are rapidly changing the face of services in ways that enable us to glimpse the future. The directions this work is taking make it relatively easy to predict several phenomena: anticipatory service, remotely performed services, services based on machine-to-machine (M2M) communication and the so-called Internet of Things, the deployment of robotics, and the integrated design of servicescapes around the needs of employees and customers alike.

Anticipatory Service

Organizations like GE Medical, Otis Elevator, and manufacturers of heavy-duty trucks have employed technology for many years to predict and anticipate the need for servicing their products. Sensors on an elevator provide the continuing measures that enable engineers to monitor wear and other functions in ways that make it possible for Otis's service teams to provide maintenance on a timely basis before owners have to order it. Technology increasingly will allow a growing number of organizations to anticipate the need for service for products that to a greater and greater extent are simply computers capable of communicating their own service needs to technicians waiting to take their calls.

Remotely Performed Service

It is becoming increasingly clear that any service involving primarily the transmission of information and knowledge will, sooner or later, be performed to some degree on a remote basis. This will have a profound effect on the quality experienced by users as well as competition among service providers. Access to advice or instruction from the "best in the world" will quickly raise the standards of those being served remotely. Furthermore, it will set in motion a process by which increased competition will raise the standard even higher, putting a number of service providers at a distinct competitive disadvantage and even putting them out of work and out of business. Mediocre hospitals and educational institutions of higher learning are already feeling the pressure that will grow in other service industries as well.

Service Based on the Internet of Things and M2M Communication

In recent years so-called big-data systems have been sweeping up raw data (not information) from a variety of machines, computers, mobile devices, and other sources in ways that allow the application of advanced analytic methods that yield information about how humans behave and things work. These methods can automatically trigger actions that provide competitive edge. With increasing frequency, they involve machines and devices speaking to one another (M2M). Jahangir Mohammed, founder of Jasper Technologies, says that "when things are connected, they become a service." His firm has produced software that "allows companies to manage and monetize those services." For example, the software will enable stolen Nissan automobiles to send out location signals directly to law enforcement agencies. Or it will turn General Motors' automobiles into remotely controlled Wi-Fi hotspots by linking its technology with that of AT&T to enable passengers to do whatever they now do on their computers or mobile devices, but in their automobiles.

The possibilities for services delivered through the Internet of Things are vast. In a few years, these services will become so numerous that we will take them for granted. They will enhance productivity in ways that will be credited both to service providers and manufacturers.

Deployment of Robotics

Some people have speculated about the use of robots to deliver services. It will increase, but it will be confined largely to those services not involving face-to-face contact with customers, such as warehouse order processing. The adoption of robots faces several challenges. The first, of course, is a customer's unwillingness to interact with a robot for anything but a simple transaction, such as withdrawing money from a bank account, an application that has had nearly universal success. A more complex set of challenges involves interaction on the job, especially where robots are employed alongside humans in a team-like setting to deliver services requiring both the efficiencies of robotics and the judgment of humans. According to one analysis, "robot researchers are confronting some fascinating questions that are much less about tasks that robots can perform than what social and interpersonal capabilities they might need to persuade their human colleagues to accept them."[18]

Although their use may be slow to develop, robots nevertheless will increasingly be used in services such as medical surgery and security. In such cases, they will increase productivity with an attendant loss of some service jobs.

Integrated Servicescape Design

In the future services will be designed with a greater emphasis on the customer experience rather than on marketing, operational, or financial satisfaction. In a sense, services increasingly will be designed from the inside out, starting with the customer. The concept of the servicescape will become more and more important in this process. Practitioners will consider how technology, networks, and facilities design intersect to enable service providers to deliver the desired customer experience. Integrated design will increasingly become the name of the game here.

THE ULTIMATE TEST

We can't emphasize strongly enough that an overarching criterion in the design and implementation of any kind of support system is whether it produces a win for employees, customers, and investors. If the answer for any of these parties to a service is no, it may well be a signal that redesign is in order, no matter how large the benefit to one of the parties or the sum of the benefits to all three.

Support systems are changing at warp speed, driven primarily by changes in technology. As this occurs, wide generational differences, as usual, will be seen in the ability of managers to appreciate and envision the potential of the future. These differences explain why change is being led by young entrepreneurs rather than more senior managers in large, established organizations. The operational question for the future of the large service firm is not how it can be made more entrepreneurial. It is rather how to transport new ideas generated outside the box of the large organization into the service of the mass of customers served by the service giants. Will this be done primarily by acquisition or by a process in which the giants will be displaced by the upstarts?

Up to now, much of our discussion has assumed that services are delivered to customers. The question has been "What can we do for customers?" Going forward, the question increasingly will be "What can we do with customers?" and even "What can customers do for us?" As it turns out, they are often willing to do plenty, as we will see when we turn next to the ways in which service organizations are tapping in to the extraordinary value of customers as owners rather than just people and organizations to be targeted.

CHAPTER 7

Services Marketing:

Foster Customer Ownership

What great service leaders _know:_
satisfying customers is not enough.

What great service leaders _do:_
they take steps to develop a core of customers who are owners.

We'll be up front about it. The purpose of this chapter is to convince you that much of conventional marketing theory and effort is misdirected, especially when applied to the marketing of services. Because such marketing effort is insufficiently focused, it is not just wasteful, but it overlooks the fact that no more than 10 percent of the customers of many, perhaps most, service organizations represent _all_ the profit. They are what we have come to regard as "owners"— customers who are loyal and engaged and who provide referrals, ideas for new services, and suggestions for ways to improve the service encounter. A core of owners, as few as one in 20, can replace most conventional marketing activities.

WHAT HAPPENS WHEN CUSTOMERS
BECOME OWNERS

We saw what happens when employees act as owners in chapter 4. Mabel Yu stood her ground and even faced ridicule as she helped her employer, the Vanguard Group, avoid buying exotic, risky investments before the economy crashed in 2008. Customers can also have a significant impact on service cost and value when they act as owners and co-creators of service. They do that at La Villa Gallarati Scotti in northern Italy, one of more than 30 château-style seminar and meetings venues operated by Paris-based Châteauform'. A seminar there in which one of us (Heskett) taught provided a reminder of the power of the customer in creating value in a service.[1]

A warm welcome to the villa was followed by a tour of the public rooms, the bar, and the restaurant, given by a married couple who were carefully selected to manage the facility and encouraged to think of themselves as owners of the château. Only one thing appeared to be missing during the tour: staff. As it turns out, only a small staff is needed to deliver the service.

Guests were told not to worry about a tab for food, wine, recreational materials, or even the bar. There was no tab. The all-inclusive daily charge was precisely that. Instead, guests were to make themselves at home, fix themselves a drink at the bar, or find themselves a midnight snack from a table set up in the kitchen. In short, it was the kind of place with just the kind of service many people like. But wait a minute. This is do-it-yourself service, in which customers help make it work, contribute labor, and at the same time reduce costs. Why do they do it? Probably because they enjoy the novelty of providing services that are usually performed for them. But they are willing to do it as well because they are invited, along with the married couple managing it, to take responsibility for the property and regard it as their own.

The all-inclusive, do-it-yourself format is just one of a number of practices that align to produce high levels of employee and customer satisfaction and loyalty—as well as good financial results, as we will see in a moment. Together, the practices differentiate Châteauform' from operators of other executive-development centers, providing important sources of leverage and edge over competitors operating more conventional meeting venues.

At this point, you may be asking yourself what this has to do with marketing. After all, customer participation in co-creating a service or leveraging value over cost mostly concerns operations, not marketing. But it's what happens next that provides the connection. Châteauform' relies heavily on satisfied customers to sell the service to newcomers. The attention-getting "headline" in the referral may be the unusual experience—fixing your own drink at La Villa Gallarati Scotti. But the conversation quickly turns to the quality of the overall experience and the results it produces. It helps explain why Châteauform' realizes more than half of its business through word-of-mouth referrals, added evidence of the power of customer ownership.

The Châteauform' example sends a strong message that putting customers to work in the co-creation and marketing of a service may be a great source of leverage and competitive edge. Châteauform' has distinguished itself by developing unusually high proportions of owners among its clientele. These are customers who fall at the extreme end of what we call the "ownership curve."

THE OWNERSHIP CURVE

The nature of customer ownership is best described in the context of six different types of customers, arrayed on what can be called a *customer ownership curve* (figure 7-1). It reflects the influence that value, trust, and loyalty (developed by a dedicated workforce of owner employees) have on customer ownership and lifetime value.

Figure 7-1 The Customer Ownership Curve

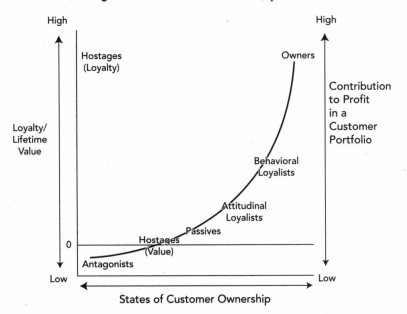

Source: Adapted from the "satisfaction-loyalty curve" in James L. Heskett, W. Earl Sasser Jr., and Leonard A. Schlesinger, *The Service Profit Chain: How Leading Companies Link Profit and Growth to Loyalty, Satisfaction, and Value* (New York: The Free Press, 1997), at p. 87.

As we move from left to right on the customer ownership scale, and from bottom to top on the loyalty/lifetime value scale, an ownership relationship with customers increases at an increasing rate. Current or potential customers who populate the ownership curve experience various amounts of value (results combined with the quality of the service experience) and react in a variety of ways to what they experience.

First, there is a group of customers who perceive little value from the service encounter and develop little trust in the provider. Clearly, their expectations are not met. Some remain passive, telling no one but vowing not to repeat the experience. Others take action, telling others about their bad experiences and dissuading some from trying the service.[2] We used to call them "terrorists," but events since 9/11 have convinced us that *antagonists* is a better term. Antagonists can be damaging to the growth of a business. If too many decide to act early in the life of an organization, they can put it out of business. It's critical that they be identified, perhaps through the complaint process or through listening posts, so that efforts can be made to at least neutralize their feelings. As we see in figure 7-1, antagonists represent negative lifetime value to a service provider.

Passive customers, whether or not they have had positive or negative service experiences, populate the middle range of the curve. Regardless of their experiences, they don't tell others and don't exhibit high loyalty. They make up perhaps the largest proportion of customers on the curve. One particular group of passives can be costly to a service organization. They are the *opportunists,* who time their purchases to take advantage of promotions, only to return to passive status. For this group price is the primary influence on value. Passives may exhibit a particularly vexing characteristic: they believe and tell researchers that they are going to repurchase, whether or not they do. It's this behavior, for example, that we think poses a problem for measures such as the popular Net Promoter Score that may rely on false expressions of customers' intent to repurchase. This behavior has been termed *attitudinal loyalty.*[3]

On the right side of the diagram are behavioral *loyalists*—customers who react to positive service encounters with repeat purchases that can, over time, be a substantial source of profit. They exhibit both attitudinal loyalty (belief that they are loyal) and behavioral loyalty (actual repurchase).[4] Like the passives, they only occasionally tell others of their experiences, even though they may respond positively to the question "How likely are you to recommend this service to a friend?" This too presents a problem for the accurate measurement of profitability resulting from loyal customers. Those who do follow through with recommendations to friends are the *owners.*

One type of customer doesn't fit on the ownership curve. We call them *hostages* because we know of no other word to explain why they exhibit high levels of loyalty with lowered levels of lifetime value. These are customers who perceive themselves as trapped in a relationship that they would terminate if it were easy to switch service providers. They complain to anyone who will listen, creating negative value for their service provider. As industries such as cable television and network service providers consolidate, the number of hostages grows.

We've purposely drawn the curve in figure 7-1 to suggest that owners are the ones who propel an organization's performance to new heights. These are loyal customers who not only express a willingness to recommend an organization, but they do it, and they do it with some influence over others. In doing so they become an important arm of the marketing effort for a service organization. This is not all that owners do. They are also most likely to suggest ways of improving the service encounter (if only the service provider will listen, a matter addressed below). It doesn't stop there. Organizations have tapped into the enthusiasm of owners by involving them in operational decisions. For example, taking a cue from Southwest Airlines, which has been doing it for years, several organizations now invite customer owners to help interview and select some of the frontline people who will be serving them in the future.

Our explorations of the economics of ownership in several organizations in different businesses suggest that the lifetime value of an owner is worth from 80 to 100 passive customers. In fact, owners and loyalists provide more than 100 percent of the operating profit (offsetting losses from the remaining customers) in many service organizations—even though together they may represent no more than 10 percent of the customer base. This was the conclusion we reached when we analyzed the data supplied to us by Caesar's Entertainment, as described below.[5] Curious about whether these ideas apply to other kinds of services, we asked Lanham Napier, former CEO of Rackspace Hosting, a website hosting and management company that relies heavily on customer referrals, to provide us with similar estimates of the value of a customer owner at Rackspace. With a couple of assumptions, a few calculations and little hesitation, he confirmed our notion by concluding that a customer owner at Rackspace is worth about 80 less-engaged customers.

Where the economics of customer ownership are so significant—and we believe the potential is widespread—it is important to know how owners and loyalists are developed from the merely passive middle of the typical base of customers.

DEVELOP CUSTOMERS AS OWNERS

Great service leaders know the organization must take action to either reinforce customer ownership or encourage it. The baseline for this effort is the delivery of excellent service on a consistent basis, the subject of much of this book. Beyond that, it includes efforts to define and track customer owners; put customers to work; provide multiple, personalized service levels; and rethink how the marketing/operating budget is to be allocated.

Create Consistent Value for Targeted Customers and Those Who Serve Them: The Starting Point

The value of results delivered to customers determines their willingness to repurchase; it also potentially determines their loyalty. But it is the consistency with which value is delivered that determines their trust. Trust forms the base of a pyramid of behaviors that encompasses customer engagement (willingness to refer), loyalty (actual repurchases), and ownership (number of referrals of new customers and suggestions for new ways of doing business).

What are the most important elements of value to a customer? Two things are becoming increasingly clear. It is only tangentially about the product or service being acquired. It is only partially about price. And in many cases it doesn't involve purchases at all.

First, customers tell us that a primary goal is to realize results or solutions, regardless of whether that requires products and services or not. That knowledge was the cornerstone of the effort to transform IBM from a product-oriented mainframe computer company to one delivering turnkey information-processing solutions to clients on a global basis, regardless of whether IBM products were mobilized to do it. In many cases, the solution allows a client to avoid acquiring hardware, software, and related services altogether, instead renting a capability provided by IBM. As mentioned earlier, the management of Pitney-Bowes similarly transformed the company from a manufacturer and seller of mailroom equipment to an operator of mail rooms for other businesses.

Second, customers care about how results are achieved, as well as the quality of the experience. It has led several to conclude that we indeed live increasingly in an "experience economy."[6] If results are the baseline requirement for value for customers, the quality of the experience is often the differentiating factor that determines whether a customer will return or recommend a vendor to someone else.

Together, results and the quality of the customer experience are at the core of a customer's decision to repurchase a service. But none of this has much business value unless efforts are made to track customers who exhibit ownership behaviors in order to reinforce relations with them. It's well worth the effort.

Define and Track Customer Owners

Increasingly, information systems are being designed to track customer behaviors. But tracking is not enough. Someone has to be able to use the information to craft individual "conversations" with customers intended to make owners feel special.

At Victoria's Secret, the retailer devoted to creating memorable experiences for its customers for lingerie, each of a thousand stores now has access to a current database of the purchases of its loyal customers. A new "bra launch" is the occasion for the preparation of individual invitations to attend an after-hours reception, product introduction, and fitting for loyal customers. The company's sister organization, Bath & Body Works, lacks such detailed information about purchasers of its lower-value beauty products, and instead relies on the judgment of its store managers and employees to distribute free samples of new products to their better customers. While both approaches have proved effective, the future of success-ful service delivery will clearly depend more and more heavily on the effective tracking of customer owners.

Put Your Best Customers to Work

We're convinced that the overwhelming majority of customer loyal-ists (using terms from figure 7-1) want to serve as owners if given a chance. Unfortunately, too many marketing organizations ignore this, preferring instead to listen to admonishments by their sales arm not to disturb loyal customers with requests for referrals and suggestions. Research we conducted at Caesar's Entertainment sug-gests just how wrongheaded this is.[7]

Caesar's Entertainment, one of the world's largest operators of gaming casinos, under the leadership of one of our former col-leagues, Gary Loveman, developed what is arguably the world's largest customer loyalty program. As a reminder, it's called Total Rewards, and it is based on the concept of the lifetime value of each member to Caesar's.

For our study of customer ownership, we were able to access more than 4,000 of Caesar's customers. We asked them the standard Net Promoter Score question ("Based on your experiences, would you be willing to recommend Caesar's to others?"). But we also asked them questions indicating actual ownership behaviors over the previous 12 months, as well as other things they might be willing to do to help Caesar's improve its operation. What we found is remarkable.

First, we found that the company's most valuable customers (Seven Stars and Diamonds) referred 20 percent more Total Rewards members to Caesar's on a per capita basis than its less valuable (Platinum and Gold) customers, even though the two groups registered roughly the same "willingness to recommend." What they did was more important (and accurate) than what they said they would do if given the chance. Their recommendations also carried more weight, producing 32 percent more new recruits than lower-value Platinums and Golds. As you might guess, more Seven Stars and Diamonds were recommended by people just like them than by Platinums and Golds. The result was that their recommendations in total yielded new members with a 73 percent greater estimated lifetime value than members referred by Platinums and Golds.

There is more. Sixteen percent more of these high-value, busy, wealthy, probably high-ego Seven Stars and Diamonds were actually willing to attend a meeting to discuss new service ideas for Caesar's to improve its business than their lower-value fellow members. But most surprising of all, in response to our question, 39 percent more of them indicated that they would be willing to take time off to help Caesar's in the interviewing and selection of its frontline employees. Adding up the contributions of the relatively small number of Seven Stars and Diamonds in our sample (roughly 5 percent of the total), we concluded that during just the year that we studied them, the total came to more than the collective lifetime value of those making up the other 95 percent of our sample. Even allowing for overreporting, the differences were dramatic. Each Seven Star and Diamond member was easily worth more than 80 Platinum and Gold Total Rewards members. This program helps explain why the organization was purchased by two private-equity organizations in

2006 for a price three times the company's market value just five years earlier.

Results of this research led us to the conclusion that when loyal customers are asked to provide referrals to potential customers, their loyalty is not diminished. It suggests that one of the highest priorities of a successful service organization is to convert loyalists to owners. In some of the most successful service organizations, marketing management appears to play a facilitating role. Customers themselves supply much of the selling effort.

Provide Multiple Service Levels

In order to make Total Rewards work well, Caesar's has to be able to deliver more than one level of service—and that is not easy. It is assisted not only by information technology that makes available up-to-date information on each Total Rewards member but also by the servicescape in its casinos and the way its network of casinos and the information they generate is managed. As we saw in chapter 6, support systems can play a large role in facilitating service differentiation, even when it is difficult for humans to do so. But support systems can't do everything. Employees have to be hired and trained not only to deliver differentiated service levels but also to sell the benefits of loyalty to customers who may complain that they are being discriminated against.

Questions have been raised about policies that provide multiple service levels. They include issues of fairness and whether or not they repel as many customers as they encourage. What researchers have found is that varying service levels are accepted by customers who understand what people have to do to qualify for each level of service. What really irks customers is the same service provided at highly varying prices, such as in the airline business.

Differentiated services associated with frequent-flyer programs in the airline business establish high loyalty levels that are negatively affected only through changes in scheduled departure times or customer lifestyles (apart from poor service).[8] Airline passengers' loyalty is explained in part by the relatively poor treatment they receive when they fly on airlines they don't normally patronize—airlines on which their frequent-flyer status is low. The experience reinforces their preferences for the service on the airlines they fly frequently. It also reminds them that not everyone experiences the level of service they have come to expect on their "home airline."

This type of passenger experience illustrates the inept way in which many airlines use their passenger information today. In a world of better management, information showing a reservation by a first-time (or infrequent) passenger, particularly in business class, would trigger extra one-time perks by an airline in an effort to demonstrate its best service level and the benefits of customer loyalty. This could be an equally effective way of putting information to work in using multiple service levels as a means of marketing the service. But it requires that management be willing to scan and put to use already-available information, as well as frontline cabin attendants who are willing and able to welcome a first-time passenger and potential customer owner to a new flying experience.

Rethink How the Marketing/Operating Budget Is Allocated

There is room for debate about the allocation of funds designed to change the shape of the ownership curve. The question is, what kind of attention should be given—and with what priority—to each customer type as part of the process of creating budgets for service operations and marketing? We have insufficient research and little public data on which to base a conclusion; priorities may be influenced by individual circumstances. But at the very least, it appears that you should give high priority, first, to neutralizing antagonists who can do great harm to an organization's reputation and brand. Second, you can gain particularly high payoffs from catering to existing owners as well as efforts to convert loyalists to owners. Further down the list of priorities, recognizing how lack of choice can represent negative value, you might make an effort to free the hostage customers by offering them alternatives or quality services. It is less clear how much money should be spent trying to convert passives to loyalists; surprisingly little research has been done on what should be an important question for marketers.

This brings us to the potentially high return on investment that is often ignored: converting other organizations' owners and loyalists. Some industries offer greater opportunity for converting competitors' customers than others. The airline industry, for example, offers numerous opportunities for it. The nature of the business is that it is hard to meet or exceed customers' expectations every time. Service is slow. Facilities are crowded during peak times. Flights are cancelled due to mechanical problems. These are perfect opportunities for efforts to convert loyalists from one competitor to another. A restaurant operator with whom we are familiar regularly carried coupons offering a free meal when visiting competitors' establishments. Whenever he observed or overheard a customer registering dissatisfaction with the service or the food, he would produce a coupon and invite the dissatisfied customer to his restaurant for a free meal, often with the comment that "no one should have to put up with the service you just received."

CUSTOMER LIFETIME VALUE: TRANSFORMING MARKETING EFFORT

Châteauform' employees are rewarded for the loyalty of their clientele. In addition, they naturally benefit from the referrals that satisfied clients at all of the company's châteaus make to potential new clients. Customer loyalty and referrals are the two most important sources of what has come to be known as *customer lifetime value*—the true measure of the value of a customer. There are other sources, of course, such as higher margins on added purchases and reduced costs of marketing. Together, these contributors to customer lifetime value can add up to surprisingly high levels of economic success.

Lifetime Value by the Numbers: Supporting Research

Work by one of us (Sasser) and one of his former MBA students, Fred Reichheld, is widely credited with provoking a renewed interest in customer lifetime value.[9] Based on an examination of nine companies in nine different service businesses, they concluded that, in addition to an initial purchase, customer loyalty produces a stream of revenue from (1) added purchases of the same product, (2) purchases of new products, (3) added profit from price premiums that loyal customers are willing to pay for new products, and (4) reductions in the costs of serving loyal customers. As customer and supplier become more familiar with each other, customers even begin to contribute to the quality of the experience for themselves and others by helping provide the service and training of new customers.[10] The list of benefits also includes increased profits from purchases by new customers referred by loyal customers, termed the "loyalty ripple effect" by Dwayne Gremler and Stephen Brown,[11] and increased profits from ideas for new processes or products suggested by loyal customers who act like owners. Reichheld and Sasser found that customer profitability is invariably greatest in the year before a loyal customer ultimately defects. As a result, in the nine businesses they studied, they calculated that by extending a relationship with a customer from five to six years, companies in the sample could increase lifetime profits from customer relationships by up to 85 percent.

Why Estimate Customer Lifetime Value?

Anyone who subscribes to the findings of this research has to give serious thought to the possibility that new business, at least in the short run, is less profitable than repeat business. This leads to a conclusion that marketing budgets should include ample funds for the retention of existing customers, even if it means reducing budgets for the generation of new business. In the absence of measures of customer lifetime value, this can be a hard proposition to sell. Thus, efforts to estimate customer lifetime value constitute more than an academic exercise. The process is especially useful if it is used as a way of underlining for senior managers the importance of what they do in serving existing customers. It is anything but academic at Caesar's Entertainment, where focusing on customer lifetime value is a way of life.

The act of estimating customer lifetime value sensitizes marketing and other managers to the importance of positive customer experiences. More importantly, it is a way of convincing top managers that significant investments can be justified to improve customer service, something that is not always obvious to them. Client lifetime value is not a useful day-to-day measure of success. Rather, it is a number that, if estimated occasionally, alerts people at all levels of an organization to the importance of achieving the right level of customer service as part of a marketing strategy.

The Estimating Process

Calculating comprehensive customer lifetime value requires a number of pieces of information. They include the following for each major category of customer: (1) average length of relationship with the customer, (2) the customer acquisition cost, (3) year-to-year sale of (basic and related) products or services over the length of the relationship, (4) the margin of operating profit on sales, (5) the increase in margin or operating profit attributable to the development of improved practices and better knowledge during the relationship with the customer, (6) the flow of operating profit associated with new product or service ideas provided by the customer, (7) the number of new-business referrals per year attributed to the customer, and (8) the flow of operating profit from new referrals (repeating steps 1 through 6 for each piece of referred business).

Because much of this information is not normally tracked, the process often requires assumptions on the part of those estimating a lifetime value. This has the benefit of personalizing the estimate—making sure employees "own" it.

Putting Customer Lifetime Value to Work in Marketing Services

We mentioned earlier that Caesar's Entertainment's Total Rewards program is based on member lifetime value. Information gained from members of the company's Total Rewards customer-retention program is used in its operations to provide differentiated, customized services that recognize customer loyalty at its casinos. But the information is also used for marketing.

Total Rewards is the foundation for Caesar's Entertainment's marketing efforts to its existing customers. Depending on each member's profile and preferences, the company fashions various complementary packages designed to recognize patronage and preferences as well as encourage ownership behaviors. And it works, as they say, in spades.

Much of the success of any effort to build customer ownership starts with enlisting employees as owners. This is particularly true where the service encounter between customer and employee is personal and face-to-face. In a companion survey to the study we described at Caesar's Entertainment, we found that 54 percent of the organization's employees had recommended their company as a place to work to two or more of their friends.[12]

MAXIMIZE BENEFITS FROM LISTENING POSTS

Breakthrough service organizations make use of every available opportunity to listen to customers, as well as their own employees. In the past, this included survey data, complaint letters and phone calls, and requests for information or assistance. Today's technology has made available an added array of methods such as websites, social networks, feedback services, and polling devices for doing this. At Amazon, for example, the channel is simple and direct. An e-mail to jeff@amazon.com puts a customer in direct contact with Jeff Bezos, CEO. If the e-mail is sufficiently provocative, the escalation process begins with the appropriate executive. As Jeff Wilke, senior vice president for North American Retail at Amazon, put it, "Every anecdote from a customer matters. . . . We research each of them because they tell us something about our processes. It's an audit that is done for us by our customers. We treat them as precious sources of information."[13]

Employees are at the heart of a strategy of developing organizational *listening posts* to detect shifting customer interests and needs. Most often this includes personnel at customer-service centers (don't think of them as merely "call centers"), who are valued for their abilities to identify needs for new products and services, as well as resolve customer problems. Unfortunately, too many organizations assign minimum-wage personnel or, worse yet, outsourced organizations to handle customer requests and concerns. The result is the loss of information of incalculable value to those designing new products and services. Consider what one of us (Heskett) experienced recently.

The problem involved the operation of a cable television service provided by Comcast. At the outset of the phone call to a service representative, the caller was asked if he would participate in a survey after the call. As an advocate of listening, of course Heskett said he would. The call went miserably. After 30 minutes of confusing conversation with the Comcast representative, the caller was rushed to the end of the conversation. Obviously, the representative was facing some kind of limit on the length of the call. A somewhat puzzled, frustrated caller was then asked for his feedback. At the outset, a voice on the automatic polling device thanked Heskett for his cooperation in what would be a two-minute poll. The first question was "On a scale of 1 to 5, with 5 being the most favorable, how would you rate your recent service experience?" The caller responded with a "1," whereupon the polling device thanked him for his cooperation and hung up, leaving the caller to ponder why Comcast had taken the trouble to sponsor the survey at all. In the process, a useful listening opportunity was lost, and a bad-service story was created for telling and retelling (and writing about).

A good listening strategy includes methods of ensuring that the results of frontline listening reach those who are responsible for new product and service development. One of the most effective of these is the requirement that those responsible for marketing research and product development periodically take calls from customers.

Build an Organization around Listening: The Case of Intuit

Intuit, the largest provider of personal financial software in the world, was literally built on listening posts. From its earliest days, Intuit's co-founders, Scott Cook and Tom Proulx, followed a strategy typical of the software industry: putting good but imperfect, 1.0 software on the market, then relying on users to identify bugs and ways of improving it. The strategy required mechanisms to be set up to solicit feedback; people, who had to be hired and trained, who could interpret the feedback; and an organization that could hand off suggestions fielded by frontline personnel to those designing later versions of the same software.

This strategy has yielded successful annual updates of existing software packages such as Quicken (for personal finance) and QuickBooks (for small business management), producing a stream of sales over several years and thereby enhancing the lifetime value of Intuit's customers. The success of the strategy requires that users of the imperfect software don't defect to competitors. That, in turn, makes it important that the updates are of acceptable quality and contain the new ideas suggested by users.

Intuit ensured the success of this strategy by organizing itself as one big listening post. From the very outset, it hired people with skills and interests in interacting with customers, then provided them with product knowledge and training—not only in the use of the software, but also in the laws and regulations related to problem areas users might encounter. Most importantly, these people were trained and paid well for their listening skills. Working out of customer-support centers, they have always been regarded as sources of ideas, product development, and marketing effort, rather than merely a necessary cost.

Ideas are also collected at another listening post staffed by marketing research personnel. Users are brought to Intuit's offices and given new software to install on company computers while Intuit's marketing research executives watch, asking questions about why users did something a certain way. In addition, they engage in "follow-me-home sessions," where researchers actually accompany purchasers of Intuit's software back to the home or business, observing everything, from unwrapping the product to installing and using the software.

The flow of ideas from customer-support centers and marketing research listening posts then extends to a group of software engineers who are hired to make the product simple for users. In an occupation where engineers typically want to work on complex software and applications, those who are driven to make things simple are a rare breed. They also have to be willing to take over the phones at the customer-support center to listen personally to customers' ideas.

That's the core of a simple organization comprising customer support, marketing research, and software engineering. With this kind of organization and listening, the company doesn't have much need for sales. Satisfied customers provide the sales effort through word-of-mouth recommendations. And product manufacturing is outsourced. All of this makes for an organization that has grown into a profitable business with a $20 billion valuation—one of the few that has successfully outcompeted giant Microsoft over the years, at least in the field of personal finance software. Intuit is proof that a strategy built on listening posts can work and work well.

Decide How to Track Results

A number of measures have been developed to assist listening by tracking such things as employee and customer satisfaction, loyalty, and ownership.[14] Whether an organization gauges results through use of a Net Promoter Score or some other metric is not of huge importance to us. We're also less concerned about what is measured than the fact that measures be employed consistently (using the same question) and frequently. Any measure has some value in tracking important dimensions of service performance over long periods. Measures are likely to have the most value if they reflect the kind of listening that triggers useful change in policies and practices.

Develop Listening Capability

Developing listening capability requires that organizations (1) hire frontline people with the capability to listen and learn; (2) create listening posts, opportunities for the organization to hear about new ideas from customers, employees, suppliers, and others; (3) provide training in how to listen and incentives for employees to serve effectively as listening posts; (4) develop ways of organizing the information collected; (5) create incentives for communicating the information to those who can do something about it; and (6) organize and take other steps to ensure that those on the receiving end use it. This is how Intuit and great service organizations like it ensure that they stay ahead of competitors—who either don't listen, or just as bad, who listen but don't hear.

REDUCE CUSTOMERS' PERCEIVED RISK: THE SERVICE GUARANTEE

Earlier, we discussed the use of service guarantees to engage customers in efforts to control quality. The guarantees serve a second important purpose as well in helping to market novel services or those involving perceived risk.

Service guarantees for marketing purposes are distant cousins of entrepreneur Josiah Wedgwood's satisfaction-or-your-money-back guarantee on his pottery in the United Kingdom in the 18th century, as well as Richard Sears's money-back mail order assurances in the United States in the 19th century. They are related to the warranties that were first introduced by automobile dealers early in the 20th century. Warranties were the dealer's way of assuring people buying their first automobile ever that their new purchase would serve them well for the period of the warranty—something of real value at a time when new automobiles broke down frequently. Service guarantees serve the same purpose for high-risk service purchases—they are the warranties of the service world.

In helping managers decide whether or not to offer a service guarantee, Christopher Hart has posed several questions: (1) Is the proposed guarantee substantial enough to be meaningful to customers? (2) Is it meaningful to the one offering it; for example, is it potentially so costly that its invocation by customers could put the company out of business?. (3) Is the guarantee unconditional; that is, can it be invoked on the say-so of the customer alone? (4) Is the guarantee easy for the customer and service provider to understand, invoke, and collect on?[15]

Service guarantees may be explicit or implicit, depending on their purpose. For example, if the objective is to provide outstanding service recovery or information for quality-control purposes, the decision may be to employ an implicit guarantee. Ritz-Carlton, for example, does not advertise the fact that its housekeepers have the authority to spend up to $2,000 correcting concerns that may be raised by guests. Even its most loyal guests probably don't know about it.

However, if the purpose of a guarantee is largely marketing, an explicit guarantee may serve the purpose best. For example, Scott Cook and Tom Proulx at Intuit decided to take an audacious tack by offering their first product, Quicken, to users with an unconditional service guarantee. They decided that they had to do it to induce customers to try an unknown product with no credibility.

If customers didn't like Quicken for any reason, they could get their money back, whether or not they returned the software. It required confidence in the product on their part. It placed a heavy burden on them to ensure the quality of their product. Not only didn't the product come back, but neither did requests for refunds. Instead, satisfied users who might have never tried Quicken began telling their friends to order the software. Intuit's star was launched on the back of a service guarantee that could literally have put its co-founders out of business. Guarantees have also been successfully employed to market services to people who have had poor experiences with competitors. What better time to tap into the opportunity that competitors offer along with their inferior service?

A service guarantee, combined with highly effective listening devices, created a large cadre of customer owners among users of

Intuit's software products. As a result, Intuit is a company built on the recommendations of its customer owners to potential buyers, rather than on extensive advertising or a large sales force. In a sense, it calls into question some traditional marketing concepts, illustrating the power of new approaches to marketing that will characterize future service organizations.

REAP THE ULTIMATE BENEFIT OF LISTENING: NEW STRATEGIC DIRECTIONS

Customer ownership can literally save a business. We've seen it happen more than once. For example, the leadership of Rackspace Hosting steered the company out of near bankruptcy on the advice of a customer.[16] At a time when the company was about to fail, offering website design and management services with declining margins to a wide range of clients, one of its better clients suggested that Rackspace focus on the increasingly complex problems faced by companies relying primarily on their websites. As a result, the company developed a premium service, staffed by "customer fanatics," who provide 24/7 support so good that it is able to command premium prices.

Much the same thing happened to Diane Hessan, the founder and CEO of a struggling start-up, Communispace, in 1999.[17] Hessan founded her company based on software that enabled members of large organizations to share ideas, converse with one another, and develop best practices via internal online "communities," hence the name of the company. It was an interesting idea, except that people in organizations adopting Communispace software didn't seem to want to share, at least not in the way that Hessan had envisioned. A customer saved her from an almost certain fate.

Tom Brailsford, a market research director for Hallmark Cards, concluded that the Communispace service wasn't going to work for his Gold Crown (greeting card) store managers either. And Hessan listened to him as he suggested to her that instead of creating employee "communities," her software could be used to create online consumer focus groups, designed to provide faster, less expensive answers to questions facing marketing managers than they could realize by more traditional means. As a result, Communispace created its first online focus group—150 women with young children—for Hallmark. It was so successful that Hessan completely rethought her business model, creating what she refers to as a "consumer collaboration agency." Now employing more than 500 people around the world, Communispace has created more than 600 online communities for 200 clients, with a higher than 90 percent client retention rate.

What happened at Rackspace Hosting and Communispace is especially remarkable for several reasons. First, it required leaders who were willing to listen (not a common trait for many in leadership positions). Second, it required that leaders suspend belief regarding the strategic direction of their respective organizations. This is hard to do. They had given a great deal of thought to the directions their organizations should take. They could easily have lost objectivity on the subject. In fact, many have, ultimately riding an idea into oblivion. They could have let their egos, their pride of authorship, get in the way of common sense. Instead, they listened to their customers, and found a way to please their employees and investors—a win-win-win.

THE CHANGING FACE OF SERVICES MARKETING

Organizations like Châteauform' spend little or nothing for advertising. They don't have to because their clients do their marketing for them. Customers "own" the properties while they visit them. And they act like owners. As we mentioned earlier, they account for substantially more than half of the company's business, both through return visits and recommendations to other organizations. The future will see a growing number of organizations relying on similar strategies. The reason is evolutionary: they will be the survivors. They are great places to work, offer real value to customers, and provide high returns to investors—again, win-win-win. Other organizations will seek to emulate their business models.

This raises the question of the role traditional marketing will have in service organizations in the future. It will be a world in which highly loyal customers co-create service experiences with employees while taking primary responsibility for business development activities—typically the province of marketing. In this environment the primary tasks of marketing will be to allocate effort and budgets toward current and potential owners while using more conventional marketing techniques to maintain a brand's recognition and credibility. Further, marketing management will have to cooperate with peers from operations and human resources in this effort, sometimes even playing a secondary role. All of this suggests a quite different role for marketing than that studied traditionally by aspirants to marketing management jobs.

Before we get too deeply into this view of the future, however, we must note that others see the idea of customer loyalty, at least as currently understood, as largely a thing of the past. According to this view, for years consumers have been guided in their purchase decisions by brands, recommendations from personal friends and family members, and their own experiences. This guidance has enabled them to choose based on a perception of the value of a product or service relative to alternatives. In the future, however, they will be able to navigate through the thicket of information by means of search devices, smartphone apps, customer reviews, Internet feedback sites, and advice gleaned from social networks. As a result, they will be better informed and more willing to switch brands and products than in the past.[18] By extension, the phenomenon will significantly reduce the value of brands, customer retention, and customer lifetime value.

This thesis represents an extreme view, one that assumes that customers will take valuable time not only to "shop" many of their purchases but also to periodically update themselves with the latest shopping apps and other technologies. It also downplays the importance of past experience on customer loyalty, which is of much greater importance for services than for products. It gives greater credence to the advice of unknown reviewers on Internet sites of unknown degrees of objectivity than to that of trusted acquaintances. While it is useful in suggesting trends in behaviors, we don't believe this view of the impact of technologies on customer loyalty (and others predicting the impact of technologies on consumers) will play out to the degree its authors predict. However, it may provide an added incentive for organizations to adopt the concepts for building employee and customer loyalty that we've discussed throughout this book.

A LOOK TO THE FUTURE

Customer ownership is one concept that will transform marketing efforts in the future. Three others discussed in this chapter, shown with asterisks in figure 7-2, will continue to contribute to the transformation. They include a laser-like focus on customer lifetime value to drive differentiated service offerings, a high priority on the creation and maintenance of listening posts, and the creation of service guarantees that help reduce customers' perceived risks.

Together, these changes suggest that the marketing of services in the future will bear little resemblance to conventional efforts of the past. As organizations place greater reliance on customers as owners who assume much of the responsibility for both co-creating

Figure 7-2 Services Marketing in the Future

Conventional Marketing Strategy Emphasis	Future Marketing Strategy Emphasis
Product	Results + Quality of Experience Service Guarantees/Risk Reduction*
Customer Trial and Repurchase	Customer Ownership*
Price	Value
Place	Service Encounter/Servicescape
Marketing Research	Listening Posts*
Market Segmentation	Customer Lifetime Value*

* Concepts discussed in this chapter.

and marketing services, traditional field selling and advertising will make up a smaller portion of the marketing budget. Traditional selling and advertising will be aimed primarily at maintaining an organization's brand recognition and credibility. As a result services marketing jobs will potentially involve more interesting efforts to engage loyal customers to become owners. The task will be shared with those who are responsible for assembling and deploying the resources critical to the service—operations and human resource management. Success will require that these functions be closely coordinated in the effort.

Clearly, the world of services is a rapidly changing and expanding one. Just as successful services marketing will require the merging of organizational boundaries, so too will it obscure the clear lines between customer and supplier, partnering organizations, and even competitors that have marked the limits of an organization in the past.

Our great service leaders understand this. But what kinds of responses will these shape-shifting changes require? And what role will leadership play in these changes? These are the questions we address in our final chapter.

CHAPTER 8

Leading for the

Future of Services

What great service leaders *know*:
their current beliefs about the future of services are wrong.

What great service leaders *do*:
they build agile service organizations
that learn, innovate, and adapt.

When he was asked recently about the future, Herb Kelleher, CEO emeritus of Southwest Airlines, who was well known for cultivating a freewheeling image to go with Southwest's culture, commented that, "I've always tried to look a little bit ahead, at least when I'm sober—and when I'm not, I look way ahead!"[1]

Fourteen views of the future of services that we've expressed or implied throughout the book are presented in the sidebar. To these we have added a 15th to reflect the discussion to come. All were formed while we were fully sober!

If there is one thing we're certain about, it is that some of the observations in the sidebar are wrong. We just don't know which ones. To make matters more interesting, we're convinced that the leaders with whom we engage don't know either. What's just as

(continued on page 194)

The Future of Services in a Nutshell

1. The migration of jobs from manufacturing to services has nearly run its course in developed economies. It will continue in less developed economies, including China's.

2. Jobs in business and professional services will increasingly provide the foundation for a vital middle-class society, assuming the role that manufacturing jobs have played in the past.

3. The transfer of jobs across borders will be facilitated by the Internet. Service industries that will be particularly vulnerable to this phenomenon will be remotely performed education and medicine, as well as online retailing.

4. Manufacturing strategies will continue to migrate from the production of products to the delivery of results through a package of goods and services.

5. Continued application of the strategic service vision framework will blur the distinctions between manufacturing and service activities until they become indistinguishable.

6. Increasingly, competitors seeking advantage in service industries will do the following:
   a. Focus on more-definitive assessments of the results and experiences sought by employees and customers
   b. Seek to leverage value over cost in developing operating strategies that provide competitive edge
   c. Design support systems that enhance human capability to achieve operating breakthroughs

7. The service profit chain framework will become a way of life for those who design operating strategies in support of a strategic service vision. It will do the following:
   a. Influence the measures used to make up managers' balanced scorecards
   b. Be used to justify the importance of building employee and customer loyalty in the face of networking technologies

8. A larger proportion of service workers will be employed in higher-paying jobs in organizations with high-retention operating strategies; conversely, many jobs in organizations

employing low-retention strategies will be replaced by new technologies.

9. Technology will replace the most boring, least value-adding service jobs. This will do the following:
   a. Contribute to continued productivity increases in services
   b. Moderate growth in service-sector employment
   c. Generally raise job-satisfaction levels among service workers

10. Technologies will advance service strategies designed to provide such things as anticipatory service and remotely performed services.

11. The resources needed to deliver service results will increasingly be shared and crowdsourced in an "informal service economy" in which services are designed to (1) utilize unused and previously wasted capacity, (2) employ an increasing proportion of independent contractors versus conventional employees, and (3) use the full capabilities of the Internet. The trend will last until the service trifecta underlying this trend can no longer produce wins for contractors, their customers, and investors.

12. Co-creation of services by customers and those who serve them will be accelerated, facilitated by increased use of the Internet. This trend will be limited by the extent to which customers perceive themselves to be rewarded sufficiently in terms of costs, time savings, and unique results.

13. Services marketing strategies increasingly will rely on (a) listening posts not only for fielding customer complaints and suggestions but also in the design of new services and (b) a small core of customers as owners to help market their services versus more traditional forms of marketing.

14. Organizations employing both/and thinking and win-win-win analytics for assessing new service designs will rise to the top of their respective industries.

15. Survivors in a competitive environment in which uncertainty and transient competitive advantage are common will be those able to create and sustain learning logics, mentalities, and mechanisms necessary to produce repeated transient versus sustained competitive advantage.

important is that they can't be certain how these changes are going to affect their jobs or organizations.

The most insightful service leaders are asking themselves and those around them questions such as these: What changes for leaders at all levels when an organization can only hope to achieve transient advantage in a rapidly changing competitive landscape? How do organizations address a competitive world that is dominated by services that are co-created and marketed with the help of customers to a base of potential users "freed" by Internet-driven mobile technologies? What happens when a service is organized and operated largely with crowdsourced resources? What will it take to lead organizations that are capable of delivering seamless service globally?

We wouldn't have thought to ask ourselves most of these questions just a few years back when leaders were encouraged to seek sustainable competitive advantage, were expected to supply all the answers, were trained to lead organizations with armies of employees seeking lifetime jobs rather than independent contractors, conducted marketing research to determine whether customers would like products and services they had already designed, and by and large led international organizations in which national subsidiaries were fiefdoms. No one really knows what the future holds—the *what* remains uncertain. But, having reflected in the first seven chapters on what great service leaders know and do, we're much more certain about the *how*—concepts that will help leaders deal with uncertainty as well as those qualities that will distinguish leaders of the next transformations in services.

Why concentrate this attention on the leadership of services? It's not just because of their dominance in today's developed economies. We believe that because of the way they are created and delivered, many services represent the canary in the coal mine for leadership generally. Three stories illustrate what we're talking about.

CHANGING THE RULES OF THE GAME

Sixteen years ago, one of us (Schlesinger) taught an MBA class at the Harvard Business School based on a case that had been developed on a new company with about $100 million in sales. Its name was unusual but not as eye-catching as many of the other start-ups just beginning to raise big money for tech-centered ventures. The issue of the day was whether the company's market potential for a direct distribution service from an online site would be sufficient to sustain it and, if not, where the company should look beyond its current business to expand revenue.

Students wrestled with the issues, weighing various ways of expanding the product line and rejecting most, but concluding that the company had a reasonable shot at survival even though competition would be fierce and there were only a limited number of product categories that would lend themselves to the business model.

At the end of the class, the CEO in the case, a guest in the class, began by complimenting class members on the depth of their analyses, then chided them for their lack of confidence in his business model and their limited vision of the future. He then disclosed his vision for the company. It was "to sell everything to everyone everywhere."

Upon hearing the story 16 years later, another of us (Sasser) recalled that his family thought nothing of having 50 pounds of dog food regularly delivered by this same company, still based in Seattle, to his summer home in a remote part of Maine at a price competitive with the grocery store 15 miles away. Of course, the class guest was Jeff Bezos, founder and CEO of Amazon.com, now a behemoth with more than $75 billion in annual sales. The company sells an outrageously broad line of products—including many that the MBA class rejected—directly to customers globally.

Bezos saw something that others didn't. Among those who saw

the same vision were few who could achieve it, and none as well as Bezos and his company. A venture called Webvan spent $375 million of other people's money in barely more than two years trying to distribute groceries directly. Kozmo.com went through $250 million in 37 months endeavoring to provide free delivery of "videos, games, DVDs, food, Starbucks products, and more" with no minimum order in a maximum of one hour—essentially selling $10 bills for $5—in selected areas of 11 US cities.

All three of these enterprises were in a get-big-fast mode, developing markets through attractive offerings supported by customers' trust that promises could be met. One of them made it through the business sound barrier by enlisting its customers to help enhance the information on its website (through product reviews) and providing them with the mind-blowing means (a groundbreaking "1-Click" website feature) to buy its offerings.

But selling everything to everyone everywhere isn't easy. Amazon investors still complain that the company's leadership devotes too much of its profits from the core to selling more and more kinds of products, thereby depressing profits. While complaining, however, they buy the company's stock. They do it because, among other things, they assume that Bezos's longer-term vision of continued large-scale innovation ensures top management support for the implementation of new ideas, both successful and unsuccessful. As a result, Amazon's stock has continued to appreciate in spite of often meager profits.

Jeff Bezos doesn't have all the answers and can't always see the future all that clearly. (After all, $60 million of Amazon's money went into the ill-fated kozmo.com.) That doesn't stop him from trying things that may position him and his company for the future, then investing rapidly and heavily based on information yielded by the experiment. It's this spirit that produces rapid innovation. It will characterize efforts to achieve 30-minute delivery in selected markets, one of Bezos's current goals. Whether Amazon employs drones, as Bezos has suggested, or some other method, it's unwise to bet against him and his philosophy of constant experimentation, fast learning, and the rapid introduction of innovation.

Amazon has changed the competitive world and market potential for entire industries. It has changed customers' expectations and the way they think about all kinds of services. In the process, it provides insight into our view of what it takes to lead transformations in services.

The leadership task at Amazon has, among other things, been centered on creating and sustaining an internal culture of frugality and low cost with a strong emphasis on customer service, low prices, and value. Its operating strategy is based on building trust with customers while engaging them in the enhancement of the service, managing (not without mishaps) important relationships with service partners, and creating realistic expectations among investors.

Its business model focuses on the customer, driven by a headquarters culture centered around one of its 14 leadership principles that advises everyone to "Have Backbone: Disagree and Commit." It produces a working environment that is described as "notoriously confrontational" and "famously demanding" and yet one in which "you are learning constantly, and the pace of innovation is thrilling."[2] The model isn't ideal for everyone, however. The nature of Amazon's business, with its demanding deadlines for picking and shipping orders has, at times, necessitated long hours on the job that some frontline employees regard as too demanding. This has, for example, resulted in attempts in Europe to unionize Amazon's distribution centers.

Investors are not at the forefront of the model, however much they may have benefitted from it. And suppliers such as book publishers have often felt the pressure that a customer-centered mission can produce—one in which Amazon negotiates, as Walmart's leaders have said for years, as an agent for the customer.

Although it has changed the rules of the game for the distribution of any number of products, Amazon's investors and some of its employees may be the first to claim that it has not achieved the service management trifecta. Its win-win-win is still a work in progress.

DELIVERING INNOVATIVE RESULTS GLOBALLY

Jeff Bezos's ideas for 30-minute delivery on demand may well have been influenced by a company that couldn't be more different than Amazon—a Mexican cement and concrete company, CEMEX.

When the late Lorenzo Zambrano returned to Monterrey, Mexico, after having earned an MBA at Stanford University in 1968, he went to work for his family's business, a cement manufacturer called CEMEX. Given his newfound knowledge, one of his first requests was for a company computer. His father, who was CEO, denied the request after inquiring why he could possibly need a computer. Why would he want one? What would he do with it? It fueled Zambrano's determination to modernize the company's information systems if ever he assumed its leadership, which he eventually did, in 1985.

It didn't take long before CEMEX's general managers throughout the world were equipped with computers. Zambrano didn't stop there. His company was one of the first in the world to ensure that families of general managers were supplied with computers as well, and one of the first to adopt the Internet as the standard for the worldwide communication of new ideas critical to the company's learning and development. It was all part of what came to be known as "the CEMEX Way," which was elemental to the company's core values and culture that emphasize a "one-company organization" comprising managers interconnected by information technology, common background, and education. This enables them to exchange ideas, exchange jobs, jointly develop innovations, and manage anywhere in the world with a minimum of start-up time.

But why cite an example of a cement company? The answer is that CEMEX doesn't produce cement, at least not in the minds of its leadership. Lorenzo Zambrano never thought the company sold cement or concrete. He thought about it in terms of the results achieved from the products it sells: roads, airport runways, and hospitals made from CEMEX materials. He didn't stop there. In his mind CEMEX provided (and provides today) such things as efficient transportation (on roads made with highly durable, easy-to-maintain concrete) and good health (delivered in hospitals constructed of disease-resistant materials).

The entire CEMEX organization is encouraged from the top to listen for new ideas. A form of concrete that contributes to germ-fighting hospital buildings? CEMEX will explore it. Concrete with varying weights, densities, and strengths? CEMEX has already developed it. A guarantee of delivery of ready-mix concrete to contractors—who are normally plagued with unreliable service—within 20 minutes of the promised time on the crowded streets of Mexico City or Guadalajara? CEMEX has found a way to do it—and develop the systems to provide anticipatory service and ensure that it can be done again and again. A housing crisis among Mexico's poor? CEMEX will help organize groups of poor citizens to make collective plans to build homes with the technical assistance of architectural advisers provided by the company. And it will provide the means by which Mexican workers outside the country can transfer funds to their families in Mexico in low-cost ways that ensure they will be used for home improvements that they specify in advance. Does this sound like a *cement* company to you?

Managers from more than 50 countries feed their ideas and those of their customers into an "idea bank" that is managed by the company's Innovation Committee. One reason they feel confident that the ideas will be considered seriously is that all of them have at one time or another gathered in the same room somewhere in the world to participate in seminars that are also about building the CEMEX learning network. They know that their efforts will be recognized by a top management team that gives a high priority to learning. They trust their colleagues. And they trust the process. Face time at meetings around the world, many of them involving executive training, is intended, among other things, to build the trust on which a learning organization thrives.

Cement manufacturing can be a boring industry with few learning opportunities and little change. Fortunately, managers in this organization don't regard it as a cement manufacturer. CEMEX is an exciting company in the business of solving problems and delivering results, one that is constantly changing what it does and how it does it. It is what has come to be known as a *learning organization*.

Organizations like CEMEX don't just happen. They're influenced by leaders who foster transparency, communication, and the trust that follows. It's a formula intended to deal with a future in services that will be dominated by changes in information and communications technology, globalization, competition, the very nature of service work, and the role of customers in devising and delivering services.

CEMEX encountered real difficulties in the face of declining demand during the Great Recession. After all, it is a company that is operating in a cyclical industry buffeted by change as well as by the expropriation of its properties (in Venezuela). But it has found a way to succeed by concentrating on the delivery of results—not products or services—in the 50 countries in which it operates.

CEMEX provides an interesting example of a "one-company organization culture" fueled by the CEMEX Way—by which services may be developed and marketed globally in the future. Its initiatives are part of a larger landscape of innovative efforts that will raise the competitive bar for services. This should be a cause for celebration for leaders who have patience and perseverance and are able to accept the challenge of what it takes to build a learning organization. It should be a cause for concern for their competitors.

Is CEMEX a manufacturing or service company? We would argue it is neither; it is focused on delivering value made up of results and experiences. It defies definition in traditional terms. However, it is typical of a growing number of organizations with similar focus. And it illustrates what it takes to survive and thrive, especially in terms of the kind of leadership it requires.

CEMEX also reminds us that the lines between manufacturing and services are becoming blurred. This merging of identities will likely surround an increasing number of companies, rendering obsolete our current ways of categorizing organizations and activities. Further, questions will be raised about the very boundaries of a learning organization.

TESTING THE BOUNDARIES
OF THE LEARNING ORGANIZATION

Omnicom—maybe the largest company that you've never heard of—provides marketing services to its clients, many of whose products are marketed globally. Omnicom is not a household name. It's a corporation with more than 300 profit centers—many of which are household names (like BBDO and Ketchum) to their clients—offering services that range from conventional advertising agency work to advice for digital and social network marketing strategies. (In this respect, it couldn't be less like CEMEX, and its one-company philosophy.) Up to now the business has specialized in giving expert advice, a lot of "telling."

Just because Omnicom's global clients see the organization as a source of ideas for seamless global marketing doesn't mean that these same clients are well organized to implement them. Whether they realize it or not, they need help in organizational design as well as marketing services. Some clients see Omnicom as an enforcer of change in their own marketing organizations as well as a source of marketing ideas. If only Omnicom's operating units were prepared for the challenge. After all, this is an organization that is expert in delivering the conventional services of the past through individual agencies. Now it is entering the Land of Oz future of coordinated, integrated, global marketing hand-in-hand with its larger clients. In some cases it is sharing its most talented employees with them. The task involves teaching as well as doing. It requires more listening and learning and less of the telling that Omnicom's experts have been so good at for so long.

In a sense, leaders of Omnicom's many subsidiaries are teaching and learning at the same time. In order to help clients develop learning organizations, leadership of the parent has to achieve the same goal. To pursue it, the holding company as well as its larger subsidiaries sponsor extensive internal education and management-development programs. Their primary goals are to bring together managers for a common experience that includes the propagation of a core set of beliefs such as the importance of service profit chain relationships and of listening (and learning) versus telling behaviors. Like at CEMEX, the internal training programs provide opportunities for face-to-face networking that will come into play when the same managers are asked to coordinate their efforts on behalf of global clients.

In addition to stepped-up internal learning and an emphasis on listening, Omnicom has taken steps to implement an organizational solution as well. It has created jobs for managers, hired and paid by Omnicom, who represent large individual clients. They share office space with their client (not their employer), represent the client in relations (including negotiations) with Omnicom's companies, and even have authority to recommend services offered by Omnicom's competitors. In nearly every respect, they are members of the client's organization. In this case, how should organizational boundaries be drawn? Or does it matter? It suggests that service in the future will increasingly require that old organizational concepts be revised to accommodate new realities.

John Wren, chairman and CEO of the parent company, plays a low-key role in all of this. He is much less well known than Jeff Bezos or Lorenzo Zambrano. And in many respects, he is well suited to lead a company whose organizational boundaries fuse among subsidiaries and overlap with clients. He spends most of his time on three things: (1) acquiring companies whose people bring to Omnicom new talents that reflect new directions in the business, (2) ensuring that there is sufficient support for decentralized decision making as well as organizational learning, and (3) allocating resources in ways intended to maximize shareholder return. In addition, he spends some of his time deflecting dispute-resolution requests from leaders of Omnicom's subsidiaries. The message often is "Work it out among yourselves, and let us know what we can learn from the way you resolved it."

Amazon, CEMEX, and Omnicom are representative of a small group of organizations that, through the vision and efforts of their leadership, represent several aspects of the future of services that we are predicting. They share some things in common: (1) they are breaking new ground in their industries, (2) they base their businesses on results for clients, (3) they create high expectations in the minds of customers that are hard to meet and even harder for competitors to meet, (4) they are pressed just to stay a step or two ahead of the people they serve, (5) they support learning through formal education as well as less formal efforts, and (6) they engage in boundary-spanning strategies, whether across industries (Amazon), across manufacturing and service activities (CEMEX), or across organizational and national boundaries (Omnicom). Together, they help us understand the kinds of organizations that will produce demands for great service leadership in the future.

CURRENT QUESTIONS FOR ASPIRING LEADERS OF THE FUTURE OF SERVICES

Current trends that will loom large for services in the future suggest the nature of both changes in the competitive environment and responses needed to successfully execute strategies that produce at least transitory advantage. We say current trends, because they will change. Nevertheless, elements of these strategic logics suggest several of the most important questions that have to be asked as strategies are shaped and reshaped today. The role of leadership is to ensure that these questions, among others, are being asked repeatedly. The first concerns the way in which services are created, marketed, and used.

Is There Customer-Centric Collaboration in Creating, Marketing, and Using the Service?

Service design is being affected by the development of more and more capable information and communications technology (including social networking and interactive software). Increasingly, services ranging from banking to medicine are being delivered through mobile devices. Devices that can fit into our pockets "contain" everything from our entertainment to our money. But new technology is not the headline of the story. The real importance of this for services in the future is that technology will encourage the increasing involvement of customers in the design, co-creation, marketing, and intelligent use of services. The very process of doing this will help create a core of customers who are psychological owners not waiting to be asked for suggestions and assistance in referring potential new customers to the service. It will be a primary responsibility of great service leaders to ensure that such customers and their ideas are cultivated.

To What Extent Are Resources Being Crowdsourced?

Just as organizations will rely on customers to design, sell, deliver, and consume services, they will rely increasingly on the crowdsourcing of talent and other resources, engaging contractors to help produce them. At the same time that crowdsourced organizations extend their boundaries, involving more and more people, they will count fewer employees, in the traditional sense of that term, in their ranks. Many of their working assets will belong to others. It will be harder to define the boundaries of the organization.

One start-up that illustrates the next generation of the kind of crowdsourcing we envision is called Instacart. At the time we are writing this, it comprises 10 people working out of a San Francisco office. The company offers home delivery of grocery items and other products sourced from a variety of stores by hundreds of contract shoppers, members of "free agent nation."[3] Contract shoppers are paid in commissions and gratuities. They are guided by Instacart's software through the aisles of designated stores all the way to the front doors of customers, to whom they deliver in their own vehicles. In a sense, the service is a reaction to Webvan, kozmo.com, and Amazon, providing a wide product line with little of the fixed expense of owned infrastructure. It is little more than a small band of engineers maintaining and enhancing their software. We don't know if Instacart will be successful. It faces challenges of maintaining the cooperation of retailers as well as the quality of its contract shoppers. But if it fails, it will not take hundreds of millions of dollars of other people's money with it. Or will it? Given the small investment required for truly crowdsourced services, others will come along with improved versions of the same model. That will require the Instacarts of the world to buy up potential competitors, helping explain why it is in the process of raising more money.[4]

Are Resources Being Shared?

Increasingly, individuals in the developed world are putting their idle assets—their automobiles and their spare rooms—to work. For example, Uber is little more than a dispatch service centered around a website that enables those seeking rides to "hail" drivers and their automobiles for what amounts, in the minds of taxi operators, to what they themselves do. The valuation placed on this company as we write this is more than $41 billion.[5]

Or consider a venture begun when two entrepreneurs put three air mattresses on the floor of a San Francisco apartment, called it "Airbed and Breakfast," and rented them out during a sold-out convention week for hotels in the city. It progressed rapidly to a website that enables anyone in the world to list a spare room for rent to anyone else in the world. It offers accommodations even more unusual than airbeds on the floor, such as backyard tree houses, under the brand Airbnb. The distrust that can accompany sharing is addressed by enabling hosts and potential renters to check one another out on Facebook or other networks, refer to reviews provided by previous users of a particular space, and purchase insurance protecting themselves against damage or theft. That is apparently enough for users of the service. Hosts in tens of thousands of towns and cities and more than 190 countries currently list rooms, according to the founders. Peak usage on a nightly basis at the time we write this now exceeds 200,000 room nights, a number equivalent to that of global hotel chains such as Marriott or Hilton. Now Airbnb's strategy is to create "a full-blown hospitality brand, one that delivers a seamless end-to-end experience when its customer travels."[6] All this in an organization that owns few tangible assets. Its intellectual property, however, is valued at more than $3 billion at the time we write this.

This is just the beginning of sharing. People not only have spare rooms. They have automobiles sitting idle. Hence, they are beginning to rent to others automobiles that would otherwise be parked during a trip away from home. Extra power tools in the garage? Rent them. There are Internet-based services that make it easy. While there will be efforts by conventional service providers such as taxi companies to stop the development of some businesses based on sharing, they'll eventually have to come to terms with the power of the Internet combined with the entrepreneurial spirit that it feeds.

Sharing is a phenomenon that is thought to be concentrated among Millennials living in large metropolitan areas. It is regarded not only as economical, a source of much-needed cash for younger adults, but also the green thing to do. That prompts many analysts to write off sharing as a generational activity. But people are demonstrating that they bring everything from their beliefs to their preferences in music with them as they move through life. These people are one of the best sources of information about the future of services. As Jeff Bezos, in his own hardly subtle way, advised Airbnb's CEO, Brian Chesky, "This company is going to be massively successful as long as you don't fuck it up."[7] Much the same can be said for any number of ventures that will be centered around resource sharing.

Can the Service Benefit from a Rating Mechanism?

We've mentioned several organizations, with Amazon as perhaps the largest, that rely on some form of rating mechanism made possible by the Internet. Rating by customers has become a staple of the online shopping community. It provides some degree of legitimacy, subject to questions about how ratings can be rigged, to services whose quality would otherwise be unknown.

As we mentioned earlier, two-way rating mechanisms such as those employed now by operators of several shared services can be valuable in matching service providers and users. In a sense, they make information about the service encounter more symmetric and transparent. At the same time, they put more power in the hands of the service provider seeking to limit service to the most valued customers.

To What Degree Is the Service Anticipatory?

Speed and dependability of response times in services will continue to increase. Of greater interest to us is the growth in anticipatory services, those that are performed before a customer realizes he or she has a need for them. They will continue to be developed based on a confluence of new technology and improved logistical infrastructure.

A small number of organizations have been delivering services in anticipation of needs realized by customers. As we mentioned earlier, GE Medical representatives sometimes arrive at hospitals using the firm's CAT scan machines to "fix" a problem before the hospital administrator realizes that she has a problem. It is an extreme form of what has been known for some time as preventive maintenance. It will be carried to new extremes in the future, made possible both by new information technologies and by people who are able to read and interpret the messages they send.

The biggest new driver of anticipatory services may well be big data, in which data about individuals and organizations is collected, stored, and tracked from a variety of sources. What's new about big data is not the data itself but the techniques that are being developed to relate data from disparate sources and organize it into actionable information. The Steven Spielberg film *Minority Report* portrays a world of big data and anticipatory services in which Washington, DC, hasn't had a murder in six years because of a big data system. The system, using many sources of information, allows a "precrime unit" to arrest people before they are able to commit the murders that the system predicts. In the real world, we are becoming familiar (but not always comfortable) with the use of big data to predict all kinds of behaviors. The New York City Police Department developed and uses CompStat, a computer program that pinpoints areas most susceptible to crime so that its resources can be allocated effectively. Medical data is used to predict the likelihood that people, including actress Angelina Jolie, will contract cancer. Commercially, big data is being used to fuel predictions of purchases and sales. For example, offrs.com, a website intended for use by realtors, makes predictions about a homeowner's willingness to sell before a home is put on the market, or in some cases even before the homeowner knows she is going to sell. According to one account, offrs.com uses data from 20 different sources that describe mortgage and equity levels, the history of the property, and the backgrounds of the owners.[8]

In some cases anticipatory service will require frontline service workers who are able to interpret and act on data with little decision time. Characteristic of this use of such data is the action by the waiter at Caesar's casino who knows what to deliver to the woman at slot machine number 744 based on the guest's data in her Total Rewards membership profile. Gary Loveman, former CEO of Caesar's, calls this "active enterprise." He explains, "The revolution is this: when you check in with us in Vegas or Atlantic City, we're going to engage with you in real time during your visit through a digital device to invite you to do things with us based on what capacities we have and what your preferences have been shown to be."[9]

When Jeff Bezos announces that Amazon will provide same-day (and eventually possibly 30-minute) delivery on some items, some amount of inventory will have to be positioned to anticipate the demands of customers. Just which inventory receives that treatment will require the careful analysis of buying patterns based on the same kind of software that suggests other merchandise that customers might like once they have made a purchase.

Anticipatory service requires the study of data patterns over time to predict consumer behavior. Airlines have for years had an opportunity to do this, an opportunity that they have largely passed over. Tracking information about travelers' behaviors would enable them to predict possible defections (and the flights and airlines to which the passenger might defect). All it requires is the merging of several data files that are maintained at nearly all airlines, data files concerning passenger lists, late-arriving aircraft, lost baggage records, passenger complaints, and the like. All too recently some airlines have begun to take timely, customized actions to retain those travelers who have, for example, experienced lost luggage, several consecutive departure delays due to operational problems, recent flights on other airlines, or other predictors of potential defections.

Anticipatory service will also require closer partnering across organizations. Amazon will not be able to provide same-day delivery without closer coordination with its suppliers and package-delivery partners, whether or not routine delivery by drone comes to pass. Remember, delivery by drone is just one more technology that will, if it is permitted, become available to all of Amazon's package-delivery partners and competitors. What won't become available is the database from which delivery by drone is offered and provided.

How and to What Degree Will Data Be Secured?

Breaches of data systems by everyone from hobbyist hackers to criminals are becoming more common. These breaches are of particular concern in the service sector because that's where personal information largely is held. The information required for identity theft—a lucrative if illegal industry—resides in service firms. Financial, medical, and educational information of a personal nature is of much greater interest and value to hackers and criminals than the number of automobiles shipped from a given factory last month.

The problem has become so widespread that markets have been established for the trade of such information. They enable us to predict the next big data breaches. Recently, they have told us, for instance, that a medical record has a value that is 25 times greater than that of a mere credit card number and related information.

Even if they don't know much about data security, service leaders will have to be able to assure their customers, their employees, and themselves that all possible efforts have been made to address the nearly impossible task of securing something that by its very nature is sharable.

Will the Service Address Increasing Global Competition?

Globalization of services, and the increasing tradability of service jobs among locations, will be a product of the increasing use of communications and social networking technologies. It will encourage global competition in service industries such as professional services where such competition did not exist before. It will place a premium on strategies designed to enhance productivity and foster competitive cost structures.

As more and more jobs in the service sector become *tradable*, capable of being carried out without requiring proximity of server and customer, they will be subject to increasing international competition. Nobel Laureate Michael Spence is an articulate proponent of this thinking.[10] For example, as we've seen, Apollo Hospitals in India is concentrating on providing remote medical diagnoses and, in some cases, treatments on a remote basis, through the use of state-of-the-art technology. It is a pioneer in a practice that may lead to more tradability of jobs in medicine in the future. And this is just a start. Any service with a substantial information content— medicine, education, the maintenance of complex products—will increasingly be delivered remotely as the most expert knowledge and capability in the world is made available globally.

Increased tradability will put pressure on mediocre service providers, who were protected by geographic barriers in the past, to either improve or risk the fate of being replaced by global experts.

There is nothing very surprising about our current road map of trends with the greatest impact on the service sector. Of greater concern to service leaders is the speed at which the trends are progressing. Worse yet, if the past is any indication, the most important signpost to the future isn't even on our current road map. It may be an important technological breakthrough, extreme climate change that fosters entirely new service industries, or the different social characteristics and priorities of a generation that is just now being born. But chances are, it isn't on our list. What sets apart the service winners of the future is the fact that they are right now preparing for the certainty that our predictions here are wrong. No matter what comes, they'll be ready.

THE PRIMARY LEADERSHIP TASK: NURTURE A LEARNING ORGANIZATION

In terms of service futures, the one thing about which we are most certain is this: if organizations are to survive for long in the current competitive environment, they will have to learn and adapt with increasing speed. The ability to create and sustain learning organizations will be the most significant feature of leadership in this kind of world. Peter Senge, who has researched learning in organizations for years, sounded the trumpets of change when he proclaimed that "I believe that the prevailing system of management is, at its core, dedicated to mediocrity. It forces people to work harder and harder to compensate for failing to tap the spirit and collective intelligences that characterize working together at their best."[11] The learning organization, then, is a mechanism not only for learning and for personal development but also for enabling people to accomplish more and more meaningful work with less effort, more effectiveness in the eyes of customers, and more personal satisfaction. At the same time, it is a mechanism for dealing with the uncertainty of the future of services.

Given the significant contact between frontline employees and customers in many service industries, unusual opportunities exist to create learning organizations. Amazon, for example, may have one of the best listening devices in the history of service activities, its Amazon Marketplace service. Amazon Marketplace displays and supplies merchandise offered by more than 2 million third-party partner-sellers while collecting a commission on each sale. It has enabled Amazon to track the sales of its partners, identifying trends in popularity and discovering when to enter a merchandise category with its own offering in competition with its partners. Amazon Marketplace has become a source of conflict and controversy among its sellers. However, many can't afford to forego the marketing power of the site by withdrawing their merchandise. But note one thing: Amazon Marketplace would have much less value if the Amazon organization weren't geared to heed its lessons and act rapidly to take advantage of the information it provides. This can only happen in an organization with a culture of mutually shared values and mutual trust that is all eyes and ears, has little pride of authorship, and is geared to respond with new ways of delivering value. Great service leaders have a primary responsibility to ensure that such a culture is created and preserved.

While an overarching culture is important, it's not everything, and it doesn't happen by itself. A variety of other values, beliefs, and behaviors are needed to nurture a learning organization.

Establish Other Values, Beliefs, and Behaviors for Learning

Several beliefs and behaviors will increasingly characterize leaders of learning organizations in the future. Based on our fieldwork and experience over the years, we've created the following list out of a conviction that the perfect set of shared values and behaviors simply does not exist for an organization; what is important is that the values be accompanied by suggested behaviors, measures, and actions to be taken when the values are not met. With these caveats in mind, values and behaviors that foster organizational learning and long-term success include customer-centricity, reliability, generosity, transparency, curiosity, and diversity. Although some of these values can be found occasionally in value statements of organizations, they haven't been given sufficient attention.

Customer-centricity heads the list because it is the most important source of new ideas. We don't mean *customer* in the conventional sense of that term. We use it to mean both external customers and employees. At Southwest Airlines, the term used is *People* to include both Customers and Employees. People have been the primary source of learning, change, and continued success in that organization.

Reliability is what successful fighting forces take into battle with them. It fosters the trust critical to faster and better decisions and action. It means "doing what you say you'll do," for better or worse. A successful business at USAA has been built on reliability and trust.

Generosity is critical to the effective deployment of assets (as well as the development of human capital). It fuels the "boundary-less" behavior that provides the foundation not only for global mobility and success but also the learning and development of individual members of an organization. It means yielding up your best talent and resources for the good of the organization. It characterizes what we described going on at CEMEX.

Transparency fosters both trust and the learning that comes from "need to know" and other information. It may involve, in many instances, more than a decision maker needs to know. It's a central belief and practice at India's HCL Technologies, where, as we noted earlier, former CEO Vineet Nayar has opened his 360-degree feedback (performance) report to everyone in the organization and encourages his colleagues to do the same, along with making other efforts to disseminate useful information throughout the company.[12]

Curiosity leads to constant questioning and listening. It results from a sense that we don't know and may never know the answers but that some answers are better than others.[13] It explains why Scott Cook at Intuit leads with questions, not answers. It requires self-confidence for a leader to admit that he or she doesn't have all the answers. The candor it encourages is good for a learning organization.

Diversity of background, training, skills, and interests has been shown to be critical to the creative process.[14] It enables team members to learn from one another. Google's hiring practices, based on a person's passion and creativity, have led to a diversity of backgrounds in its talent base.

The Service Leader's Role in a Learning Organization

A leader of a learning organization plays a number of roles. We've set forth the most important in the sidebar. They reflect beliefs and practices that we've described in greater detail earlier. Number one on our list is acting out the learning beliefs and behaviors we've discussed here. A large body of research tells us that members of an organization tend to emulate the behaviors of a leader. Behavior patterns cascade through an organization all the way to those leading frontline people. We've attached a great deal of importance to certain frontline beliefs and behaviors in service organizations. If frontline people are to adopt those ways, it makes sense that the leaders must demonstrate the same beliefs and behaviors. This is the case regardless of the philosophy advocated by the leader.

We should add a word here about one term that appears in

The Service Leader's Role in a Learning Organization

Propagate, visibly act out, and enforce through measurement and action a set of values and behaviors that characterize learning organizations.

Organize for learning. Rely heavily on team efforts. Propagate a "test, then invest" mentality. If it is necessary, create separate "laboratories" for innovation and learning staffed with people who are not burdened with the day-to-day responsibility for producing short-term profits.

Mobilize the organization to foster the changes needed to preserve strategic advantage, however transient it might be.

Set specific goals and recognition for innovation, whether it is the proportion of revenue and profit from new value-centered services or some other measure.

Constantly seek ways of bringing people from various functions and businesses together for a consideration of agendas designed to foster the exchange of ideas and learning.

Allocate human and other assets across the entire organization, recognizing those that make the greatest contributions in terms of shared values and behaviors for a learning organization.

Ensure that short-term results are strong enough to provide "cover" for the learning and innovation required for long-term success, satisfying a need for "ambidexterity" in an organization.

Serve as a window to the public, providing the kind of transparency that anticipates and eliminates public surprises.

---

the sidebar, *ambidexterity*. Ambidexterity, according to Michael Tushman and Charles O'Reilly, requires leadership teams that are able to "exploit the past and discover the future concurrently."[15] It combines in one leader the ability to nurture and provide oversight for both established and new businesses. It requires patient leadership in support of innovations with long-term outputs and the impatience that fuels urgency to deliver short-term results from more established businesses. It is a relatively rare set of qualities to be found in one person, but there are those who believe that it can be learned through practice.

It should be clear by now that the characteristics essential for great service leadership differ in subtle but important ways from the beliefs and behaviors that have been honored in the past. For these traits to have maximum impact, we can never forget that they have to be aligned with elements of organizational design, policies, practices, incentives, and measures (discussed earlier) that encourage long-range innovation as well as a bias for action. That brings us back to the three examples—Amazon, CEMEX, and Omnicom—with which we began the chapter.

Our three example companies are taking different routes in pursuit of future success, and we're not referring to differences in their choice of businesses. In spite of the differences, all are encouraging leadership for learning at several levels of their organizations. Amazon hires talented people with that kind of capability and makes every effort to get the best out of them through constructive conflict that produces a stream of innovative ideas, many more than Amazon can pursue at any one time. CEMEX has created a one-company culture, the CEMEX Way, coupled with organizational devices to encourage the exchange of ideas and constant learning and innovation. Omnicom is sharing common organizational territory with its clients in an effort to foster a mutual learning process that will enable clients, and Omnicom itself, to organize for the seamless implementation of new marketing concepts on a global basis.

The leaders of these organizations exhibit different combinations of qualities. They don't fit into the neat categories or exhibit the behavior patterns described by leadership gurus. While Bezos has perhaps given more attention to the development of ambidexterity in his company, Zambrano (during his leadership tenure) and Wren have focused more on the needs for learning in industries that have followed rather rigid models for success in the past. But all have exhibited a clear value-dominant logic for their respective industries. They are religiously customer-centric. All have had visions of results and experiences that their customers and clients will be expecting several years hence.

The point here, of course, is that it is impossible to generalize on specific elements of great service leadership. What has characterized these three organizations is, however, an unusual alignment of leaders and their traits with the cultures, organizations, policies, and practices developed to execute future-oriented business concepts in three different service industries.

WHAT ABOUT SERVICE PRODUCTIVITY, QUALITY, AND WORKPLACE GAPS?

We noted earlier that the service sector, particularly in the United States, has trailed manufacturing in productivity improvements in recent years. Perceptions of service quality in many parts of the world are not improving. And employee job satisfaction is barely above the all-time lows in all of the world's economies measured recently. The question is whether the negative gaps implied by this data (see appendix) will be closed going forward.

The Productivity Gap

Manufacturing has made greater strides than the service sector in improving productivity among its workers in the United States and other developed countries. It has been more successful in substituting technology (through capital investment) and offshoring strategies for labor. It has put a damper on increases in manufacturing jobs, a factor in the decline of unionization among at least US factory workers.

This disparity has come about in spite of vast opportunities for increasing productivity in services that don't generally exist in manufacturing. For example, customers can be engaged in the service encounter in ways that reduce the input of paid labor. Hospital visitors who complete forms in advance that outline their ailments and medications save health care workers time in processing patients. Similarly, teaching patients to medicate themselves has been found to be an effective way of administering drugs—better outcomes with the use of less medication—in many medical processes. It also saves valuable labor time and costs.

One factor that has spurred productivity improvements in manufacturing has been international competition between manufacturers, with jobs arising in the most productive places and relatively unproductive jobs being eliminated. To the extent that technological advances make it possible to deliver a wider and wider range of services remotely, this same competitive force will characterize some services. The tradability of service jobs on a multinational basis will lead to an increase in global competition among some services. This competition will reduce differences in the rate of productivity increases between jobs in the service and manufacturing sectors, helping close the productivity gap.

We're not sure the gap hasn't been closed already. There appear to be issues associated with the measurement of service productivity. For years, there have been debates about how to measure productivity in information-mediated work, especially where the quality of ideas is a major factor in output. Measurement challenges have risen with the introduction of the Internet. In particular, measures of output are clouded by the fact that many services delivered over the Internet are free, overlooked in antiquated productivity measures of the value of output. Perhaps most important of all is the failure of productivity measures to include the quality of a customer's experience, an important element of the value equation.

Regardless of these measurement questions, we will see increases in service-sector productivity that rival those in manufacturing. In the minds of some, there will be a price associated with the phenomenon. Some of it may be achieved with a slowing in the increase of the number of service jobs as technology and other efforts to leverage results and the quality of service experiences over costs are employed as a substitute for jobs.

The Service-Quality Gap

Customers' perceptions of quality in various parts of the world have remained constant or declined over the past two decades. However, this may not be an indicator of declining quality levels. The problem is that quality is a moving target. Because it is defined as a function of what was experienced as opposed to what was expected, it is defined by the customer. And that definition may change with time and the accumulation of higher and higher quality service experiences.

Consider the example of airline service. Travelers continue to rate airlines poorly on the experiences that they provide. This is particularly true for economy airlines like Ryanair. As we noted earlier, people don't fly on Ryanair for the quality of the experience; they fly because of results produced for them by Ryanair's route structure and the money they can save. But these same travelers bring with them a set of standards based on experiences of full-fare airlines. This expectation overlooks the fact that European airline fares used to be prohibitively expensive for service levels that were mediocre at best. Relatively few people traveled by air, preferring to take the railroads. Today, European air travel has been democratized. In the process airports have become more congested, flights have become more crowded, legroom has been reduced, and amenities such as meals have been eliminated. At the same time, improvements to the air traffic control systems and procedures have been made, resulting in better on-time performance for airlines in Europe than ever before. So the question is whether airline service in Europe has improved or not. Customers say no. And they will probably continue to say no as more and more people take advantage of the low fares provided by economy carriers like Ryanair.

Unless measures of value beyond price are introduced, we see little chance of improvement in customers' ratings of service quality in various parts of the world. As expectations change, improvements in the value of service delivered have to change even more if customer perceptions and ratings are to improve. The likelihood of that happening is slim. But we see it being as much a problem of measurement as of trends in the actual service delivered.

The Employee Job Satisfaction Gap

The most recent Conference Board survey reported 47.7 percent of US workers as being satisfied with their jobs. If we assume that the others weren't satisfied, that leaves us with about 72 million workers dissatisfied with their jobs in the United States alone.[16] Dissatisfaction fosters job shopping. So we should not be surprised that at about the same time 86 percent of US firms reported that talent retention was a problem.[17]

Employee dissatisfaction can arise from any one of a number of sources—poor leadership, inadequate opportunities for personal development, insufficient backup support, too much work, low pay, and on and on. There are encouraging signs that the causes of job dissatisfaction are being addressed in a growing number of organizations, suggesting that we have reached a nadir in these trends that will be followed by improvements.

Without changing anything regarding the nature of the work, organizations that take a more careful approach to setting expectations will improve employees' views of their work. Engaging them in generating and implementing ideas for improvements will have a significant positive impact. Just as important will be policies and support systems designed to make frontline service providers heroes in the eyes of their customers; this is an advantage that service leaders have over their counterparts in many manufacturing industries.

Organizations have a lot to learn in the use of technology in service work. Whether it is used to enhance or dumb down frontline service work, and how it is used, will have a profound impact on its nature. In the process, work in the service sector will continue to show a bifurcation, with an increasing proportion of it carried out by more highly paid, highly trained people with technological support designed to give them expert status in the eyes of the people they serve. But at the other end of the spectrum, more jobs will be eliminated entirely than merely dumbed down.

Bifurcation of Service Jobs

Our bet is that the philosophy of "fewer, better-trained, and better-paid people winning every time" will prevail wherever the service is complex and customized and requires both judgment and empathy. The introduction of MyMagic+ at Disney World provides an example of what is happening in the world of frontline service. MyMagic+ is a new system centered around the use of guest bracelets that not only contain information that make a guest's visit to Disney World more pleasant with less time spent in waiting but also communicate information to Disney's "cast members" about each guest that enables them to personalize the way they address and serve that person.

The job of cast member at a Disney theme park is low on the jobs ladder in services. In the past some of these jobs have involved little more than greeting guests. Others have required conversational skills and an ability to listen and respond to children and their families. Armed with the information provided by MyMagic+, however, these jobs become more interesting, require more judgment, and offer the opportunity for delighting guests in new ways, all part of the unique interactive nature of much service work.

Just the opposite may occur for mass-produced services requiring little or no judgment or interaction with customers, often involving the most boring jobs. Many of these jobs will be eliminated entirely, as we saw with the toll takers on the Massachusetts Turnpike in chapter 6.

In recent years we've observed how service organizations are combating low job satisfaction by establishing realistic job expectations as well as enhancing the nature of service work by means described earlier. In the process, we have become aware of an increasing sensitivity on the part of top management to make sure that these efforts extend all the way to frontline employees. There is recognition that in many services, the frontline is the primary influence on customer loyalty, the most important influence on growth and profit. For these reasons we believe that there will be a turnaround in employee job satisfaction. It won't be dramatic. But it will slowly reflect the efforts of more and more enlightened leadership.

Closing the productivity gap and reversing negative views of employees about their jobs may appear to some to be a tall order. But we're placing our bets on savvy service leaders of today who have led the transition from the slow-moving, centralized, hierarchical, command-and-control organizations of the past to the fast-moving, decentralized, flat, enfranchised organizations needed to succeed in providing customized solutions of the future on a global basis. In many cases technology will be the catalyst for new business models that drastically change the design, production, and delivery of these customized solutions. However, the key to turning around basic negative trends will be service leaders who, instead of having strong biases and one constant strategy for the future, are maintaining an open mind about what will be necessary to put the power of their organizations to work sensing and responding to the changing needs of customers and employees in a fast-changing competitive environment with many moving parts. Their task and the results they produce are critical to a healthy society. After all, as we said at the outset, jobs in the service sector, not manufacturing, now provide the foundation for the middle class in all of the developed economies of the world.

Throughout the book, we've chosen to illustrate our views with stories from the service front lines. The primary objective was to bring our points of view to life in memorable ways. With that in mind, we have one more story left to tell.

EPILOGUE

One Last Story

We have chosen to illustrate the important points in the book with one final extended example. The story, fascinating in its own right, contains key lessons for service leaders.

In 1998 the Progressive Corporation, a personal property insurer, ran a test in Houston, Texas, of Autograph, a concept called "pay-as-you-go insurance."[1] It installed telematic devices (with global positioning and cellular communications), described by one company executive as "clunky $600 boxes the size of car stereos that had to be professionally installed," in fewer than a thousand automobiles. Their owners had volunteered to serve in a test of whether they and the company could benefit from knowledge about their driving habits: mileage driven, fast acceleration, hard braking, turning, cornering, and the time of day or night on the road. In return, they could qualify for discounts on their insurance rates. The improvement in pricing accuracy resulting from the information that the device yielded was promising, but the device and its requirements were uneconomical. To make matters worse, the *Plain Dealer* newspaper in Cleveland, Progressive's hometown, ran a story about the test, which was typical of several to follow, with comments such as "some people—even good drivers—might be creeped out by the Big Brother presence."[2] Drivers were nevertheless intrigued by the idea.

Even though the test was terminated, it convinced Progressive managers that usage-based insurance (UBI) would someday be a reality.

Progressive's leadership didn't give up. In 2004, they introduced a second-generation version of the idea, branded as TripSense, in three states. It featured a device that could be plugged in to a car's onboard diagnostic port, a device installed in all US automobiles after 1996. The monitoring device had by now become smaller and cost about $100. It had to be unplugged by the customer, who then uploaded her driving information to Progressive over the Internet. The incentive again was the prospect of lower insurance rates for those with good driving habits. However, drivers proved to be undependable in uploading their data. Many didn't follow directions. Progressive found that they tended to be drivers who didn't deserve lower rates anyway.

Under TripSense, drivers' rates could either be raised or lowered as a result of the automatic reports. At its peak TripSense was installed on several thousand vehicles, but according to one Progressive executive, "People hated it when rates were increased dramatically due to risky driving behaviors. We learned a lesson about pricing."

Because of its shortcomings, the TripSense program was replaced in 2008 by MyRate, which ultimately covered 18 states in the United States. The driver incentives for lower rates were the same, but the measuring device now cost only $60, and it automatically uploaded driving data over the cellular network. For the first time, drivers shared access to UBI rates and reports on their driving habits via their online policy accounts.

With MyRate the company learned a great deal about driving behavior and accident rates. Among the lessons were the following: (1) driving behavior is more than twice as predictive of claims costs as any other factor, (2) drivers with the most risky driving behaviors have loss costs that are about 2.5 times higher than drivers with the lowest-risk behaviors and "shouldn't even be on the street," according to one executive, and therefore (3) safe drivers subsidize a smaller number of drivers who engage in higher-risk behavior, suggesting that "the range of rates could be much wider and more personalized than they are today."[3]

Based on these lessons, Progressive tried yet again, this time in 2010 with a program called Snapshot—with automatic upload and no GPS tracking device (for privacy). Rate reductions of up to 30 percent (or $240 on an average premium of $800 a year) after a four-month monitoring period, were accompanied by an assurance that no participant's rate would be raised. Further, Snapshot was offered to everyone, whether they were Progressive policyholders or not. It was promoted aggressively in 42 states and by early 2013 had been tested by more than 1 million drivers, 70 percent of whom received rate cuts. One executive at Progressive commented that "we think we have something cool; we're carefully examining how best to capitalize on it."[4]

Why this long story? It suggests to us a number of things about the leadership mentality required for the design, delivery, and pricing of services in the future:

1. It illustrates the marriage of customer behavior, measurement, and technology in the design of services and service prices.

2. It shows how the rapidly declining cost of technology and increasing availability of ways of sharing information can make services possible that could only be envisioned just a few years ago. Service providers will be faced with the need to make prudent decisions about how benefits of cost reduction will be shared with customers.

3. It suggests ways in which management can design services that enable customers to participate in the creation, or co-creation, of those services, often on a real-time basis.

4. It provides an example of how services can be customized by the customer.

5. As exciting as co-created strategies may be, it suggests that the process takes time.

6. It illustrates ways in which services can be designed to teach customers how to be better consumers, altering their behaviors in ways that benefit themselves, the service provider, and society.

7. It shows that customer benefits have to be built in first to encourage participation; then the service provider has to determine how to make the strategy work for it.

8. It suggests the need for long-term perseverance and a learn-as-you-go mentality among great service leaders. From Autograph to Snapshot has been a 14-year journey for the Progressive Corporation, and it's not over yet.

9. Above all, it is testimony to the importance of organizational learning if service enterprises are to survive the increasing speed and magnitude of change.

Progressive's exploration of user-based insurance provides a good example of an organization's efforts to achieve the service trifecta. It took two trials to get the pricing right so that those using UBI could be convinced of its value to them on the third iteration. It wasn't until the fourth iteration, Snapshot, that Progressive was finally able to get the economics in line so that the value to the company became attractive. The development journey also illustrates how an organization learns through a "test, then invest" effort to shape an important strategic decision. UBI is not yet a fully proved concept, but if and when it is, Progressive will be at the forefront of the development because of its head start in conducting experiments that prepare it to be in the best competitive position to take advantage of the technological options, the expanding limits of customer acceptance and trust, knowledge of the features that are most and least attractive about user-based insurance, and the economic implications of various management actions.

UBI is only the latest in a long line of innovations that Progressive has introduced to an industry not known for its innovative spirit. Early on, its first-rate actuarial capability identified deep indicators that enabled the company to offer insurance to motorcycle owners at standard (regular) rates. Either its competition charged exorbitant amounts for such insurance, or they didn't offer it at all based on the high average rate of accidents for the vehicles. The secret? The answers to two questions posed to applicants for motorcycle coverage: Do you garage your vehicle? Do you have grandchildren? Progressive's actuarial team had found that those two characteristics dropped the risk of accident to levels warranting standard rates. It used this information to achieve the dominant position in motorcycle insurance that it continues to enjoy today.

At one time Progressive wrote insurance for large long-haul truck fleets. All large trucks can be involved in horrendous accidents that result in acrimony and expensive lawsuits. Again, an analysis of data found that the longer it took an insurance adjuster to reach the scene of an accident, the higher the costs. So the company instituted a rapid-response capability to get its representatives to the scene of a crash as fast as possible to tend to the needs of crash victims. Even though Progressive now confines its business to writing insurance for smaller regional truck fleets, it has carried over the lessons from the experience with large fleets to its other businesses through an Immediate Response Claims Service. According to its website, Progressive was the "first auto insurance group to serve customers at the accident scene."[5]

Because buyers of insurance shop around anyway, Progressive decided to help by posting the rates of competitors for comparable insurance coverage on its website. The practice has built credibility with its customers and leads to sales even when Progressive's rates are not the lowest.

These are just a few examples of a constant stream of innovations in a somewhat staid industry. As you might guess, Progressive's industry leadership in innovation is reflected in its own leadership, a restless, never-satisfied bunch that have been hired and coached to manage for one transient competitive advantage after another in an industry with 200 competitors. Our first exposure to it happened on Halloween, a big event at Progressive, some years ago. It was a celebration of the kind that inspired then CEO Peter Lewis to enter a meeting of his board wearing a Lone Ranger costume (his Halloween outfit) with toy six-guns blazing.

Lewis's philosophy was to create an organization that was data- and evidence-driven, in large part resulting from the creation of a world-class actuarial group. At the time, Progressive hired more MBA graduates from the Harvard Business School than the rest of the insurance industry combined. Combining bright people with good data, Lewis then supported efforts to test any new idea with the potential for producing mutual benefits for customers and the company. The assumption was that the organization could learn from failures as well as successes, and there were many of each. But credit was always given for informed risk taking.

Lewis entrusted his legacy to a hand-picked successor, Glenn Renwick, in 2001. Renwick is described internally as a "hard-working, dependable, tell the truth guy, and a consummate engineer able to keep all the plates spinning in a way that doesn't always get noticed." In short, he would never be found firing toy guns in a board meeting. He leads an organization that doesn't consider itself in the insurance industry. Rather, Progressive's vision is to "reduce the human trauma and economic costs associated with automobile accidents. We do this by providing our customers with services designed to help them get their lives back in order again as quickly as possible."[6]

What values does Renwick, an engineer by training, bring to the table in support of learning at Progressive? Under his "less sexy" leadership, reliability ("do what you say you will do") leading to high levels of trust, coupled with "almost nutty" (according to one executive) levels of transparency has fostered the sharing of ideas that produces learning and innovation. For example, Progressive is the only publicly held company in the United States that reports its finances in detail on a monthly basis. Associates feel secure in reporting both successes and failures. "The sharing of screw-ups often leads to 'can you top this' conversations," according to one executive. It also leads to learning. The level of collaboration is high, and Progressive is focusing on hiring that brings greater diversity of background to its team members.

There is no one department or center for innovation at Progressive. Instead, employees who seek to lower costs or improve service test their ideas for a customer segment against a remarkable database. Perhaps as a legacy of Progressive's industry-leading actuarial group, the company today traces revenue, claims, and expense data to *individual policies*. Such granularity facilitates the testing of ideas. The reporting system gives prompt feedback, helping the sponsor of an idea to decide whether to expand, modify, or kill it. In a sense, this is innovation by the numbers. The most successful ideas are chosen for countrywide rollout. The biggest honor at Progressive is being known as the champion of a new product or process.

In recent years Progressive has been fighting, not always successfully, to avoid becoming just another big, mature company. Growth has slowed, along with the spectacular returns to which investors had become accustomed. New ideas have, at times, faced a gauntlet of data-laden naysayers in an organization in which data is king. But learning still appears to be foremost, as evidenced by such things as the continued development of user-based insurance as well as some of the most innovative marketing efforts in all of US business.

The Progressive Corporation over the past four decades has illustrated many of the ideas associated with great service leaders and their organizations. The results show up in high retention rates for employees and customers alike, as well as bottom-line results for investors. They show up in innovations as well. We're watching and waiting for the next innovation to emerge from Progressive in this often-mundane service industry as it learns to deal with big data. This involves learning new skills to store, retrieve, and analyze usage-based insurance results. And, already, the company is planning for the day when self-driving automobiles change the face of the automobile insurance industry.

A FINAL WORD

There is an evolutionary reason why the future will see a growing number of organizations relying on ideas we've discussed in this book. They will be the survivors—great places to work, offering real value to customers, and providing high returns to investors—benefitting from the win-win-win service trifecta. And the survivors will all have leadership capable of building and maintaining organizations at the forefront of learning in their respective industries.

As we go forward, the demand for services in the developed economies of the world will outpace that for manufactured products as consumers turn to new forms of consumption to address their growing nonmaterial needs in ways that are environmentally sustainable. As we say, information will replace stuff, at the same time making the production of stuff more effective.

More importantly, the future of services will bring with it a redefinition of work and jobs in many organizations, jobs requiring more careful staffing and more extensive training to enable their occupants to exercise a wider range of faculties, jobs that are more satisfying because they have the potential for delivering results to end customers.

The leadership required to realize the potential of the future of services is at this moment being developed in a growing number of breakthrough service organizations—organizations that will supply a disproportionate amount of the talent that is up to the task we have outlined here. Because of the care with which they were selected for attitude, trained for skills, provided with outstanding support systems, and given the latitude to deliver results as they move to more and more senior leadership roles, they will be ready. They will provide a cadre of leaders capable of meeting the expectations that foster trust so essential to the development of employees and customers as owners with extraordinary lifetime value to the organization. They will be leading the learning organizations of the future. They may have little idea today just what that will require in the form of strategies and tactics. They don't have to know. But when the future takes shape, they'll be the first to react and change. They and their service organizations will be learning and ready.

APPENDIX

Service Trends

and Take-Aways

In the course of our work, we have tracked a number of global trends in the service sector. They disclose interesting patterns for service work in the developed economies of the world. Some of the most interesting are presented in the following figures. Observations that they support include those shown in the sidebar.

Of the trends mentioned in the sidebar, two highlight concerns of ours and of economists in general.

The first is the productivity gap between workers in manufacturing and services. Data in figure A-4 shows that in the United States between 1987 and 2011, productivity in manufacturing grew a full percentage point a year more than in a wide cross-section of businesses encompassed by the Bureau of Labor Statistics under "services." Both an explanation for this and a caution for the future is contained in figure A-5. It shows that inputs to production from labor have actually increased for services, from 57.5 percent in 1987 to 58.2 percent in 2011, while they have fallen substantially for manufacturing, from 34.8 percent in 1987 to 27.1 percent in 2011. If inputs from labor are so important to services, the search for higher labor productivity in services surely takes on more urgency.

(continued on page 238)

Trends in the Service and Manufacturing Sectors for the United States and Other Developed Economies

1. Since 1978 jobs devoted to services (as opposed to manufacturing, mining, and agriculture) in the United States have grown from 78 percent to 88 percent of total employment (see figure A-1). Regardless of the wistful hope that this trend will be reversed, and the manufacturing jobs that were supposed to have fueled resurgence of the middle class will return, it is not going to happen. Manufacturing jobs in the United States and many other parts of the world are going to continue to decrease as a proportion of total employment.

2. Similar trends are seen in employment patterns of the United Kingdom, France, Mexico, and China, to name just a few other countries (see figure A-2). All economies, as they develop, naturally support a higher proportion of service jobs. This is occurring fastest in the least developed economies. While nearly 90 percent of jobs in the United Kingdom and 85 percent of the jobs in France are in services, the figure now exceeds 70 percent even in Mexico. China's pattern mirrors that of other countries at an earlier stage in their development.

3. Just since 1990 the share of gross domestic product of the United States that is credited to services has increased from 70 percent to 78 percent, as shown in figure A-3.

4. Services now constitute more than 70 percent of the world's gross domestic product, suggesting that the entire world is trending toward some equilibrium point at which the share of services globally may approach or exceed 80 percent (figure A-3).

5. The service sector encompasses industries with vastly different characteristics. For example, revenue per employee (an imperfect measure of productivity at best) varies from nearly $1.2 million per employee in wholesaling (where labor as a share of expense is small) to less than $60,000

per employee in consumer services such as accommodation and food service and even business services such as warehousing and storage (table A-1).

6. Annual productivity improvements in some service sectors such as trade, transportation, and information in the United States between 1987 and 2011 roughly kept pace with those in manufacturing. However, a wide cross-section of service activities under the catch-all heading of "services" in US government statistics have lagged those in manufacturing by a full 1 percentage point per year, at least since 1987 (figure A-4).

7. As one would expect, inputs to production for services in general involve much higher proportions of labor and much lower proportions of materials than for manufacturing. But while inputs to production from labor for manufacturing have fallen from 34.8 percent in 1987 to 27.1 percent in 2011, inputs to production from labor for services have actually increased slightly, from 57.9 percent to 58.2 percent over the same period (figure A-5). It's another indication of lagging productivity improvements in service activities.

8. The United States continues to enjoy substantial positive trade balances in services (from such things as interest earned on money invested abroad; services provided to foreign visitors to the United States; and transport, communications, military, and other services supplied across borders) that have only partially offset even more substantial negative trade balances in manufacturing (figure A-6).

9. Contrary to popular belief, while average wages vary a great deal across the service sector, overall they have grown recently in the United States to exceed average wages in manufacturing (figure A-7 and table A-2).

10. Employment in the US service sector is more stable than in manufacturing (figure A-8). Although data isn't available, this probably varies greatly from one kind of service enterprise to another. And it does not take into account job shifting and turnover among employees.

This urgency is heightened by the fact that many service jobs, particularly in sectors such as health care and education, increasingly can be carried out without proximity of service provider and customer.[1] As a result, these jobs are becoming tradable, subject to international competition and pressures for increased productivity. By contrast, lower productivity increases characterize the less tradable jobs in location-based service settings such as public education, health care, and leisure and hospitality. Even these kinds of jobs are showing signs of becoming more tradable, as we have seen.

A second and even more important matter concerns us as students of management. We would like to think that frontline employees have been provided with more control over the outcomes of their work. That they've been given bigger jobs requiring more training that has improved their productivity. That support systems have been designed to enable more of them to deliver results to customers. We would like to think that they are more satisfied with their jobs. Unfortunately, what one would like to think is not always an accurate reflection of reality.

How does one explain the results of a 2014 Conference Board survey indicating that 47.7 percent of US workers were satisfied with their jobs, a figure only slightly higher than the all-time 27-year low.[2] Why did a similar 2005 study of workers in 16 countries show that only 14 percent answered that they were "highly engaged" with their work while 29 percent indicated that they were "disengaged"?[3] And why did a recent Gallup Poll survey show that only 2 percent of Singapore's workers "feel engaged by their jobs."[4] The bottom-line importance of the finding of the 2005 study was that the "highly engaged" workers said they were twice as likely to remain in their jobs as those who were "disengaged."[5]

There are several possible explanations for these disappointing findings. First, of course, attitudes toward work may be influenced by many factors somewhat outside the control of individual managers. There is one important factor, however, that isn't outside the control of management. It's job satisfaction. Satisfaction is a function of the positive or negative difference between what is actually experienced as opposed to what is expected. Low job satisfaction may be a function of unrealistically high expectations, increasingly negative experiences, or both. We've found in our research that unmet expectations are also associated with a lack of trust among employees toward an organization and a boss, which is yet another piece of the puzzle of employee dissatisfaction. Whatever the explanation, management has to take some responsibility for the condition and how to correct it.

Figure A-1 Trends in US Employment, by Sector, 1900–2013

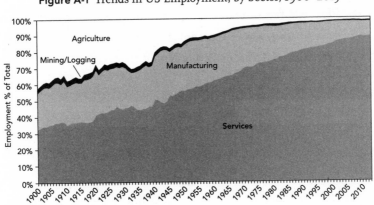

Source: US Bureau of Labor Statistics, Historical Statistics of the US, www.bls.gov/data/#employment, accessed June 20, 2014.

Take-aways: The proportion of jobs devoted to services in the United States has climbed steadily since 1900 with the exception of the periods during the Great Depression and World War II. It is approaching its ultimate share of nearly 90 percent of all jobs.

Figure A-2 Service Sector as a Percentage of All Employment,
UK, France, Mexico, China, 1969–2012

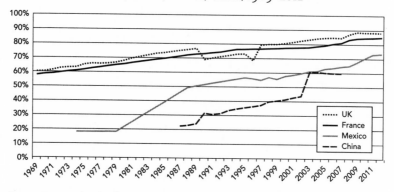

Source: International Labour Organization, ILOSTAT Database, www.ilo.org, accessed
June 19, 2014.

Take-aways: The proportion of jobs devoted to services has shown
gains in both more and less developed economies around the world
for decades. The rate of increase is greater in developing economies
like Mexico and China. It is slowing in developed economies like
the United Kingdom and France, where it is approaching the same
proportion as in the United States

Figure A-3 Share of Services in Gross Domestic Product,
US and the World, 1990–2011

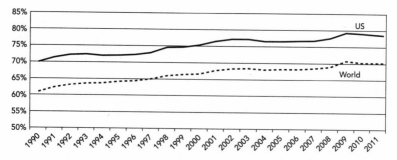

Source: World Bank, World Development Indicators, http://data.worldbank.org/data
-catalog/world-development-indicators, accessed July 8, 2014.

Take-aways: The share of Gross Domestic Product (GDP) generated by services has increased from about 70 percent in 1990 to

about 78 percent of GDP in 2011. The same pattern describes world trends, although shares of GDP from services globally have trailed those for the United States by about 10 percentage points in recent years. Comparing this data with that in figure A-1 showing employment in services at about 89 percent of the US total, it suggests that the value of output, measured in GDP, is lower per employee for services than for manufacturing in the United States. This is one way of measuring productivity, however imperfect it may be.

Table A-1 Revenue per Employee
for Various Types of Enterprises, US, 2012

Type of Enterprise	Revenue per Employee
Oil and gas extraction	$1,738,163
Wholesale trade	1,184,560
Utilities	796,943
Insurance carriers and related activities	749,774
Manufacturing	510,816
Mining	446,244
Information	384,227
Retail trade	286,887
Real estate and rental and leasing	247,760
Professional, scientific, and technical services	189,574
Transportation and warehousing	172,653
Other services (except public administration)	125,063
Health care and social assistance	110,349
Arts, entertainment, and recreation	96,273
Educational services	85,480
Accommodation and food service	59,083
Warehousing and storage	44,276

Note: Types of enterprises listed in bold print are primarily services.
Source: US Bureau of the Census, http://factfinder2.census.gov/faces/tableservices/
jsf/pages/productview.xhtml?pid=ECN_2012_US_00CADV1&prodType=table,
accessed July 9, 2014.

Take-aways: Revenue per employee varies greatly by type of enterprise in the United States. For most types of service enterprise, it is far lower than that in manufacturing. It is, however, a poor indicator of productivity because labor input (and cost as a proportion of revenue) is generally lowest in those businesses with high revenue per employee. To the extent that revenue puts an upper limit on the total labor bill, and to some degree on wages per hour, it is important in services ranging from information services to warehousing and storage. It is a reminder of the need for productivity improvements, particularly in services with low revenue per employee such as education, accommodation and food service, and warehousing and storage.

Figure A-4 Productivity Changes, Manufacturing vs. Selected Services, U.S., 1987–2011

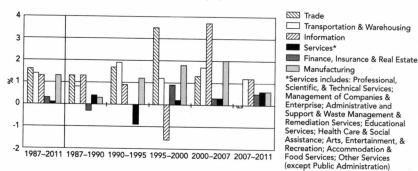

Source: US Bureau of Labor Statistics, http://www.bls.gov/mfp/mprdload.htm, accessed July 11, 2014.

Take-aways: During the 24-year period between 1987 and 2011, the average annual multifactor productivity increases in several service categories (trade, transportation and warehousing, and information) approximated those in manufacturing. However, multifactor productivity in many service jobs (encompassed by "services") hardly changed at all, explaining why productivity increases in service jobs as a whole trailed those in manufacturing. However, during the most recent period of 2007 to 2011, generally years of the Great Recession, even in jobs included under "services," productivity increases were roughly comparable to those in manufacturing.

Figure A-5 Inputs to Production from Labor, Services vs. Manufacturing, US, 1987 to 2011

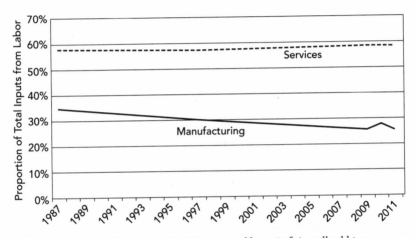

Source: US Bureau of Labor Statistics, http://www.bls.gov/mfp/mprdload.htm, accessed July 8, 2014.

Take-aways: Although manufacturing enterprises reduced labor inputs to finished products between 1987 and 2011, service enterprises were unable to do so. Data in table A-2 provides one possible explanation. It shows that the largest job growth in services in recent years has occurred among jobs in leisure and hospitality, jobs with the highest share of labor to total input and jobs that are the lowest paying. As shown in table A-1, these are also jobs in organizations that generate lower revenues per employee. This helps explain why productivity increases in services as a whole have been smaller than those in manufacturing over this period.

Figure A-6 Trends in the US Trade in Goods and Services, Balance of Payments (BOP) Basis, 1980–2011

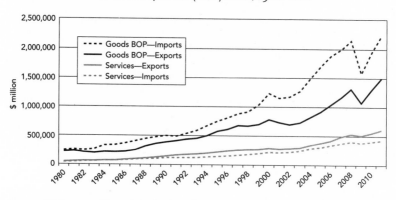

Source: US Bureau of Economic Analysis, http://www.census.gov/foreign-trade/ statistics/historical/gands.txt, accessed June 19, 2014.

Take-aways: Services have generated substantial positive trade balances for the United States for many years. Such balances, however, have not been sufficient to offset larger negative trade balances generated by manufactured goods.

Figure A-7 Average Hourly Wages in Service & Manufacturing Sectors, US, 1966–2013

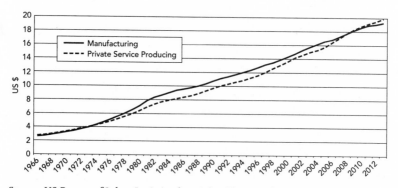

Source: US Bureau of Labor Statistics, http://data.bls.gov/pdq/SurveyOutputServlet, accessed June 18, 2014.

Take-aways: Average wages in services in the United States have steadily gained ground on those in manufacturing since 1994, and have actually exceeded them in the years since 2010.

Table A-2 US Hourly Earnings and Employment in 2013 and Job Growth, 2004–2013, for Manufacturing, Selected Services, and Extracting Enterprises

Type of Enterprise	Hourly Earnings, 2013	Employment, Millions, 2013	Job Growth, 2004–2013
Oil and gas extraction	$30.28	.2	60.2%
Information services	**27.99**	**2.7**	**–13.9**
Mining and logging	26.81	.9	46.9
Professional and business services	**23.69**	**18.6**	**13.2**
Private service producing	**19.90**	**5.8**	**–16.5**
Transportation and warehousing	**19.82**	**25.9**	**1.3**
Manufacturing	19.30	12.0	–16.1
Other services	**18.00**	**5.5**	**1.0**
Leisure and hospitality	**11.78**	**14.2**	**14.0**

Note: Service enterprises are shown in bold print.
Source: US Bureau of Labor Statistics, http://www.bls.gov/opub/eef/archive.htm, accessed June 24, 2014.

Take-aways: While, on average, service jobs pay more than manufacturing jobs in the United States, in fact wages vary over a wide range, with many jobs falling at both the top and bottom of the range. Job growth in all services has exceeded that in manufacturing, with the highest rate of growth coming in low-paying leisure and hospitality as well as high-paying professional and business services.

Figure A-8 Stability of Employment in Services and Manufacturing, US, 1901–2013

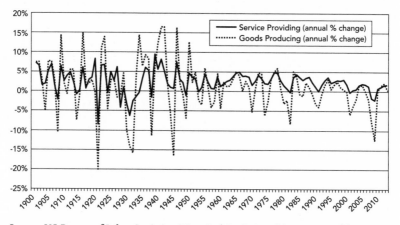

Source: US Bureau of Labor Statistics, Historical Statistics of the US, www.bls.gov/data/#employment, accessed June 20, 2014.

Take-aways: During the period shown in Figure A-8, employment in services has been more stable than that in manufacturing in the United States. Most recently, this was true as well during the Great Recession of 2008 to 2010.

NOTES

Introduction

1. Kate O'Keeffe and Josh Beckerman, "Caesar's CEO Will Step Down," *Wall Street Journal*, February 4, 2015, http://on.wsj.com/1BYc5pk.

Chapter 1

1. James L. Heskett, W. Earl Sasser Jr., and Christopher W. L. Hart, *Service Breakthroughs: Changing the Rules of the Game* (New York: The Free Press, 1990).

2. Some of the earliest work on elements of the customer value equation examined the influence of outcomes (results) and process (quality of customer experience) on perceptions of a service. See, for example, Mary Jo Bitner, Bernard H. Booms, and M. S. Tetrault, "The Service Encounter: Diagnosing Favourable and Unfavourable Incidents," *Journal of Marketing*, January 1990, pp. 71–84. This work influenced our conceptualization of the customer value equation in James L. Heskett, W. Earl Sasser Jr., and Leonard A. Schlesinger, *The Value Profit Chain: Treat Employees Like Customers and Customers Like Employees* (New York: The Free Press, 2002), p. 26.

3. Aruna Divya and Swagato Chatterjee, "The Journey or the Destination: Asymmetric Impact of Process and Outcome on Service Evaluations," Working Paper No. 478, Indian Institute of Management, accessed February 23, 2015, on papers.ssrn.com.

4. A. Parasuraman, Leonard L. Berry, and Valarie A. Zeithaml, "Understanding Customer Expectations of Service," *Sloan Management Review*, Spring 1991, pp. 39–48.

5. For example, see Charles Duhigg, *The Power of Habit: Why We Do What We Do in Life and Business* (New York: Random House, 2012). For a more extensive discussion of the employee value equation, see Heskett, Sasser Jr., and Schlesinger, *The Value Profit Chain*, pp. 157–158.

6. For an early compendium of papers on this topic, see John A. Czepiel, Michael R. Soloman, and Carol F. Surprenant, eds., *The Service Encounter* (Lexington, MA: D. C. Heath, 1985).

7. See James L. Heskett and Roger Hallowell, "Shouldice Hospital Limited (Abridged)," Harvard Business School Case No. 805-002, 2011.

8. John Mackey, in a presentation at a conference on conscious capitalism at Bentley College, May 22, 2012.

9. John Mackey and Raj Sisodia, *Conscious Capitalism: Liberating the Heroic Spirit of Business* (Boston: Harvard Business Review Press, 2013), p. 90.

10. See, for example, Valarie A. Zeithaml, "How Consumer Evaluation Processes Differ Between Goods and Services," in *Marketing of Services,* eds. James H. Donnelly and William R. George (Chicago: American Marketing Association, 1981), pp. 186–190.

11. For examples, see B. Joseph Pine II and James H. Gilmore, *The Experience Economy,* updated ed. (Boston: Harvard Business School Press, 2011).

12. Experience-creating processes at Mayo Clinic are described in detail in Leonard L. Berry and Kent D. Seltman, *Management Lessons from Mayo Clinic: Inside One of the World's Most Admired Service Organizations* (New York: McGraw-Hill, 2008).

13. Jad Mouawad, "The Frills Are Few. The Fees Are Not," *New York Times,* June 1, 2013, p. B2.

14. Ibid., p. B2.

15. See Christopher W. L. Hart, James L. Heskett, and W. Earl Sasser Jr., "The Profitable Art of Service Recovery," *Harvard Business Review,* July–August, 1990, pp. 148–156.

16. See N. W. Pope, "Mickey Mouse Marketing," *American Banker,* July 25, 1979, pp. 4–14; and "More Mickey Mouse Marketing, *American Banker,* September 12, 1979, pp. 4–14.

17. See, for example, Atul Gawande, "The Cost Conundrum: What a Texas Town Can Teach Us about Health Care," *New Yorker,* June 1, 2009, pp. 36–49.

18. Patient Protection and Affordable Care Act, Title III, Section 3021, p. 712. Link to summary of act provisions: http://www.healthcare.gov/law/timeline/full.html.

19. See David H. Maister and Christopher H. Lovelock, "Managing Facilitator Services," *Sloan Management Review,* Summer 1982, p. 22; and Roger W. Schmenner, "How Can Service Businesses Survive and Prosper?" *Sloan Management Review* 27, no. 3 (1986), pp. 21–32.

20. One of the most comprehensive reviews of these efforts is presented by Rohit Verma, "An Empirical Analysis of Management Challenges in Service Factories, Service Shops, Mass Services and Professional Services," *International Journal of Service Industry Management* 11, no. 1 (2000), pp. 8–25. In his analysis, Verma uses Schmenner's 1986 taxonomy.

Chapter 2

1. James L. Heskett, *Managing in the Service Economy* (Boston: Harvard Business School Press, 1986), pp. 5–43.

2. Sources for this section include the company website, IKEA.com, and the cases Christopher A. Bartlett and Ashish Nanda, "Ingvar Kamprad and IKEA," Harvard Business School Case No. 390-132, 1996; and Youngme Moon, "IKEA Invades America," Harvard Business School Case No. 504-094, 2004; as well as other sources cited below.

3. By February 2015, the 88-year-old Kamprad had relinquished the chairmanship of the companies controlling IKEA's brand and its day-to-day operations.

4. IKEA.com.

5. Lauren Collins, "House Perfect: Is the IKEA Ethos Comfy or Creepy?" *New Yorker*, October 3, 2011, pp. 54–65.

6. Johan Stenebo, *The Truth about IKEA: The Secret Success of the World's Most Popular Furniture Brand* (London: Gibson Square, 2010).

7. See Helen Rosethorn, *The Employer Brand: Keeping Faith with the Deal* (Gower: Farnham, UK, 2009).

8. For evidence of this, see the results of an in-depth study in James L. Heskett, *The Culture Cycle: How to Shape the Unseen Force That Transforms Performance* (Upper Saddle River, NJ: FT Press, 2012), pp. 151–167.

9. See Tony Hsieh, *Delivering Happiness: A Path to Profits, Passion, and Purpose* (New York: Business Plus, 2010).

10. Mike McNamee, "Credit Card Revolutionary," *Stanford Business*, May 2001, p. 23.

11. For a more extensive discussion of the employee value equation, see Heskett, Sasser Jr., and Schlesinger, *The Value Profit Chain*, pp. 157–158.

12. Leonard A. Schlesinger, *Quality of Work Life and the Supervisor* (New York: Praeger, 1982), pp. 1–9.

13. Rogelio Oliva and Robert Kallenberg, "Managing the Transition from Products to Services," *International Journal of Service Industry Management* 14, no. 2 (2003), p. 169. Their study was of 11 German capital equipment manufacturers at different stages of developing service offerings for their products.

14. Oliva and Kallenberg, "Managing the Transition," p. 161.

15. S&P Capital IQ, accessed July 29, 2014, www.capitaliq.com/.

16. "Horsemeat Found in IKEA Meatballs," *USA Today*, February 25, 2013, www.usatoday.com/story/news/world/2013/02/25/horsemeat-scandal/1933037.

17. We have had no relationship of any kind with IKEA.

Chapter 3

1. Heskett, Sasser Jr., and Hart, *Service Breakthroughs*.

2. Organizations that primarily deliver services represented 86.1 percent of best places to work on the *Fortune* survey from 2009 through 2013. The same is true of the customer service rankings if automobile companies (which actually deliver service through their dealerships) are eliminated from the list. This is not surprising because customer service surveys do not adequately cover business-to-business services that many manufacturers provide.

3. Michael Burchell and Jennifer Robin, *The Great Workplace: How to Build It, How to Keep It, and Why It Matters* (San Francisco: Jossey-Bass, 2011), p. 13.

4. J. D. Power and Associates, "Achieving Excellence in Customer Service," Press Release, February 17, 2011.

5. In the spirit of full disclosure, none of us are clients of USAA.

6. One of the early expositions of this idea was presented in Jim Collins and Jerry Porras, *Built to Last: Successful Habits of Visionary Companies* (New York: HarperBusiness, 1994), especially pp. 43–46.

7. See, for example, Benjamin Schneider and David E. Bowen, "New Services Design, Development, and Implementation and the Employee," in *New Services*, W. R. George and C. Marshall, eds., (Chicago: American Marketing Association, 1985), pp. 82–101; and E. M. Johnson and D. T. Seymour, "The Impact of Cross-Selling on the Service Encounter in Retail Banking," in *The Service Encounter*, J. A. Czepiel, M. R. Soloman, and C. F. Suprenant, eds., (Lexington, MA: D. C. Heath, 1985), pp. 225–239.

8. For an example of this work, see Frederick F. Reichheld and W. Earl Sasser Jr., "Zero Defections: Quality Comes to Services," *Harvard Business Review*, September–October 1990, pp. 105–111.

9. David H. Maister, *Practice What You Preach: What Managers Must Do to Create a High Achievement Culture* (New York: The Free Press, 2001). This study examined feedback from more than 5,500 respondents from 139 offices operated by 29 firms providing marketing services to clients.

10. This work was first reported in James L. Heskett, Thomas O. Jones, Gary W. Loveman, W. Earl Sasser Jr., and Leonard A. Schlesinger, "Putting the Service-Profit Chain to Work," *Harvard Business Review*, March–April 1994, pp. 164–174.

11. In figure 3-3 elements connected by dark lines and arrows are those that have withstood the challenge of confirmatory research relatively well. Other relationships shown there have received less attention from managers and academic researchers even though they may be influencing actual managerial practice.

12. See, for example, Benjamin Schneider, P. J. Hanges, D. B. Smith, and A. N. Salvaggio, "Which Come First: Employee Attitudes or Organizational Financial and Market Performance?" *Journal of Applied Psychology* 88 (2003), pp. 836–851; and J. K. Harter, F. L. Schmidt, and T. L. Hayes, "Business-Unit Level Relationship between Employee Satisfaction, Employee Engagement, and Business Outcomes: A Meta-Analysis," *Journal of Applied Psychology* 87 (2002), pp. 268–279.

13. See R. Silvestro and S. Cross, "Applying the Service Profit Chain in a Retail Environment," *International Journal of Service Industry Management* 38 (2000), pp. 24–47; R. Silvestro, "Dispelling the Modern Myth: Employee Satisfaction and Loyalty Drive Service Profitability," *International Journal of Operations & Production Management* 22, no. 1 (2002), pp. 30–49; and Timothy L. Keiningham, Lerzan Aksoy, Robert M. Daly, Kathy Perrier, and Antoine Solom, "Reexamining the Link between Employee Satisfaction and Store Performance in a Retail Environment," *International Journal of Service Industry Management* 17, no. 1 (2006), pp. 51–57.

14. David H. Maister, *Practice What You Preach*, p. 154.

15. See, for example, Fred Reichheld, *The Loyalty Effect: The Hidden Force Behind Growth, Profits, and Lasting Value* (Boston: HBS Press, 1996).

16. Corporate Leadership Council, *Driving Employee Performance and Retention Through Engagement: A Quantitative Analysis of the Effectiveness of Employee Engagement Strategies* (Corporate Executive Board, 2004), p. xiv.

17. Shad Foos, vice president of Marketing, Service Management Group, e-mail message to authors, February 10, 2015.

18. Bo H. Eriksen, "How Employee Turnover Affects Productivity" (working paper available on Social Science Research Network, ssrn.com, January 16, 2010).

19. Corporate Leadership Council, *Driving Employee Performance and Retention*.

20. Shad Foos, e-mail message to authors.

21. Ibid.

22. The study is reported in Heskett, *The Culture Cycle*.

23. Ibid., especially pp. 136–142.

24. Limited Brands, "Service Profit Chain Analysis, 2012" (proprietary internal research, used with permission).

25. Ibid.

26. Anthony J. Rucci, Steven P. Kirn, and Richard T. Quinn, "The Employee-Customer-Profit Chain at Sears," *Harvard Business Review*, January–February 1998, pp. 82–97.

27. Maister, *Practice What You Preach*, especially p. 79.

28. *Bloomberg Businessweek*, June 23–June 29, 2014, p. S2.

29. Sarah Max, "If Its Customers Love a Business, This Equity Firm Does Too," *New York Times*, July 30, 2013, p. B7.

30. Fred Reichheld, *The Ultimate Question: Driving Good Profits and True Growth* (Boston: HBS Press, 2006).

31. Robert S. Kaplan and David P. Norton, *The Balanced Scorecard: Translating Strategy into Action* (Boston: HBS Publishing, 1996).

32. Lerzan Aksoy, "How Do You Measure What You Can't Define?: The Current State of Loyalty Measurement and Management," *Journal of Service Management* 24, no. 4 (2013), p. 373.

33. Dan Maher and Dan O'Brien, "So Long, Safe Harbor: Putting the Service Profit Chain to Work," Case No. OU-184 (New York: Omnicom University, 2013).

34. Adapted from Tom Davenport, "Retail's Winners Rely on the Service-Profit Chain," *Harvard Business Review*, November 2012.

35. Itamar Simonson and Emanuel Rosen, *Absolute Value: What Really Influences Customers in the Age of (Nearly) Perfect Information* (New York: HarperBusiness, 2014).

Chapter 4

1. John Thornhill, "France's Favourite Englishman," *Financial Times*, February 9–10, 2008, p. 3 (Life & Arts).

2. Mark Cuban, foreword to *The Extra 2%: How Wall Street Strategies Took a Major League Baseball Team from Worst to First* by Jonah Keri (New York: Ballantine Books, 2011), p. vii.

3. John C. Bogle, *Enough: True Measures of Money, Business, and Life* (New York: John Wiley & Sons, 2009), p. 115. Bogle was quoting the words of a sermon given in London on the 200th anniversary of Lord Nelson's death.

4. Ibid., p. xvi.

5. Thomas H. Davenport and Brook Manville tell it well in their book, *Judgment Calls: 12 Stories of Big Decisions and the Teams That Got Them Right* (Boston: Harvard Business Review Press, 2012), pp. 143–159.

6. This and other information about Mayo Clinic in this chapter can be found in the excellent profile of the organization by Leonard L. Berry and Kent D. Seltman, *Management Lessons from Mayo Clinic: Inside One of the World's Most Admired Service Organizations* (New York: McGraw-Hill, 2008), p. 195.

7. See, for example, Valarie A. Zeithaml, A. Parasuraman, and Leonard L. Berry,

Delivering Quality Service: Balancing Customer Perceptions and Expectations (New York: Free Press, 1990).

8. See Heskett, *The Culture Cycle*, pp. 135–136.

9. Measured in SMG employee surveys as intent to be working here 6 and 12 months from now.

10. Andy Fromm, Joe Cardador, and Mark Hunter, *Latest Findings from the Restaurant and Retail Industries* (Kansas City: Service Management Group, 2006).

11. For one of the most comprehensive, see J. Richard Hackman and Greg R. Oldham, *Work Redesign* (Boston: Addison-Wesley Publishing, 1980).

12. Leonard A. Schlesinger and Jeffrey Zornitsky, "Job Satisfaction, Service Capability, and Customer Satisfaction: An Examination of Linkages and Management Implications," *Human Resource Planning* 14, no. 2, pp. 141–149.

13. Fromm, Cardador, and Turner, *Latest Findings*, pp. 13 and 18.

14. This study, reported in detail in Marcus Buckingham and Curt Coffman, *First, Break All the Rules* (New York: Simon & Schuster, 1999), was based on in-depth interviews with more than 80,000 managers in more than 400 companies.

15. No-surprises management is usually a term applied to efforts of subordinates to "manage up" by not surprising their superiors. Here we have turned the proposition upside down to reflect the reverse effect.

16. Jean M. Phillips, "Effects of Realistic Job Previews on Multiple Organizational Outcomes: a Meta-analysis," *Academy of Management Journal* 41, pp. 673–690.

17. See, for example, Chip Heath and Dan Heath, *Decisive: How to Make Better Choices In Life and Work* (New York: Crown Business, 2013), pp. 212–213.

18. See, for example, Jack Welch's account of GE's effort to disassociate itself from managers unable to manage by the company's values, in Jack Welch with John A. Byrne, *Jack: Straight from the Gut* (New York: Warner Business Books, 2001), pp. 188–189.

19. Berry and Seltman, *Management Lessons from Mayo Clinic*, p. 143.

20. Lululemon.com, accessed January 14, 2013. This and the following quote are from the same source.

21. Amy Wallace, "It's a Stretch," *New York Times Magazine*, February 8, 2015, pp. 20–23.

22. "Dining Out: Good Manners Beget Good Service," editorial, *Boston Globe*, August 20, 2012.

23. Ibid.

24. See Julie Weed, "In Turnabout, Some Companies Are Rating Their Customers," *New York Times*, December 2, 2014, p. B7.

25. Adam Bryant, "He's Not Bill Gates, or Fred Astaire," *New York Times*, February 14, 2010, p. B2.

26. Jena McGregor, "The Employee Is Always Right," *Businessweek*, November 19, 2007, p. 80. See also Vineet Nayar, *Employees First, Customers Second: Turning Conventional Management Upside Down* (Boston: Harvard Business Press, 2010).

27. See Gunter K. Stahl, Martha L. Maznevski, Andreas Voigt, and Karsten Jonsen, "Unraveling the Effects of Cultural Diversity in Teams: A Meta-Analysis of Research on Multicultural Work Groups," *Journal of International Business Studies* 41, no. 4 (2010), pp. 690–709. The authors conclude that in teams, "cultural diversity

leads to process losses through task conflict and decreased social integration, but also to process gains through increased creativity and satisfaction."

28. Amy C. Edmondson, *Teaming: How Organizations Learn, Innovate, and Compete in the Knowledge Economy* (San Francisco: Jossey-Bass, 2012).

29. See an interview of Richard Hackman with Diane Coutu, "Why Teams Don't Work," *Harvard Business Review*, May 2009, pp. 99–105; and Richard J. Hackman, *Leading Teams: Setting the Stage for Great Performance* (Boston: Harvard Business School Press, 2002).

30. Giada DiStefano, Francesa Gino, Gary Pisano, and Bradley Staats, "Learning by Thinking: How Reflection Aids Performance," Harvard Business School Working Paper No. 14–093, March 2014.

31. Kaplan and Norton, *The Balanced Scorecard*.

32. The quotation was verified by David Glass, April 10, 2002.

33. We first called this the "cycle of failure," a name that our colleague at the time, the late Christopher Lovelock, suggested we change to "cycle of mediocrity." We have further modified it to remove the stigma of even that name.

34. See Robert Kanigel, *The One Best Way: Frederick Winslow Taylor and the Enigma of Efficiency* (New York: Viking, 1997).

35. Bonnie Kavoissi, "Costco CEO: Raise the Minimum Wage to More Than $10 per Hour," *Huffington Post*, March 6, 2013.

36. Wayne F. Cascio, "Decency Means More Than 'Always Low Prices': A Comparison of Costco to Wal-Mart's Sam's Club," *Academy of Management Perspectives*, August, 2006. See also Cascio, "The High Cost of Low Wages," *Harvard Business Review*, December 2006, pp. 23–33.

37. As we completed this book, Walmart announced that it would raise the minimum wage paid to its employees, provide more regular work schedules, offer more opportunities for advancement, and focus on recruiting and retaining "better talent so it can improve its business . . . [with] better-run stores, more satisfied customers and an increase in sales and profits." Anne D'Innocenzio, "WalMart Is Raising Its Wages," *Sarasota Herald-Tribune*, February 20, 2015, pp. D1–D2.

38. Davenport and Manville, *Judgment Calls*, p. 153.

39. Ibid., p. 157.

40. Huntley Manhertz Jr., "Worldwide Trends in Employee Retention," AchieveGlobal, http://www.achieveglobal.com/resources/files/Worldwide_Trends_Employee_Retention_Report.pdf, February 2011. This study of 738 managers from several countries found that one in four planned to leave in the coming year.

41. D'Innocenzio, "WalMart Is Raising Its Wages," p. D2.

Chapter 5

1. David A. Maister, "The Psychology of Waiting Lines," in *The Service Encounter*, John A. Czepiel, Michael R. Soloman, and Carol F. Suprenant, eds. (Lexington, MA: D. C. Heath, 1985), pp. 113–123.

2. Daniel Kahneman, *Thinking, Fast and Slow* (New York: Farrar, Straus and Giroux, 2011), especially pp. 380–409.

3. Huggy Rao and Robert Sutton, "Bad to Great: The Path to Scaling Up Excellence," *McKinsey Quarterly*, February, 2014, http://www.mckinsey.com/Insights/

Organization?Bad_to_great. This excerpt is from a book by the same authors, *Scaling Up Excellence: Getting to More without Settling for Less* (New York: Crown Business, 2014).

4. John Colapinto, "Check, Please: The Challenge of Creating a World-Class Restaurant—and Turning a Profit," *New Yorker*, September 10, 2012, pp. 58–65.

5. Frances Frei and Anne Morriss, *Uncommon Service: How to Win by Putting Customers at the Core of Your Business* (Boston: Harvard Business Review Press, 2012), pp. 75–76.

6. For a more extensive discussion of service guarantees, see Christopher W. L. Hart, "The Power of Unconditional Service Guarantees," *Harvard Business Review*, July–August 1988, pp. 54–62; and Christopher W. L. Hart, Leonard A. Schlesinger, and Dan Maher, "Guarantees Come to Professional Service Firms," *Sloan Management Review*, Spring 1992, pp. 19–30.

7. The Hampton Inn example is based on company data and Christopher W. L. Hart, "Hampton Inn's Guests Satisfied with Satisfaction Guaranteed," *Marketing News*, February 4, 1991, p. 7.

8. This vignette is based on Jennifer Steinhauer and Michael S. Schmidt, "Man behind FEMA's Makeover Built Philosophy on Preparation and Waffle House," *New York Times*, November 4, 2012, p. 31.

9. For a detailed description of the Waffle House strategy, see W. Earl Sasser Jr., "Waffle House," Harvard Business School Case No. 672-101, 1972, revised 1977.

10. Steinhauer and Schmidt, "Man behind FEMA's Makeover."

11. See Kaplan and Norton, *The Balanced Scorecard*.

12. For early work on service gaps, see A. Parasuraman, Valarie A. Zeithaml, and Leonard L. Berry, "A Conceptual Model of Service Quality and Its Implications for Future Research," *Journal of Marketing*, Fall 1985, pp. 41–50. The authors concentrate on negative service gaps, but the concept applies similarly to positive gaps.

13. Ibid.; and Christopher Lovelock, *Product Plus* (New York: McGraw-Hill, 1994).

14. Jim Collins, *Good to Great: Why Some Companies Make the Leap . . . and Others Don't* (New York: Harper Collins, 2001), p. 6.

15. The organization that was second on this criterion was another that encountered significant difficulties later, Fannie Mae.

16. Rachel Beck, "Lessons in How Circuit City's Job Cuts Backfired," *San Francisco Chronicle*, January 13, 2008, p. C3.

17. Leonard L. Berry, A. Parasuraman, and Valarie A. Zeithaml, "Improving Service Quality in America: Lessons Learned," *Academy of Management Executive* 8, no. 2, 1994, pp. 32–52.

18. A. Parasuraman, Valarie A. Zeithaml, and Leonard Berry, "SERVQUAL: A Multiple-Item Scale for Measuring Consumer Perceptions of Service Quality," *Journal of Retailing*, Spring 1988, pp. 12–40.

19. See, for example, Tom R. Tyler, "Leadership and Cooperation in Groups," *American Behavioral Scientist* 45, no. 5 (Jan. 2002), 769–782.

20. For an all-too-common discussion of this, see Tracey Meares, "The Legitimacy among Young African-American Men," the Barrock Lecture on Criminal Law, Marquette University Law School, February 19, 2009, *Marquette Law Review*, Summer 2009, pp. 651–666.

21. See Jaren Lanier, *Who Owns the Future?* (New York: Simon & Schuster, 2013).

Chapter 6

1. Leonard L. Berry, A. Parasuraman, and Valarie A. Zeithaml, "Improving Service Quality in America: Lessons Learned," *Academy of Management Executive* 8, no. 2 (1994), p. 37.

2. Material regarding Starbucks in this chapter is based on Howard Schultz with Joanne Gordon, *Onward: How Starbucks Fought for Its Life without Losing Its Soul* (New York: Rodale, 2011).

3. Ibid., p. 4.

4. Alan Levin and Julie Johnsson, "Asiana Crash Probe: Is Autopilot Making Flying Less Safe?" *Bloomberg Businessweek*, July 18, 2013, http://www.bloomberg.com/bw/articles/2013–07–18/asiana-crash-probe-is-autopilot-making-flying-less-safe.

5. Michel Anteby, Elena Corsi, and Emilie Billaud, "Automating the Paris Subway (A)," Harvard Business School Case No. 9–413–061, 2012.

6. Michel Anteby, Elena Corsi, and Emilie Billaud, "Automating the Paris Subway (B)," Harvard Business School Case No. 9–413–062, 2012.

7. Catherine Shaw, "Ahead of the Curve," *Financial Times*, July 14–15, 2012, p. 1 (House & Home Section).

8. See, for example, B. Bowonder, Mohit Bansal, and A. Sharnitha Giridhar, "A Telemedicine Platform: A Case Study of Apollo Hospitals Telemedicine Project," *International Journal of Service Technology and Management* 6, nos. 3/4/5 (2005); and, for a description of the early development of the organization and its culture, Gary Loveman and Jamie O'Connell, "Apollo Hospitals of India (A)," Harvard Business School Case No. 9–396–027, 1996.

9. For a discussion of Internet-based networks, see Thomas R. Eisenmann, ed., *Internet Business Models: Text and Cases* (New York: McGraw-Hill, 2001); and Thomas R. Eisenmann, "Managing Networked Businesses: Summary Module," Harvard Business School Module Note 808–008, 2007.

10. See James L. Heskett and W. Earl Sasser Jr., "Southwest Airlines: In a Different World," Harvard Business School Case 910–419, 2009.

11. Pull networks sometimes involve the same kind of risk. For example, Craigslist, a rapidly growing Internet website, became associated with questionable advertisers that reflected poorly on its credibility and required that the operator of the site begin screening its advertisers for acceptability.

12. Management at McDonald's continues to struggle with this issue. In mid-2013 it announced that two franchisees in Detroit would discontinue their practice of serving halal beef and chicken products to a predominantly Muslim clientele when they were sued for allegedly selling as halal meats products that were not halal.

13. For an early development of this concept, see Bernard H. Booms and Mary Jo Bitner, "Marketing Strategies and Organization Structures for Service Firms," in *Marketing of Services*, J. Donnelly and William R. George, eds. (Chicago: American Marketing Association, 1985), pp. 47–52. Booms and Bitner define a *servicescape* as "the environment in which the service is assembled and in which the seller and customer interact, combined with tangible commodities that facilitate performance or communication of the service."

14. Mary Jo Bitner, "Servicescapes: The Impact of Physical Surroundings on Customers and Employees," *Journal of Marketing* 56, no. 4 (April 1992), pp. 57–71.

15. See Mark S. Rosenbaum, "The Symbolic Servicescape: Your Kind Is Welcome Here," *Journal of Consumer Behavior* 4 (2005), pp. 257–267.

16. Observations here summarize the results of many research projects conducted in restaurants and other service venues. See, for example, Bitner, "Servicescapes"; Mary Jo Bitner, "The Servicescape," in *Handbook of Services Marketing & Management*, Teresa A. Swartz and Dawn Iacobucci (New York: Sage Publications, 2000), chapter 2; and Eric Sundstrom and Irwin Altman, "Physical Environments and Work-Group Effectiveness," *Research in Organizational Behavior* 11 (1989), pp. 175–209.

17. Howard Schultz, *Onward*, pp. 121–122.

18. Joan O'C. Hamilton, "Will They Eat Our Lunch?" *Stanford Magazine*, January–February, 2014, https://alumni.stanford.edu/get/page/magazine/article/?article_id=67459.

Chapter 7

1. Information concerning Châteauform' in this chapter is based on personal observation, the company's website, http://chateauform.com/en/chateauform/maison/29/la-villa-gallarati-scotti, promotional material, and a case by Benoit Leleux, Winter Nie, and Anne-Sarine Courcoux, "Chateauform' (A): How to Grow and Maintain Service?" Case No. IMD-3-1660, International Institute for Management Development, October 25, 2006.

2. Various studies have shown that customers with a negative perception of a service are significantly more likely to tell others than those with a positive perception.

3. See M. D. Uncles, G. R. Dowling, and K. Hammond, "Customer Loyalty and Customer Loyalty Programs," *Journal of Consumer Marketing* 20, no. 4 (2003), pp. 294–316.

4. Ibid.

5. See James L. Heskett, W. Earl Sasser, and Joe Wheeler, *The Ownership Quotient: Putting the Service Profit Chain to Work for Unbeatable Competitive Advantage* (Boston: Harvard Business Press, 2008).

6. See B. Joseph Pine II and James H. Gilmore, *The Experience Economy: Work Is Theatre & Every Business a Stage* (Boston: HBS Press, 1999).

7. The research was first described in Heskett, Sasser, and Wheeler, *The Ownership Quotient*, pp. 17–18.

8. One of us participated in a discussion in the late 1970s at a neighborhood restaurant in Cambridge, Massachusetts, with airline executives who described a set of ideas that would later lead to the introduction of one of the early programs, AAdvantage. Little did we realize at the time how effective frequent-flyer programs would become in building loyalty.

9. Frederick F. Reichheld and W. Earl Sasser Jr., "Zero Defections: Quality Comes to Services," *Harvard Business Review*, September–October 1990, pp. 105–111. Reichheld subsequently expanded on these ideas in his book *The Loyalty Effect*, especially pp. 33–62.

10. See, for example, S. J. Grove and R. P. Fisk, "The Impact of Other Customers on Service Experiences: A Critical Incident Examination of 'Getting Along,'" *Journal*

of Retailing, Spring 1997, pp. 63–85. Other ways in which customers contribute to the quality of the experience are suggested in C. A. Lengnick-Hal, "Customer Contributions to Quality: A Different View of the Customer-Oriented Firm," *Academy of Management Review*, July 1996, pp. 791–824; and David E. Bowen, "Managing Customers as Human Resources in Service Organizations," *Human Resource Management*, Fall 1986, pp. 371–383.

11. Dwayne D. Gremler and Stephen W. Brown, "The Loyalty Ripple Effect: Appreciating the Full Value of Customers," *International Journal of Service Industry Management*. 10, no. 3 (1999), pp. 271–291.

12. Heskett, Sasser, and Wheeler, *The Ownership Quotient*, p. 18.

13. Brad Stone, *The Everything Store: Jeff Bezos and the Age of Amazon* (New York: Little, Brown, 2013), p. 327.

14. See Reichheld, *The Ultimate Question*; and Timothy L. Keiningham, Bruce Cook, Tor Wallin Andreassen, and Lerzan Aksoy, "A Longitudinal Examination of Net Promoter and Firm Revenue Growth," *Journal of Marketing*, July, 2007, pp. 39–51. Reichheld, in his work, maintains that he has found no correlation between growth and customer satisfaction; Keiningham and his colleagues conclude that customer satisfaction is a better measure of growth than the Net Promoter Score.

15. Christopher W. L. Hart, "The Power of Unconditional Service Guarantees," *Harvard Business Review* 66 no. 4 (July–August 1988,), pp. 54–62.

16. A more complete version of this story can be found in Heskett, Sasser, and Wheeler, *The Ownership Quotient*, pp. 184–189.

17. What follows regarding Communispace is based on Michael Winerip, "Experienced Hands, Still Valued," *New York Times*, March 7, 2010, p. ST2; and Diane Hessan, conversations with the authors.

18. See, for example, Itamar Simonson and Emanuel Rosen, *Absolute Value: What Really Influences Customers in the Age of (Nearly) Perfect Information* (New York: HarperBusiness, 2014).

Chapter 8

1. Jennifer Reingold, "*Still* Crazy after All These Years," *Fortune*, January 14, 2013, pp. 95–96.

2. Quoted material is from Brad Stone, "The Secrets of Bezos: How Amazon Became the Everything Store," *Bloomberg Businessweek*, October 10, 2013, http://www .bloomberg.com/bw/articles/2013-10-10/jeff-bezos-and-the-age-of-amazon-excerpt-from-the-everything-store-by-brad-stone; see also Stone, *The Everything Store*.

3. See Daniel H. Pink, *Free Agent Nation: The Future of Working for Yourself* (New York: Warner Business Books, 2001).

4. See Brad Stone, "Crowdsourcing Your Grocery Bags," *Bloomberg Businessweek*, July 15, 2013, pp. 32–33; and Ryan Lawler, "Instacart Could Raise a Big New Round of Funding Valuing It At $400 Million," techcrunch.com, posted April 17, 2014.

5. Douglas MacMillan, Sam Schechner, and Lisa Fleisher, "Uber Snags $41 Billion Valuation," *Wall Street Journal*, December 4, 2014, http://www.wsj.com/ articles/ubers-new-funding-values-it-at-over-41-billion-1417715938.

6. See Austin Carr, "Inside Airbnb's Grand Hotel Plan," *Fast Company*, April

2014, http://www.fastcompany.com/3027107/punk-meet-rock-airbnb-brian-chesky-chip-conley.

7. Ibid.

8. Michael Pollock, "Figuring Out Who Is Set to Sell Their Home," *Sarasota Herald-Tribune*, April 6, 2015, pp. 1A and 13A.

9. Gary Loveman, quoted in Heskett, Sasser Jr., and Wheeler, *The Ownership Quotient*, pp. 109–110.

10. Michael Spence, *The Next Convergence: The Future of Economic Growth in a Multispeed World* (New York: Farrar, Straus and Giroux, 2011).

11. Peter M. Senge, *The Fifth Discipline: The Art and Practice of the Learning Organization*, rev. ed. (New York: Random House, 2006), p. xviii.

12. Bryant, "He's Not Bill Gates, or Fred Astaire," p. B2.

13. See Peter M. Senge, *The Fifth Discipline*, p. xviii.

14. See Stahl, Maznevski, Voigt, and Jonsen, "Unraveling the Effects of Cultural Diversity in Teams" pp. 690–709.

15. Michael L. Tushman and Charles A. O'Reilly, III, *Winning through Innovation: A Practical Guide to Leading Organizational Change and Renewal* (Boston: Harvard Business School Press, 1997), p. x.

16. Ben Cheng, Michelle Kan, Gad Levanon, and Rebecca L. Ray, "Job Satisfaction: 2014 Edition," *The Conference Board*, June, 2014.

17. Manhertz Jr., "Worldwide Trends in Employee Retention."

Epilogue

1. Autograph is described in more detail in Francis X. Frei, "Progressive Insurance (A): Pay-As-You-Go Insurance," Harvard Business School Case No. 602–175, 2008.

2. Teresa Dixon Murray, "Auto Insurers Ramp Up Monitoring Your Driving in Exchange for Cutting Your Rate," *Plain Dealer*, May 27, 2012, http://www.cleveland.com/business/index.ssf/2012/05/auto_insurers_ramp_up_monitori.html.

3. Information in this paragraph is based on a report, Progressive Corporation, *Linking Driving Behavior to Automobile Accidents and Insurance Rates: An Analysis of Five Billion Miles Driven*, Progressive Corporation, 2012.

4. Progressive executive, interview with the authors, March, 2013.

5. "Progressive Firsts," https://www.progressive.com/progressive-insurance/first/, accessed May 15, 2013.

6. "Core Values," https://www.progressive.com/progressive-insurance/core-values/, accessed June 2, 2014.

Appendix

1. See, for example, Spence, *The Next Convergence*.

2. Cheng, Kan, Levanon, and Ray, "Job Satisfaction."

3. Towers Perrin, *Towers Perrin Global Workforce Study* (New York: Towers Perrin, 2005).

4. Bruce Einhorn and Sharon Chen, "Singapore Confronts an Emotion Deficit," *Bloomberg Businessweek*, November 26–December 2, 2012, pp. 24 and 26.

5. Towers Perrin, *Towers Perrin Global Workforce Study*.

ACKNOWLEDGMENTS

Among the many executives who have influenced this book, we would like to single out a few who have inspired us, assisted us in the preparation of case materials, or otherwise helped us in ways in which they are probably unaware. They include Colleen Barrett, Jeff Bezos, John Bogle, Scott Cook, Andy Fromm, Diane Hessan, the late Jacques Horowitz, Tony Hsieh, Bill Hybels, John Jamotta, Craig Jelinek, Ingvar Kamprad, Herb Kelleher, Gary Kelly, Arkadi Kuhlmann, Gary Loveman, John Mackey, Lanham Napier, Bill Pollard, Prathap Reddy, Howard Schultz, Carl Sewell, Fred Smith, Tom Watson, Jack Welch, Leslie Wexner, Ed Wise, John Wren, Mabel Yu, and the late Lorenzo Zambrano.

We have learned a great deal in working with two champion developers of case materials, Dan Maher and Dan O'Brien. Our associate Erika McCaffrey provided invaluable help in organizing the data in the appendix, finding obscure information, and otherwise helping us verify facts. Paula Alexander and Jacqueline Archer helped us make our work presentable.

Over the years, we have benefitted greatly from the work of colleagues who examine service phenomena around the world. With the certainty that we will leave someone out, those who have had probably the greatest influence on us include Lerzan Aksoy, Leonard Berry, Mary Jo Bitner, David Bowen, Stephen Brown,

Richard Chase, Tom Davenport, Bo Eriksen, Timothy Keiningham, A. Parasuraman, Frederick Reichheld, Benjamin Schneider, Peter Senge, Raj Sisodia, Rohit Verma, Joe Wheeler, and Valarie Zeithaml.

Among colleagues who are or were at Harvard Business School with us, we must recognize the work of Christopher Bartlett, Dennis Campbell, James Cash, Tom DeLong, Amy Edmondson, Tom Eisenmann, Frances Frei, Roger Hallowell, Christopher Hart, Luis Huete, Tom Jones, Robert Kaplan, Nancy Koehn, the late Christopher Lovelock, David Maister, Youngme Moon, Ashish Nanda, Charles O'Reilly III, Jeffrey Rayport, Roger Schmenner, Robert Simons, Michael Tushman, and the late D. Daryl Wyckoff.

We are indebted to the support of the four Harvard Business School deans under which we have done our work: John McArthur, Kim Clark, Jay Light, and Nitin Nohria. We have dedicated the book to John because of his recognition of the importance of the need to understand the service sector at a time when it received little recognition as an accepted field of study and research in academic institutions. It was his foresight and encouragement that motivated us to push ahead.

We have been lucky to partner on this book with a publisher who exemplifies the characteristics of breakthrough service we write about. The people at Berrett-Koehler have worked hard alongside us to produce a book that the reader will value and the authors can be proud of. Special thanks to Neal Maillet who believed in the idea of this book, shepherded us through the Berrett-Koehler organization, and most importantly, introduced us to Nic Albert who has worked hand in hand with us, and substantively improved our manuscript.

Those closest to our work are, of course, our families. We are particularly indebted to our lifelong partners—Marilyn, Connie, and Phyllis—for tolerating our absence and distractions during the preparation of the book.

INDEX

ABOUT THE AUTHORS

Heskett, Sasser, and Schlesinger were the founding members of the Service Management Interest Group at Harvard Business School, where they partnered on the research that resulted in the publication of *The Service Profit Chain: How Leading Companies Link Profit and Growth to Loyalty, Satisfaction, and Value* (1997) and *The Value Profit Chain: Treat Employees Like Customers and Customers Like Employees* (2003) and the production of two video series, *Achieving Breakthrough Service* and *People, Service, Success: The Service Profit Link.*

James L. Heskett is UPS Foundation Professor of Business Logistics, Emeritus, at the Harvard Business School, where he has taught courses in marketing, business logistics, the management of service operations, business policy, service management, general management, and the entrepreneurial manager at various times since 1965. In addition, he served in several administrative positions at HBS, including that of Senior Associate Dean in charge of the MBA and other academic programs.

Heskett is the recipient of several awards, including the John Drury Sheehan Award for contributions to the field of logistics and the American Marketing Association's Lovelock Award for lifetime contributions to the field of services marketing.

Heskett has served on a number of for-profit and not-for-profit boards, including Cardinal Health, Office Depot, and Limited Brands and was the founding President of Logistics Systems, Inc. In addition, he has consulted for a number of firms in Europe, Latin America, and Asia as well as the United States.

Earl Sasser Jr. is a Baker Foundation Professor at Harvard Business School and has been a faculty member there since 1969.

Sasser developed the School's first course on the management of service operations in 1972. Sasser has taught a variety of courses in the MBA program, including Production and Operations Management, Decision Making and Ethical Values, The Operating Manager, and Service Management.

Leonard A. Schlesinger returned to the Harvard Business School as a Baker Foundation Professor of Business Administration in July 2013 after concluding a five-year term as the 12th president of Babson College. At HBS he teaches the first-year MBA required courses Leadership and Corporate Accountability, and FIELD 3 (Integrative Intelligence) as well as a second-year elective course, General Management: Processes and Action.

Prior to Babson, Schlesinger was at Limited Brands, now known as L Brands, where he served in executive positions from 1999 to 2007, most recently as Vice Chairman and Chief Operating Officer. From 1985 to 1988, he was Executive Vice President and Chief Operating Officer at Au Bon Pain.

His earlier academic career includes 20 years at Harvard Business School, where he served as the George Fisher Baker Jr. Professor of Business Administration. Courses taught included Organizational Behavior, Human Resource Management, General Management, and Service Management.

Berrett–Koehler
Publishers

A community dedicated to creating
a world that works for all

Dear Reader,

Thank you for picking up this book and joining our worldwide community of Berrett-Koehler readers. We share ideas that bring positive change into people's lives, organizations, and society.

To welcome you, we'd like to offer you a free e-book. You can pick from among twelve of our bestselling books by entering the promotional code BKP92E here: http://www.bkconnection.com/welcome.

When you claim your free e-book, we'll also send you a copy of our e-newsletter, the *BK Communiqué*. Although you're free to unsubscribe, there are many benefits to sticking around. In every issue of our newsletter you'll find

- A free e-book
- Tips from famous authors
- Discounts on spotlight titles
- Hilarious insider publishing news
- A chance to win a prize for answering a riddle

Best of all, our readers tell us, "Your newsletter is the only one I actually read." So claim your gift today, and please stay in touch!

Sincerely,

Charlotte Ashlock
Steward of the BK Website

Questions? Comments? Contact me at bkcommunity@bkpub.com.

Certified

Corporation
bcorporation.net